Harrier Hawks
Fly High

(Subtitled:
An Ultra-Living Quest fc
2007 State Championship)

By Andrew Gideon

By Andrew Gideon

<u>Copyright Page</u>

Disclaimer

All resemblances to people alive or dead are completely intentional in this book. This is a work of non-fiction. People offended by reality and thoughts of running or hard work are advised to buy the book and then burn it. In fact, please buy 3 or 4. Burn away, and then buy more. The more, the merrier as part of the proceeds (26.214%) (26.214 miles = marathon distance) from the sale of this book supports the Thompson Falls Cross Country program.

I would like to thank the runners and families involved for living life to the fullest (Ultra-Living) and for giving my fingers inspiration to race across the keyboard to produce this championship book. It was, is, and always will be an honor to have been part of the 2007 Thompson Falls XC program.

Bible quotes are used in this book – and by a public school teacher, nonetheless. (waahhh) Separate Church and State!~ So sue me. And then remember what this country was founded upon.

The opinions expressed in this manuscript are mostly the neurotic, I mean, neuronal transmission of my brain to keyboard. If other people added comments, they are labeled as such. These entries were written journal style – nothing was changed after the fact, except for grammatical or stylistic purposes.

Kurt Vonnegut said, *"We are what we pretend to be, so be careful about what you pretend to be."* For the next 220 pages, I pretended I was a best-selling author and knowledgeable running coach.

___Dedication___

___To Shane Donaldson, Jacob Naegeli, and Ryan Sol___

Thank you for running!
(Shane doesn't understand why Coach Gideon would say this!
Shane, Thanks for running!)

Thank you for giving
the dream of a State Championship
to your teammates and coaches

Thank you for answering the call to that dream

___To the Naegeli family___

Run until you drop, then run more!

___To Cross Country runners___

Our sport is your sport's punishment.

By Andrew Gideon

Themes

Please run, don't walk, a mile in our shoes. You, dear reader, are about to encounter life in its various forms. Be forewarned, learning and life will race before your eyes.

What, what, what, a reader asks, will be in this book?

(1)   Advice to buy the book first and ask questions later.

(2)   Running a mile in someone else's shoes is a learning experience, regardless of shoe size.

(3)   Ultra Running, Ultra Marathoning, and Ultra Living are synonymous.

(4)   Learning is an ongoing process; running should also be.

(5)   Family is important. A second family, if possible, is also just as important. Maybe this second family can get me some more Christmas presents ☺.

(6)   A lot of names are mentioned – to read this book successfully, don't picture every person and name every time – some personalities will leap out, while some elements require just knowing that people (humans) are involved - high school students / people living every day life with dreams and struggles.

(7)   4-H ➔ Head, Heart, Hands, Health - in that order; thank you Beca.

(8)   Seven runners toe the line on a cross country team at a State Meet. A team is only as good as # 7. We are really also only as good as our # 8 - 13 runners, our coaches, and our mascot.

(9)   Our society is only as good as you, the reader, decide to be. So set some higher standards! Then go to work and start running.

(10)   It takes work, not random luck to succeed in life. Faith in God is also something that people should consider – NOW!

(11)   Girls are different than boys, seriously.

(12)   The eyes are the window to the soul. See what is in the soul of a high school cross country team by….

(13)   …turning the pages please.

Prologue
Cross Country Fall 2006

(This was printed in the 2006 Thompson Falls yearbook)

In ten weeks of the cross country season, the members of the team ran 7009 miles. At approximately 975 calories per hour, the team burned 6,833,775 calories.

For that effort, the boys earned 4th place at State, while the girls placed 6th.

Shane Donaldson placed 2nd, while Jacob Naegeli finished 3rd. These two earned All-State honors. These two student-athletes paced the teams and guided them in a successful direction. Their dedication to this slothful sport inspired Ryan Sol to improve from 44th place in 2005 to a 17th place finish in 2006.

For the girls, Ciara Normandeau, Beca Gunderson, Delcie Peters, and Monica Conlin are all listed in the top 11 finishing times for the Thompson Falls Hall of Fame. Check out these times at www.thompsonfalls.net and find out more about the cross country season.

The nicest thing about the student-athletes competing in cross country is that they truly are student-athletes. High grade point averages are maintained and the members are the nucleus of many successful extra-curricular activities such as 4-H, Envirothon, Student Council, National Honor Society, and Science Olympiad.

Maybe the team could burn 10,000,000 calories next year and win state. It is a possibility for both boys and girls teams in the fall of 2007. This 46% increase in effort will get the team over the 10,000 mile mark, and coaches Sarah Naegeli, Bob Reall, and Andrew Gideon will be able to drink their lattees (200 calories with 11 grams protein for each tall lattee, non-flavored) as the greatest coaches of all time in Thompson Falls.

Run Blue Hawks run and keep on soaring above the rest.

Monday, 8-13-2007, Running with Scissors

Team mileage today: 136   runners: 18   Avg. per runner: 7.6

It has been noted that mothers have warned of the dangers of running with scissors. I, on the other hand, am saying it is perfectly well and good to run with them, and not only that, but run fast too.

Understand that when my own two kids (Jaxon, Kaden) get up in the morning, I pack them in breathable antibiotic filled bubble wrap. If they play outside in the heat of a Thompson Falls summer, I cover myself with honey and carry a flyswatter to ensure they don't get stung by a bee. Dad will take the stingers! On hand at bath time is an inflatable life preserver ready in case my boy's lifejacket fails in the one inch of water. Can you say and spell facetious?

However, I'm not dealing with my own kids; I'm working with youth *in loco parentis.* Loosely translated for humorous effect, this means crazy person in place of normally dysfunctional parents. I teach and coach, so I have serious and comical "control" over some student-athletes.

Today each of our Thompson Falls High School cross country harriers received a pair of individualized scissors for the first practice. Yes, they were told to run with them and keep the scissors in view throughout the season. (No athletes were harmed in this experiment.)

What in heaven's name *in loco parentis* is a coach doing teaching kids to run with sharp objects? It is dangerous, dumb, and highly delinquent (CRAZY) for a professional educator to goad our poor little misunderstood and hormonally-challenged children to run with scissors. Really, I should be ashamed. I'm going to call the principal; ha ha, the phone lines were cut! ☺

Is it crazy to willingly put a body through the pain of a three mile race? A five mile run? An eight mile jog in 90 degree heat? A marathon (26.214 miles)? A 50 mile ultra-marathon?

Today, our first day, Shane, Jacob, and Ryan, the boy's leaders ran 13 miles. Delcie and Beca, the top two girls, ran 11. That's crazy; they should have been home watching Oprah, soap operas, and MTV4.

Actually, it is crazy not to run!

Steve Prefontaine, a University of Oregon and US Olympic athlete (1972), said, "*To give anything less than your best is to sacrifice the gift.*"

Every person is blessed in different ways, but most people take their health for granted. Bodies need exercise so the soul and mind can function at a top ability, but most people sacrifice this gift.

That is crazy!

Our Harrier Hawks Fly High. They are extreme enough to put themselves on the starting line. (Lao Tzu – "the journey of a 1000 miles begins with one step.") Our harriers will push their bodies limits to test how far they can fly. (Webster's "harriers" defined: (1) any of various slender hawks having long angled wings and long legs and feeding chiefly on small mammals, reptiles, and insects. (2) a runner on a cross country team.) The first definition fits the Thompson Falls Blue Hawk Harriers well. We will dine on Tigers (Darby), Rams (Loyola), Colts (Colstrip), and even Indians (Poplar) this season. It is not politically correct to dine on Indians – even in cowboy / red neck country.

Our athletes are crazy enough to run in 90 degree heat, run in the rain and stomp on mud puddles, do mile interval repeats until they throw up, be on the honor society, student council, Science Olympiad, 2006 State Champion Envirothon team, and mostly, be crazy enough to be amazing leaders in a world desperately in need of someone who will choose to run with scissors.

Who are these crazy Hawks and what are they doing in the Thompson Falls High School (TFHS) running world? It is time to list the glory hounds who love to see their name in print. These are the 17 kids who showed up on the first day of practice, 8-13-07. At least six more are still on family vacation or haven't had a physical yet.

The eight boys: Shane (senior, 2nd place State B cross country (XC) last season, leg turnover to make the Tasmanian Devil jealous), Jacob (senior, 3rd place State B XC in '06, from an amazingly beautiful family), Ryan (senior, traveled on a 10 day tour of Europe with Jacob and two other TFHS students this summer), Matt (senior, a remarkable wrestler who should weigh 98 pounds, but he insists on eating once a week, so he weighs 123), RT (senior, parents: this young man is teaching your child to ride a bike off cliffs into shark infested river waters. Video evidence and Ryan's scar on his shin prove this), Bryant (senior, he eats and dreams of building rockets), Mike B (sophomore, his knee hurts, but we will rehabilitate it or give him a bionic knee), and Kyle (sophomore, 7 foot 11, okay, only 6 foot 2 ¾ - but he looks 7-11 to junior high kids).

Notice all the listed seniors – the future is NOW for them.

The seven girls: Beca (sophomore, a beautiful stride when she gets the baton as the anchor leg on the 1600 relay), Monica (sophomore, missed ½ of last season with a strained Achilles), Mariah (freshman, Jacob's sister and a quaint 4-H quilting queen), Delcie (junior, a gifted writer and loves the outdoors), Amanda (junior/senior, working on graduating in three years), Lacey

By Andrew Gideon
(sophomore, quiet, great babysitter for my two kids), and JP (sophomore, knows the 3-R's of a Montana education: running, reading, and ranching).

Two junior high boys also showed up on the first day.

Each athlete has a little snippet after his/her name. In no way are our Hawk Harrier personalities static. In fact, the listed athletes are extremely dynamic and offer the world a variety of character traits to spice up life, not only for self, but for others as well. All the world is a play, said Shakespeare, and these Hawk harriers pull the puppet strings of life.

If these Hawk harriers do not emit a proper amount of enthusiasm and energy from a reader, then it is not the fault of characters – rather, my bland vanilla writing would be at fault.

Today's message of the day we (coaches) sent to our athletes was to "train the brain." Our athletes must train the brain to handle the heat of Thompson Falls, Montana, in August and September. At 2300 feet, we live in a banana belt and often have the highest temperatures in the state. Side note: Montana currently is burning down from too many forest fires, so if you don't hear from us again....

Our athletes must train the brain to push past physical limits. No pain, no gain is an often quoted athletic proverb, and this certainly fits for XC. Muscles, tendons, joints, and, most certainly, 3.5 pounds of blood soaked sponges of brains will be stressed to the limit by our Hawk Harriers over the next 68 days of the season.

Mile repeats in 90 plus heat (or drenching rain) are not fun (unless one has scissors!). Eight mile runs are not enjoyable after putting up with the English teacher (oh, that's me – one of three English teachers at T Falls High School). Three mile races are just long enough to pain the endurance threshold of any person willing to take up the challenge.

Our athletes must train the brain to realize our team shorts are nice. Yes, some skin on the upper leg shows, and these short shorts were a rage in the 50's-80's, but coach, c'mon. Lighter and skimpier is better for runners, so train the head! Shane, you look good in skimpy shorts.

My mind is trained to enjoy running, talking, and being surrounded by the Hawk Harriers; they will train their intellects to enjoy the company of other scissor-bearers. Run Hawks Run.

To emphasize "train the brain," the coaching staff handed out two articles from _Runner's World_ (March 07 pages 63, 65 and April 07 p. 43, 44). We talked about realizing life is what our brains are trained to think: that person is attractive, my job is great, this book is the greatest, and, of course, coach, 15 miles of 400 repeats was not enough to tax my body, could we please run more. Our brains should be trained to enjoy where we live, appreciate the people in our lives, take pleasure in what we do, and live up to every day life challenges (taxes, sickness, and school lunches).

Today at 3:30 pm, a car wrecked in TFalls. As I was writing sports articles at the local paper, the *Sanders County Ledger*, a reporter brought in pictures – teenagers were involved at 80 mph, two blocks from the school. My instant thoughts went to my wife and children (I knew they were out walking) and the cross country team. I prayed none of "my" people were involved.

Luckily?? None of "my" people were involved. One passenger died, the driver of the vehicle survived, and three total people went to the hospital. The driver had been a member of the 2005 Thompson Falls Blue Hawk cross country team for a little while. It can only be written that he didn't finish that season.

If we could have hooked him on running faster, buying into the concept of a Blue Hawk family, and learning to find the depth of a running soul, could that have prevented this accident? This book will follow this situation.

Running can transform lives in a positive direction. There is some bearing with this belief currently going on in prisons. A <u>Runner's World</u> article from February 2007, "Inside Track," discusses the idea of running as a form of rehabilitation. Goal setting and achieving, as well as a positive outlet for getting rid of anger or aggression are discussed. The prisons note initial positive proof. This is definitely on the right track, just as the Harrier Hawks are after day one!

On Monday evenings and Wednesday mornings in summer 07, as well as some races, we ran together. 17 total runners logged mileage with me! I ran 139 miles with Shane (boys leader), and 39 with Beca (girls leader). Overall, Shane ran 227 and Beca 181; they were the mileage leaders for each sex.

8-14-2007, just the facts, get serious

Team mileage today: 139   runners: 22   Avg per runner: 6.3

My attempt at yesterday's writing humor deserves an apology. Dear reader, please apologize for not seeing humor in life and laughing all the way to the store to buy a second copy of this book. Coaching and teaching is a serious business, and it should always be treated as such. No monkey business in today's writing; there will not even be a smile on the author's face.

Thompson Falls is a Class B school with an enrollment of 215. Montana classifications include AA (826+ students, grades 9-12), A (340-825), B (120-339), and C (0-119). 8.4% of our high school student body joined in today's workout. Four junior high boys also participated.

There is an often cited saying that 10% of the people do 90% of the work. Our Hawk harriers are that 10%.

Today's workout consisted of a one mile warm-up, stretching, one mile race preparation, a two mile time trial, and various cool downs based on abilities. In addition, seven boys labored on an extra four mile interval workout after the timed two mile. The interval workout was one mile easy, then 0:45 hard, 1:30 hard, 2:15 hard, 1:30 hard, and 0:45 hard, with equal amount of rest in between.

By Andrew Gideon

Head Coach Sarah Naegeli designed a one mile course on school property. Time trials take place here; this is the same workout we did on day two of cross country last season. The intervals, a new workout this season, occurred on forest service trails on the north end of TFalls.

Two mile times are reported per se: name 2007 time (2006 time).

Boys: Shane 10:19 (10:58), Jacob 10:29 (10:45), Ryan 11:01 (11:36), Mike M 11:49 (dnr – did not run), Coach Gideon 11:57 (11:47), RT 12:02 (12:12), MK 12:14 (dnr), BM 12:14 (dnr), Bryant 12:39 (12:53), Matt 12:51 (13:18), Kyle 14:56 (16:07), and Mike B 15:30 (dnr).

Girls: Beca 13:44 (13:30), Monica 14:37 (14:06), Delcie 14:40 (14:22), Mariah 15:20 (dnr), JP 16:41 (dnr), Lacey 17:43 (dnr), and Amanda 19:26 (dnr).

Observations: (1) all the boys improved their times, (2) none of the girls improved their times, and (3) Coach Gideon was slower (Ack, time marches forward~!). This is our first instance of the difference between the sexes.

Remember that nine runners ran at least 10 miles yesterday; 4 girls and 5 boys had a double session the previous evening. Therefore, stiff legs greeted those trying to run hard at 7:30 AM. Our harriers are to be admired for pushing themselves into an uncomfortable zone. Last year there was not a Monday night double session, so these times are very good – for both the boys and girls.

Then seven boys ran more! That's ridiculous, except one coach was bizarre enough to do the workout too. The lucky seven were Shane (crushed it), Jacob (excellent pushes), Ryan, Bryant, Mike M, BM, and MK. The last three listed were at their first workout; we wanted to see what was in their legs. They spent all of summer hiking up and down hills four to ten miles per day.

Note to reader: This is top secret information. Coaches: please use the exact same workouts with your runners. Do not adapt to the skill and fitness level of individual athletes. In fact, I lied about today. We actually ran 299 team miles (13.6/runner), and did 3 x 3 timed miles. If the 3 mile set was over 20 minutes, each harrier had an extra 1000 pushups and 1000 sit-ups.

We mean business in Thompson Falls, Montana.

Mothers might warn against running with scissors; in fact, no less than two adults even said that to me on Monday!

Other things mothers might say: If you don't eat your vegetables, then you won't grow up big and strong. If Johnny jumped off a bridge, would you be crazy enough to jump too? No mother, of course not, unless we were on a train bridge with the train bearing down on us and the water was less than 20 feet away, with little current, and decent depth. Actually, I'm pretty sure at least 90% of our cross country kids have jumped off cliffs (into water) (in the summer).

Mom: "If Johnny does drugs, will you do drugs?" Reply: "No mother."

I would go out on a thin and dead limb and say that 0% of our cross country harriers use/abuse drugs. They are good kids.

For now, let's ask the right questions.

Let's ask something like, if Shane Donaldson wins the state championship, is another Thompson Falls runner going to follow him and win the state championship too? If Jacob Naegeli puts in extra effort and works his brown nose to the grindstone, will another Hawk Harrier put in extra effort, brown nose, and become Valedictorian too? If Ryan Sol earns a nomination to the Air Force Academy, will he influence others to do this also?

No mother, of course not, that would be as crazy as running with scissors. *"We don't need no education."* (Pink Floyd) We certainly don't need someone out on a thin limb with snippety scissors having kids analyze what really is crazy in our society.

Wednesday, 8-15-2007, recovery day – The Island
Team mileage today: 106   runners: 22   Avg. per runner: 4.8

I didn't type anything today. I actually am typing the 15th's entry on Thursday. Bad, poor, undisciplined author! Who writes incomplete sentences!

Why the delay, and why tell us, we wouldn't have noticed anyway.

I didn't write. Here is my childish reason: although my given name is Mr. Andrew Coach Gideon, my two kids, Jaxon (2 years, 10 months, and 30 days old) and Kaden (1 y, 2 m, and 6 d), know me as *Jungle Gym*. They climb all over me as if I were brand new playground equipment. They drool, bite arms, and kick and/or elbow in places that are protected by laws; mostly, they take advantage of my pathetic attempts to be a disciplined parent. I should walk around with sawdust, wood chips, and sand 2 meters deep on all sides of me, so when I shed them to the ground attempting to breathe, they would be protected.

Back in the day (nerve grating cliché telling me I have aged), kids played and rode bikes without protective helmets, goggles, and knee pads.

Both my kids are sick – one with 104 degree fever (Jaxon) and another with an ear infection (Kaden). I couldn't walk anywhere without them clinging to me. My wife escaped the stress for two reasons: (1) to get a break from the nerve-racking cries of sick kids, and (2) to help her sister clean a house as her family moves into TFalls.

So I held Jaxon and Kaden all day. They cried and whimpered from sickness – it might have been from an odor called "running too many days with only baby drool to bathe in." (cologne product pending).

So we watched *Four Minutes*, a 2005 ESPN movie, about Roger Bannister's life. Bannister was the first person to crack the four minute mile barrier on May 6, 1954. On 29 May 1953, less than a year earlier, Edmund Hillary was the first person to arrive on Mount Everest's summit. I cried when Bannister broke 4:00 – even though running history had already been completed. Crazy – I also shed tears for the movie *Endurance* as well. I am a "man" who teaches and coaches high school students and attempts to raise two kids? A man who cries...in today's world – a sign God created man as opposed to evolution!

What does that have to do with coaching cross country?

11

By Andrew Gideon

It means that even in the midst of everyday responsibilities, people will achieve great obstacles. Somehow with two young children who were sick, I was able to help coach 22 kids in cross country. The 22 kids also have individual lives, work responsibilities, and stresses to deal with as they surmount every day obstacles in their own lives. Hillary and Bannister conquered things (4 minute mile, Mount Everest) that were thought impossible to humans.

Preaching – Luke 1:37, *"For nothing is impossible with God."*

TFHS XC "impossible" goal – WIN STATE.

Today = "recovery" day - the theme of most running programs is "stress and recover." A runner will stress the muscles, tendons, joints, and then give time to recover. Monday was LSD (long slow distance), Tuesday was tempo / intervals, so Wednesday was recovery. Each cycle of stress and recover will strengthen the body (and brain!).

This coach set up a course on our town's "island." The island is surrounded by the TFalls dam, and is a nice place to hike, walk, and attract visitors and their money to our town.

The main island loop is slightly over ½ mile of twisting rock-filled, root-gripping trail. Scenic overlooks exist with visitor information boards. There are three picnic tables, countless amounts of empty beer cans (despite the sign saying "no alcoholic beverages"), and copious amounts of garbage. Yes, copious!

The runners ran two miles easy to the island (the junior high kids were driven to nearby Power Park and only had to run ½ mile). After the team arrived, I explained the rules for a contest, and we took a loop around the island. 26 water bottles (26 miles in a marathon) were placed in visible places near the trail.

Our 22 Hawk harriers were divided into three teams. Numbered bottles were placed randomly (picnic tables, at the tower on the hill, etc). Three bottles had smiley faces. Cross country is scored similar to golf – lowest score wins, so you want to get the water bottles at the picnic tables, the tower, and others before the opposing teams do. There were also 12 questions typed up from the visitor interpretation signs, and categories for picking up garbage and aluminum cans.

Our runners retrieved water, aluminum cans, garbage, or answered a quiz question and returned as swiftly as possible – until all bottles were found.

The three teams were divided evenly by speed, sex, and junior high kids. Team names were Kenyans, wanna-be-Pre's, and "Too Fast for Loyola." Loyola is a private school in Missoula that dominates Class B sports and has won 5 of the last 7 Boys Class B state cross country titles. They won in 2006; however, it will be 5 of the last 8 years after 2007, thanks to the Thompson Falls Bluehawks

We collected a garbage bag full of trash and ½ of a grocery sack of crushed cans (donated to the local Whitepine 4-H club). We had a fun recovery day and emphasized team skills and motivational sayings.

Each water bottle had a saying on it, such as "Will run 4 doughnuts," "love to run," "love to train," "sharp scissors run longer," and "Hawks fly."

There were other sayings like "eat, sleep, run," "love to read," and "…victory laps." They even earned the right to drink the water bottles they found.

Winners: the team! Actually, it was an enjoyable exercise for the entire squad, but the "winners" were the "Too fast for Loyola" team.

Thursday 8-16-2007, Smoke and Mirrors

Team mileage today: 137 runners: 20 Avg. per runner: 6.9

More than 500,000 acres have burned in Montana this month so far, with at least 12 current live fires. Flames 22 miles from Thompson Falls have burned 85,000 plus acres, while a fire within ¼ mile of my wife's parent's house in Placid Lake has burned 21,000 plus acres. This state has had too much heat, not enough rain, and too many environmentalists who refuse to let us create healthy forests and jobs. So smoke has hampered many areas of Montana.

In Hamilton, 140 miles from Thompson Falls, Mark Albert coaches the Hamilton, Class A, cross country team. Despite starting practice on the same day as us, the Broncs (school mascot) have yet to practice outside because of unhealthy air quality. Mark and I graduated from Sentinel High School in Missoula, MT, Class AA, in 1986. We both played on the State Championship 1986 Boys Basketball team, the Sentinel Spartans. Mark underwent cancer treatment in 2001 for Hodgkin's lymphoma. Mark ran his first marathon (26.2 miles) on July 15 in Missoula, evidence he trampled the disease into the ground.

Speaking of first marathons, my brother Steve also jogged the Missoula route in July. The times: Mark 4:14:23, Steve 3:44:12, and author 3:14:20. This was my 8th career marathon.

I emailed and called brother Steve to ask about Darby's smoke. He coaches in Darby (20 miles from Hamilton), but he is being his usual tight-lipped, I ain't giving no information that you can use to better your coaching or your book. Darby is Class B, so they compete against us. I find it hilarious that I outline every detail of our training, while he rarely gives me information.

Maybe I should employ a smoke and mirrors concept. I should try it with the silly customer who bought this book to learn about running, life, and high school students. Ha, ha!

"Smoke and mirrors is a metaphor for a deceptive, fraudulent or insubstantial explanation or description." (Wikipedia)

With all of Montana's smoke, a *smoke and mirrors* approach should be employed. I should lie about our workouts to reporters and other coaches. Athletes should be brainwashed to believe that hard work, summer mileage, trained brains, stress and recover are all concepts that lead to success. Our kids are falling for this "smoke and mirrors."

Laughable advice: hard work helps a person succeed. Running more in the summer and getting stronger helps cross country runners become stronger. Ha, ha, ha, ha, foolish kids, foolish student-athletes have succumbed to believing in the smoke and mirrors we are employing. Here's another good one – good

By Andrew Gideon

grades and success in school will help you in life! Ha, if only we could convince the dropouts who will most likely earn minimum wage for life of this silly topic.

I visualize the reporter in Helena, Montana, on October 20th.

Reporter: How did you get your kids to run so well and be too fast for Loyola?

Coach: Smoke and Mirrors! We misled all of our kids into believing worthless concepts such as believing in your teammates, running until you drop and then running more, and challenging yourself to be the best. And they fell for it, ha, ha, ha, ha, ha, the fools! When will they realize all of us adults, teachers, and coaches just make stuff up to get you from climbing all over us and calling us Jungle Gym!!! We preached for them to eat healthy and drink plenty of fluids. We made up deceptive wisdom such as get to bed 10-15 minutes earlier every night (15 minutes times 68 days is 17 more hours of sleep between now and October 20th). We asked them to study and most of them are on the honor roll. Incredulous, that's what I say. As if healthy body = healthy mind = healthy life, right!!!!! Mr. Reporter, why we won state: smoke and mirrors, smoke and mirrors.

However, TFalls is not free of smoke – it rolled in and blanketed us like a covered mirror.

Our Bluehawk harriers had a great 3-5 mile workout with hills this morning. According to ability, each athlete ran a different amount. We were done by 9 am and ingested healthy air.

By 10 am, burnt wood, and Los Angeles type smog blanketed our moods like an evil step-mother.

How will the team survive? How will we respond? Hamilton has had to run inside because of unhealthy air, and we may need to make accommodations like indoor bikes, local gym clubs/treadmills, and yoga.

Yoga? Yes, I've typed too long, time for a break.

One girl (Delcie) and five boys (Shane, Jacob, Ryan, Mike M, and Patrick (1st practice)) were requested at an evening double session. Along with Coach Gideon, these six ran another four miles in the smoky Montana evening.

Coach Gideon ran with Delcie and Patrick and discussed running form and techniques. We had four good examples running ahead of us, so we could study their running form: is the body lined up and moving forward, where are the knees, ankles, and feet going? How is the leg turnover? We took a 30 second count (Patrick 41, Coach Gideon 44, Delcie 44), and then talked about leg turnover and separating the lower half (quicker turnover, stride length) from the upper half (lungs and brain, let the foot strikes be quicker as the brain and lungs stay relaxed). The second set showed an increase for all three runners: Patrick 44, Coach Gideon 47, and Delcie 46. The key number to the count is 45. 45 on one leg times 2 legs times 2 (30 to 60 seconds) is 180. Leg turnover should be at

14

least 180. If it is not, then drills can be employed to help increase this critical aspect of running economy.

Practice was originally scheduled in town, but it was changed by Coach Naegeli because of air quality (or so she says – really she just wanted it at her ranch). The Naegeli family lives 11 miles west from TFalls; this is where we had the 7:30 am workout as well.

We had several back up plans in place – exercise bikes at the Gideon house with a running movie was one of them. The other one was the local gym club, Bear Muscle Fitness. I called the owners and talked with them about use of their three treadmills, 2 stair climbers, and 2 incumbent bikes. The owners had no problem with working with the high school students, as long as a waiver was signed by the parents. Thanks for the offer.

8-17-2007, Ice baths

Team mileage today: 120   runners: 20   Avg per runner: 6.0

What is the advantage of ice baths? Won't our scissors freeze?

After a workout, runners have micro tears in muscles and abuse of tendons, joints, as well as an increased lactic acid build up. Icing the body drains blood, along with some lactic acid. After 10 minutes, legs become cold and stiff. Jumping out of the ice, whether into a hot shower or just normal air temperature, increases blood flow to affected areas. New blood will energize the legs. This new blood will flow in and out quickly, pulling with it even more lactic acid.

Rugby players in England and female runner Paula Radcliffe are proponents of this technique. Study www.paularadcliffe.com for her methods. She currently owns the world record in the 10K road race (30:21) and Marathon (2:15:25), so maybe one could give her ideas at least a shred of respect~!

RICE – Rest, Ice, Compression, Elevation – people around sports have heard of RICE. If this works, then the same concepts of ice baths also will work.

Our beloved Naegeli family has a home made backyard pool. It was formed by the labor of shovels, digging, and crazy Naegeli ideas. This pond is dug from the earth and has a black tarp for a holding tank; welcome to Red Neck Montana! Red Neck alert: relax and remember what I said about the Naegeli family on page two, "...an amazingly beautiful family." This family farms, does 4-H, makes quilts, gets good grades, works on emergency management in Montana, hays and bucks bales at all hours of days or nights, runs hard, coaches well, and makes themselves productive citizens. So what if they have sun burnt necks!! I hope my two kids learn from the Naegeli family.

So today, we had our third consecutive workout on the Naegeli farm (7:30 am and 7 pm yesterday, 7:30 am today). Shane, Jacob, and Ryan all ran 6 miles and biked three, switching bike riders every 1.5 miles; Coach Gideon ran the nine miles with them. Another group of three runners with painful knees rode another bike and switched riders every six minutes, going around four miles total. Other workouts ranged from 2-6 miles.

By Andrew Gideon

After the workout, the team jumped into the Naegeli pool for a ten minute ice bath. While it may not have been ice, it was pretty close. The pool was drained and refilled the previous evening – so water coming out of the hose in the 54 degree Montana evening couldn't have been more than 40-44 degrees.

The ice bath is a necessary evil. It helped prevent injuries as I trained for the July Marathon – my icing ranged from the local State Park to the icy Thompson River to the in-town picnic area (Wild Goose Landing) to my own bath tub, complete with ice chunks/freezer ice.

Coach Bob Reall (yes, we have three coaches) is also a firm believer in this treatment for runners. Please read this information:

"2007 Lancaster Bob Reall Invitational
Lancaster High School   September 22, 2007 - 10:00"

Having an Invitational Cross Country Meet named after a person is a measure of respect – especially if the person is still alive!!!! Here is some information from the internet that Al Gore invented in a losing attempt to be President (he should have invented better voting machines).

Bob *"Reall was the boys cross country coach at Lancaster High School from 1962 through 1991. He was the boys cross country coach at Columbus Whetstone in 1961 and the boys track coach at Columbus Eastmoor High School in 1963. Bob's cross country teams won two state cross country meets, 13 district/regional meets, and 15 conference meets. He coached five individual state cross country meet winners. Reall was named State Cross Country Career Coach of the Year in 1984."* http://www.oatccc.com/halloffame/1993.html

Bob read and corrected this information – bad website – the perfect internet failed! Bob coached Lancaster from 1963-1991 and had 16 League titles and 23 District titles. 20 of his teams went to State. In that respect, Ohio is much more competitive than Montana. Qualifying for a Ohio State Meet is a hard process, similar to basketball tournaments – only so many teams make it. In Montana, every team runs at State.

Naegeli family - ice. Paula Radcliffe - ice. Bob Reall - ice. Ice baths – love them or hate them, but you'd better believe in them. Ice Hawks Ice.

Note on 8-13 entry – I had other people's children run with scissors. Last night Jaxon, my own son, was racing through the house with a sucker in his mouth. He was made to take it out because it is perilous to scamper with suckers in the mouth. I asked Jaxon, "Running with suckers in your mouth, are you? Why don't we just give you some scissors too." His response: "yeahhhhh!@"

Child services, we have a problem parent.

8-18-2007, Saturday, on your own

We had a great first week of practice. 23 different runners contributed mileage, while possibilities for more participants exist. Fourty-six student feet pounded pavement (and trails); there was good team interaction and clean air that other Montana communities did not have. Our Bluehawk harriers only had one injury that slowed a runner down; JP turned her ankle (Thurs.) and could not finish the workout. She did run Friday, yeah for that!

There are other injuries for us to keep an eye on. Monica lost one-half of her 2006 season to a left Achilles problem – her left ankle, Achilles, and knee currently bug her. We beg her to ice and run on soft surfaces, and on Friday part of her workout was on a bicycle. Matt has a stomach that produces too much acid and causes him to occasionally throw up; plus he also has a hip problem. We didn't include Matt in double sessions because of the hip, and the coaches have given him information on how to reduce stomach acid for runners (if he finds good and easy nutrition for his stomach, this can also help his wrestling). Mike B, Shane, Ryan, and Mariah had part of their workout on Friday on bikes because of knee complaints.

Thompson Falls is on their way to a good season after the first week, but injuries may play a roll in how the season ends. Therefore, coaches need to keep a close eye on them.

Our Hawk coaching staff has challenged the runners to push harder, run faster, and train the brain. I am a believer that leaders should guide by example, so I signed up to run the October 13, Le Grizz Ultra-Marathon (50 miles). Ouch.

My longest training run ever was a 4 hour 5 minute, 30 miler in Seattle in October 1994...until today.

My personal workout today was 31 miles (4 hours 26 minutes). My workout consisted of intervals of running 27 minutes and walking three. This 27-3 strategy should help me achieve the *Le Grizz* 50 miler on October 13th. (more information - www.cheetahherders.com). A walk break and mental intervals will help me compete for the required amount of time. It worked okay. Miles 13-14 were run in 16:22, while miles 29-30 slowed down to 18:10. I ran loops of 8 and 7.5 and then took a ten minute break at my house. I repeated the loops and my second eight (miles 15.5 to 23.5) set was one minute faster than the first eight.

An ice bath was a reward within a half-hour of finishing. The carpet was a soft landing for recovery. I was hungry enough to eat food scraps off the floor; my kids considered my dead body a new trampoline. Those elbows are knees are always welcome, although the kid's smiles were better.

Coach Reall (readers please note: Coach Reall volunteers; he has never been paid for his work at TFHS. Thank you Bob) advocates ice baths, is in the Ohio hall-of-fame, and has a race named after him. I take ice baths and just hope to have a grave named after me someday. Today's 31 miler almost put me there, but after several hours and an ice bath, I bounced back.

Sunday will be a blessed day of rest.

Sunday 8-19-2007, A blessed day of rest

There is no rest for the wicked. This phrase originates from Isaiah 48:22 in the Bible, "'*There is no peace,*' says the Lord, '*for the wicked.*'" This same phrase is repeated in Isaiah 57:21.

By Andrew Gideon

My son is named Jaxon Isiah Gideon. He is named after Isiah Thomas (Indiana Hoosier, Detroit Piston, basketball legend) and with the thought of Isaiah 40:31 in mind. This verse reads, *"But those who hope in the Lord will renew their strength. They will soar on wings like eagles; they will run and not grow weary, they will walk and not faint."*

Once again, does this author stray from important book themes?

No. Connect the dots dear reader, connect the dots.

I ended Saturday with "a blessed day of rest." My subtitle today reads *"A blessed day of rest."* God and the Bible can give a soul rest. Our athletes should be resting after a great week of work. The verses read well for runners, *"...will renew their strength...will run and not grow weary."*

There is no rest for the wicked – what does that mean? Here I am, typing away at the book and doing research on what it will take to win it all this year for the boys. I studied the website of www.mhsa.org and cross country site (MHSA – Montana High School Association).

Can our boys win state? These questions and more will be answered on October 20, 2007 – 62 days from now.

1996-1999: Poplar boys won State B. 2000-2004 and 2006: Loyola Sacred Heart won State B. Manhattan won State B in 2005. Readers can guess who our competition is!!!!!

Boys' team scoring at state last year for: Loyola 93, Colstrip 97, Poplar 99, Thompson Falls 128, Cut Bank 130, Lame Deer 136, and Manhattan 168.

Loyola (located in smoky Missoula, MT) had runners place at 7, 10 (senior), 12, 25, 39, 64, and 93. Top five returnees score 147.

Colstrip had runners placed at 8 (sr.), 11, 16, 19, 43 (sr.), 47, and 127. Top five returnees score 220.

Poplar had runners placed at 4, 13, 18, 24, 40, 52, and 79. #40 and #79 were seniors. Top five returnees score 111.

TFalls runners placed 2 (Shane), 3 (Jacob), 17 (Ryan), 50 (Matt H), 56 (MK), 63 (Bryant), and 111. No seniors ran, but our #111 could not compete this season due to a bad back. Top five returnees score 128.

Cut Bank had runners placed at 1, 6, 30, 45, 48, 88, and 94. Seniors for Cut Bank were 1, 6, 30, and 94. Only three returnees exist.

Lame Deer had runners placed at 9, 21, 29 (sr.), 33 (sr.), 44, 89, and 115 (sr.). So they have four possible returnees.

Manhattan had runners at 5, 14, 22, 61, 66, and 100. A seventh runner wasn't listed, and there were no seniors, so their top five returnees score 168.

Based on these numbers, the top three are Poplar 111, Thompson Falls 128, and Loyola 147. However, many things need to be considered. What athletes logged summer running mileage? Who transferred into a school or moved out? Injuries are bound to happen when athletes are pushing the limits, but we pray, "No injuries to our team, Lord, no injuries to our team. Please!"

There will be a battle, and it will be fun.

Did I forget about the girls and their potential to move up from 8th (2005) to 6th (2006) to ??? (2007)? No!

Our top two girls were Beca #23 and Delcie #44. CC injured her back and could not compete this year, and she placed #21 last year.

Of the listed girls for the 2006 State Meet, only six of the top 30 scorers were seniors.

Monica was #50 and JP #78, while our other two competitors at State chose not to compete this season (one moved).

Four of the five teams ahead of our girls return at least two of their top three scorers.

Moving up from 6th will take a tremendous amount of work and discipline from our girls. I hope and pray it happens and we stay healthy. I would love to see Beca, Delcie, and Monica earn top 15 (finish in the top 15 runners) for All-State honors – last year that meant a time of 20:15 or better. Our career best time at Thompson Falls is 20:13 (2000 Kellyn Gross). We shall go to work and see the results.

Monday 8-20-2007, Much Ado about Nothing

Team mileage today: 102   runners: 15   Avg. per runner: 6.8

Hurricane Dean roars through Jamaica and conjures up images of Hurricane Katrina and New Orleans. We recall 1836 dead in that August 2005 United States devastation.

In other parts of the world, India floods since June 2007 have forced over 1 million people to evacuate with 600,000 homes partially or fully damaged.

In Utah, six miners were trapped recently, and two rescuers died trying to save them.

In other parts of the world, on August 17, 2007, 181 miners were trapped in China.

On 9-1-1 in New York, terrorists attacked the twin towers; the death total reached 2974.

Elsewhere in the world, 3637 US soldiers have died in Iraq.

In 2004, there were 29,569 gun deaths in the US. (My point with this fact is that we do more damage and killing to each other than terrorists ever will).

Egocentric is the word of the day – we make much ado about nothing. We strive to teach, coach, live, and improve our lives. Focus on the task at hand is a great lesson. However, occasionally we need to look up from our tiny ant lives and get a perspective that I am one – and there are 6 billion other "ones" in existence in the world.

Forest fires in Montana, who cares? Why should I even mention these on the 8-16 entry? In my egocentric view of the world, I realize that four houses in Montana have evacuees that are direct relations to me. The fires are on my mind and I pray for rain; the war in Iraq is on my mind because of several former students of mine that are fighting for our freedom in this world.

By Andrew Gideon

So, Monday dawns with selfish thoughts of our Hawk Harriers: What will we do with our free will and how will our fight be today?

Monday morning arrives with clouds and only 15 runners.

Cooler weather is appreciated after the hottest summer in memory. Rain from the clouds would be nice for the fires burning in Montana.

15 runners – kak, ack, and blivits! With our world outlook, how will our team improve if we don't all show up to fight?! $15/23 = 65\%$ fight today = D.

One athlete is shopping, four are off hiking for five days in the mountains as an assignment, one will probably play grade school soccer, and two are at a funeral.

Part of life is appreciating your situation and being happy with the people around you. So, for these 15 runners today – thank you for coming – for those not here – you are missed.

Run, run as fast as you can – we are the Gingerbread men. We must study why this crusty critter runs.

Run Forest Run. Examining what could drive Forest Gump to run so much and so far is important to the theme of this book.

Run away, run away (Monty Python) – we must scrutinize if running away (and then back) in our quest for the XC Holy Grail is worth it.

I tried to run with as many kids as possible this morning. The leaders Shane, Jacob, and Ryan ran 7 Gingerbread Man miles and talked about food their first 20 minutes. I drifted back with RT and listened to his ankle pop every step he took. Matt and I discussed eating to help his stomach acid and breathing pattern. He ran with a labored 2-2 breathing pattern (in two steps, out two). I talked with him about relaxing his breathing by taking a more controlled, deeper second breath, and exhaling a little harder on his second out breath. If the breathing relaxes, lungs, shoulders, legs, and mind can follow. Of course, the mind leads the control of the breathing, so around and around in circles we go.

Delcie and JP were my next partners. Another English teacher asked me on Sunday about an incident where a bee flew up Delcie's nose, and I couldn't recall this event. So today I asked Delcie about it, and indeed, a bee soared up her nose as a freshman at a track meet. Run away, run away from the bee. She was glad that it didn't sting her.

JP turned her ankle Thursday, but ran six miles on Friday and three on Saturday, so she is A-OK. The nice thing about JP this year is that she has two extra weeks of training. Last year she didn't have ten practices until the season's third meet; this year she will be able to compete at all our meets. Delcie recalled cheerfully that JP won the JV meet in Ronan last year in her first career meet.

Monica, Mariah, and Mike B were a trio running and biking together to relieve some knee pressure and pounding. All three ran strong and well today. Monica is on our mind as we lost ½ of her 2006 season to an Achilles injury; we don't want that to happen again. Mariah has done a lot of knee exercises in the past six months for rehabilitation and strength. Mike B is a project in the works – his brother Dave ran with us last year and told us to work Mike hard.

Amanda was the last one in as somehow Lacey escaped my path (she rerouted herself to sneak home for a second). So I ran a few miles with Amanda and talked about running and pushing forward. She ran 7 miles today – 66 minutes for the six mile route – a career long run.

All of this challenging running – we are training brains to handle stress and improve. But when we, meaning these kids, get into society and the "real world" - will this running help them? Relationships, disease, death, taxes, jobs, and children – what part of our running program will help them deal with these issues – how does it all tie together?

Mini-answer: Endurance, patience, and a positive healthy energy outlet come to mind.

I do want a State Championship for the boys; I do want several girls to set their Personal Records (PR's); I do want beautiful blessings for all of them in life. Analyze the following: did 102 team miles today help some neurons to handle life in a slightly better way? Only time will tell.

Much ado about nothing; State Championships, 50 mile runs, ACT & SAT scores, and all I want is to go home and eat breakfast and savor my lattee.

Double session run at 7 PM: Jacob, Shane, Ryan, and Delcie ran the two mile connector from Harlow Road to Blue Slide Road. Two miles out and two back made for a nice rolling four mile jaunt. Ryan showed me this trail on the first day of summer 2006, and I have loved it since. Good scenery, some shade, curves, and a soft surface make this a great place to run.

Coach Bob drove and waited patiently for us; the owner of the property saw him and requested that we not use/run on it because of all the bad people who leave garbage, shirts, and other miscellaneous junk; apparently some people don't know Montana's campsite rules: pack it in, pack it out. So because of rotten apples, the good ones don't get to use it.

Don't tell Bob or the owner, oops, I'm telling now, this route is too good not to use again. Maybe we will pick up two bags of garbage for the owner, he can thank us, and only the T Falls harriers will be allowed on his property.

Here's some inspiration for all runners. In 1993 I ran my first marathon in 3:14:48. In 2008, 15 years and 15,000 miles later, I ran a marathon in 3:14:20. So, with 15,000 extra miles and 15 years experience, I improved one second per mile. Ha! My words of perspiration surely didn't help motivate our harriers to go the extra mile. However, this does show that even the smallest improvement can be made. I put up the good fight to make progress. 2 Timothy 4:7 ➔ *I have fought the good fight, I have finished the race, I have kept the faith.*

Tuesday, 8-21-2007, Paradise

Team mileage today: 110   runners: 19   Avg. per runner: 5.8

21

By Andrew Gideon

In small town Montana, people have to perform multiple jobs. I substituted several weeks for local sportswriter John Hamilton while he fought fires. When he came back, I inherited the job as cross country sportswriter for the *Sanders County Ledger*, the weekly paper.

For this week's article (23 August 2007), a reader needs to know that Paradise, MT, is on some maps and is 33 miles east of Thompson Falls.

Paradise for T Falls runners   *by Andrew Gideon*

667 miles. The Thompson Falls cross country team ran a combined 667 miles during the first week of practice. One step at a time, the Blue Hawk harriers produced ten trips to Paradise and back.

Head Coach Sarah Naegeli has been with the program for all ten years of its existence and has recorded thousands of miles in her notebooks. She was the assistant in 1998 and has been the head coach from 1999-present. This season's numbers are a good indication of why Coach Naegeli looks forward to the 2007 season.

On the girl's side, there have been some seasons without a full team (seven runners can compete at the State Meet). Sarah stated, "We were worried about not having a full girl's team, but seven high schoolers showed up." Among those seven girls are Beca Gunderson, who placed 23rd at State last year as a freshman, and Delcie Peters, #44 overall for Class B girls last season. Added to the leadership of Beca and Delcie are two sophomores, Monica Conlin, who finished at #50, and Jeffreyanne Parker, who ran 78th. The numbers 50 and 78 may not seem impressive to the average reader, but Monica lost one-half of her 2006 season due to Achilles problems and was fortunate to just compete at State. Jeffreyanne missed the first two weeks of 2006 due to family vacations and 4-H responsibilities. Jeffreyanne ran 31 miles her first week of the 2007 season, compared to zero at this time last year. These lady Hawks hope to improve their 6th place 2006 team finish, and their young talent and efforts so far places them on the right road.

Coach Naegeli was eager to sound excited about the boy's side of the team as well. Four seniors are in their fourth season running together: Shane Donaldson, Jacob Naegeli, Ryan Sol, and Bryant Normandeau. "These runners had a great first week of practice on top of good summer mileage," coach Naegeli said. Her hopes for a trophy at the end of the season also rest on the shoulders (and legs) of seniors RT Brown, Matt Hojem, Mike Morris, as well as juniors Mike Kidwiler and Patrick Jamison.

Assistant Coach Bob Reall commented on the solid depth of the team. All the coaches feel great that in addition to the nine juniors and seniors, there are four underclassmen out as well.

Coach Naegeli's enthusiasm could be a sign of the runner's high – too many endorphins on the brain after hard workouts. Six different athletes ran double sessions because of logging high summer mileage. During the first week,

Shane, Jacob, and Ryan hit 50 miles for the boys, while Delcie led the girls with 43.

> *The team adjusted several practices because some athletes are involved in student council. The Thompson Falls student council is a great leadership opportunity and has been rated as one of the top councils for Class B for years. On Wednesday the team picked up a full bag of garbage from the island and aluminum cans for the Whitepine 4-H club. Several other athletes volunteered to help a business move, with a donation made to the cross country team for the effort.*

> *The first week of practice produced great and positive results. Hopefully the team can earn more trips to Paradise with their feet, such as throwing coach Naegeli into the water in Helena after winning state. A little bit of heaven, glory, ecstasy, delight, and joy (synonyms of paradise) is a welcome sight in any life, but the cost to acquire heaven isn't a lottery ticket; a choice to say yes to being a servant of hard work gets one to Paradise one step at a time.*

On a positive note, CC received a doctor's clearance to run this year. If you recall (or even if you don't) (8-19 entry), she placed 21st at State last year. She will be a welcome addition. However, we have a coach's responsibility to realize her back is not "perfectly healthy." Her back X-ray indicates that she is missing some cartilage that she should have. Eventually her back will probably have to be fused – and she will have some pain in her life. Therefore, we will manage her daily efforts accordingly, and we might have to baby her workouts. We want her back to survive another 60 years of life, and running it into the ground over the next nine weeks isn't high on our priority list. However, we do want her time, her work ethic (she puts her nose to the grindstone, and her feet to the ground), and her healthy attitude.

Dostoevsky stated, "Originality and the feeling of one's own dignity are achieved only through work and struggle."

8-22-2007, double sessions

Team mileage today: 117   runners: 19   Avg. per runner: 6.2

The TFalls Blue Hawks had another island romp today. We cleaned up more garbage and aluminum cans, while having a "recovery" and "fun" workout.

Our fun day workout teams were named the Galloping Gatorade Girls (7 girls), the "Industrious Ice Incubators," and the "Hallowed Harrier Hawks."

I originally suggested to Head Coach Naegeli we name our girls the "Hottie Harriers." Sarah has a daughter on the team, so I ran this name by her, coach Naegeli said no. My wife also said, "No. You can't call high school girls that as their teacher and coach." Sarah agreed, so I came up with a silly alliteration of Galloping Gatorade Girls. Later, Sarah asked our girls about the moniker "hottie harriers" – the girls would not have been offended. I want the general public to know that we tried to be politically correct; you are welcome.

By Andrew Gideon

Ice baths need to be emphasized and "Industrious Ice Bathers" does not have the required alliteration – thus, the "Industrious Ice Incubators" were born.

Some runners will be "Hallowed Harrier Hawks" by season's end, so that is appropriate.

It took awhile to set up the island course so our kids could have this relaxed competition; when school starts, these type of "fun" activities just won't happen.

"Industrious Ice Incubators" won today to join last week's "Too Fast for Loyola" as the winning teams on our island recovery days. Lesson learned after 2 weeks – ice baths makes us too fast for Loyola.

Slightly different rules existed today, but the main idea was to find water & PowerAde bottles, as well as "hawks" (I borrowed an ostrich and two other stuffed animals from my kids for the "hawks").

Double sessions were held today, even on a recovery day. At 5:00 pm, four boys (Shane, Jacob, Ryan, and Matt) and three girls (Beca, Delcie, and JP), along with two bikers, ran an easy three miles. We ran from Power Park along the river, through the woods, across the highway, and to the State Park. Once there, we jumped into the water for icing and cool down. RT and Bryant rode their bikes straight down the boat ramp into the H_2O. Entertainment can be cheap, but I warn readers that RT and Bryant are strictly amateurs, so don't try this at home.

Double sessions strengthen our minds and legs. However, doubles are also a sign of leadership and extra commitment. We fed the runners pizza, so they probably lost their amateur status. Actually we found the pizzas fully cooked on the side of the road (yes, good old Montana road kill pizza). The harriers were fortunate to have the dinner because Jacob is on the team and Coach Naegeli loves to see her son eat healthy before he had to go to a student council meeting at 6:30 pm. Other runners just benefited.

This is our last double session day due to school starting.

Thursday, 8-23-2007, Black Hawk Down

Team mileage today: 98   runners: 22   Avg. per runner: 4.5

There was a movie with a release date of 18 January 2002 about a 1993 Black hawk helicopter crash in Somalia. Since the US is fighting in Iraq (160,000 troops), it was an appropriate movie for the theatres to make some money for some enterprising Hollywood types.

www.thetruthseeker.co.uk/article: At a price of $7 million each, the United States has lost at least 27 helicopters in Iraq. What a bargain!

On Monday, 8-20, I discussed the large scale picture as a backdrop to our own silly efforts to move life in a positive, far-reaching direction. An Aldous Huxley quote says, "There's only one corner of the universe you can be certain of improving and that's your own self."

24

How much are our Black Hawk runners worth - surely more than $7 million each!!! PowerAde 99 cents; new running shoes $102; Blue Hawk harriers, priceless (copyright infringement noted). ☺

On Monday, 8-13, a car crash in TFalls killed an 18 year old girl who had just moved into the area from Connecticut. The car was traveling at a high rate of speed in the city and crashed into a tree. Since it was the first day of practice, my thought immediately went to members of our cross country team with hope that none of "our" kids had been injured. I also knew that my wife had taken our two boys for a walk in the stroller, less than a mile from the crash site.

I had been in the *Sanders County Ledger* office (local paper) when pictures of the crash were brought in. Rumors and names could not be confirmed, but speculation, along with pictures, fueled too many thoughts of loved ones. I hoped and prayed it was not "our" or "my" family – but at the same time, was I really praying this could happen to others?

I don't really want to lose any member of my family (wife Deborah, two kids Jaxon and Kaden) or my 2nd family (the cross country team). I came too close last year when Kaden was delivered on the highway three months premature. My wife's life was in danger, along with Kaden's (he spent the first two months of his life in the Neonatal Intensive Care Unit (NICU)).

When death is close, life can seem even more valuable. My boy Kaden struggled to breathe because his brain was not communicating properly with his lungs to breathe.

Transition to cross country – runners fight breathing during hard workouts, during long runs, and while laughing at my humor (TFHS XC – it's an ab workout!). Working on understanding breathing comes at several levels. I appreciate sweet breath after a race is over, and this should carry over to the fact that I appreciate the sweet breath each day of life. Substitute you, my runners, and people for "I" in that last sentence – with the key word "should" in front of appreciate – people should appreciate sweet breath. Every breath is a gift.

Transition from breathing to injuries to today's title, *Black Hawk Down* - we want to push each athlete's limit, yet keep each harrier injury-free. JP missed part Thursday to a turned ankle, but bounced back to do doubles yesterday. We are keeping an eye on many more.

Our most serious current injury is Mariah Naegeli; she did not finish Tuesday's three mile timed run and kept to the bike on Wednesday. The coach's daughter has tried to rehabilitate her knee with exercises for several sport seasons now. It seems to be a chronic problem. With the addition of CC on Tuesday, we have eight girls, but we really can't lose anyone.

Just say NO!!!! to priceless BlueHawks down.

On Thursday evening, Mariah was stung by a bee. That's her 3rd sting of the year, and, sadly, she is allergic. Mom (Coach) had a sting kit handy because we were practicing at her house, 12 miles from TFalls, for a little scenic variety.

By Andrew Gideon

The bees, mostly yellow jackets, have been ferocious during this terribly hot summer. In my family, Jaxon leads with two stings (one today), while Kaden received his first stinger in the calf tonight at home while Dad was goofing off running. My wife and I both have one sting.

Austin K injured himself – on his bike. He braked incorrectly and skinned his elbow, knee, and hand. He is an 8th grader and will miss Friday's practice. Bike riding is a freshman class in TFalls.

BM taped his legs for shin splints and completed only ½ of the workout.

Yes, dear reader, we used the Naegeli ice bath/pool and it was cold after our running tonight. The Blue Hawks had a competitive relay race with each participant running two stints of a long mile. One team won, but I couldn't tell who; really the Hawk Harriers as a unit won with this workout. Each runner also ran two warm-up miles and at least one cool down mile.

John Bennett, age 19, was charged with *"negligent homicide and criminal endangerment in connection with the death of Christina Gomez-Debruyker during a truck-tree crash on August 13...He is being held in the county jail pending arraignment. Bail has been set at $100,000...Gomez-Debruyker, 18 had just moved to the area from Connecticut."* *(8-23 Sanders County Ledger).*

Friday, 8-24-2007, agony vs. glory

Team mileage today:　100　runners: 18　Avg. per runner: 5.6

"We told our guys to hold on for 30 minutes of agony for 12 months of glory." - Coach John McDonnell, after Arkansas won the 1993 NCAA Cross-Country title.

On Thursday and Friday we had teacher meetings. Students report Monday. We must ask the self a question, "self, why must we interrupt something as beautiful as cross country and summer with the agony of school?" If we must do school, then it becomes much better having something like cross country to look forward to and positive kids to end the day with.

So we pace ourselves on the fields and running routes, and we pace ourselves in the classroom as well.

Is school really agony?

For kids who work long farm hours, slave at summer jobs for minimum wage, or hike 4-10 miles per day in the mountains, sitting in a school desk listening to a runner / teacher with too many endorphins on the brain – that's easy. Listening to a teacher and using the brain becomes the way to move life in a positive direction. The agony of school is worth the glory of an insurance-paid future. The agony of a school book is worth the glory of higher paying jobs. The agony of homework is balanced by the glory of hope for a better life.

The agony of a six mile training run is worth the glory of a better time at a State Meet.

The agony of defeat motivates one to forget the agony of de-feet!

The agony of de-feet is very real: blisters, pains, aching arches (despite arch supports), and an occasional split nail with blood for toughness sake. De Hawk-feet are working hard.

Jacob, Shane, and Ryan, and I ran a superb 10 miles in 85 degrees at the Naegeli ranch. This route defines *cross country* – we cut through various property, angled beside ponds, ran on mountain trails, and mostly stayed away from road.

The rest of the team ran for 60 minutes on country dirt roads near the Naegeli ranch. It was a long hot run, but for a Friday evening, it was a good way to end the week. The Naegeli ice pool was appreciated by this coach and runner.

Weekend 8-25, 8-26-2007, Real life heroes, and #1 runners

Ralph Waldo Emerson said, *"A hero is no braver than an ordinary man, but he is braver five minutes longer."*

He obviously wasn't referring to XC athletes. In our case, a hero is no braver than an ordinary man or woman, but he is braver 30 less seconds!

Heroes abound in our society. I had three main heroes as a kid: Jim Rice (baseball, Boston Red Sox), Isiah Thomas (basketball), and Jim Zorn (football quarterback, Seattle Seahawks, (note: named head coach of the Washington Redskins in early 2008)). Later on, Prefontaine (University of Oregon, USA Olympics) and Kenyan runners became people to admire. Kenyan runners include Daniel Komen (current two-mile World Record holder 7:58.61), Paul Tergat (World Records in the 1/2 marathon (59:17) and marathon (2:04:55)) and of course, Gideon Mutisyn (it's all in the name!). Paula Radcliffe has been mentioned as a hero for women's runners: World Records in the ½ marathon (1:05:40) and marathon (2:15:25).

An aside on World Records – Thomas Dold (Germany) holds the mile record for running backwards in 5:46.59. He set that record 7-18-04. Maybe we should have several of our runners try backwards! Go look on the internet for running backwards world records!

Coach Bob stated he ran a backwards ½ mile in 2:48 in high school.

Heroes: Often times the people under our noses are the last we think of. It took me 23 years to realize my mother and father were heroes, 25 years to realize God and the Bible were heroes I needed, and negative nine months to be fascinated with my own children as heroes.

What would a reader think of a coach/teacher having his student-athletes be heroes? Hold yourself down and keep hold of those scissors in a safe manner, because I'm writing it: some heroes in my life are on this cross country team.

This is my 41st season coaching sports. On my resume are the twenty one seasons of basketball (eleven boys, ten girls), seven seasons of track, and ten seasons of baseball; I am also currently in my 3rd year of cross country coaching. Thinking over my coaching career, several teams jump into my brain as truly special: a junior high boy's team (10-0 record) that eventually had four boys

By Andrew Gideon

play for a State AA Championship high school team in Missoula, a 1992 Libby Logger legion baseball team with three amazingly talented eighteen year olds, and this cross country team.

So as part of my hero respect, I am analyzing their characters and putting down personalities in a lasting form.

Our #1 runners are Shane Donaldson and Beca Gunderson.

Shane is a diminutive runner who thought he might be a sprinter in junior high. Coach Naegeli corralled him into the correct stall of long distance running, and Shane has even branched out to run four half-marathons, including a 1 hour 22 minute, 4th place finish, at the Missoula Half-Marathon on July 15, 2007.

Shane's current best times are 4:41 (1600 meters), 10:12 (3200m), and 15:57 (three miles). His goals for this year include breaking 15:30 (cross country) and 10:00 (8 dizzying track laps). He wants to win the State Meet for XC this season (he missed last year by one second, leading the race the entire way, only to be passed by a longer legged runner in the final 75 meters).

With a 3.89 GPA (4.0 scale), one can see that his brain works well in a school environment. Shane's favorite class is English, while his favorite teacher is Doug Padden. Bob Reall claims the spot as the top coach in Shane's life, which is a good fit to his favorite sport to participate in of cross country.

His parents (Bruce and Laura) both graduated high school in Arkansas and somehow found their way to Thompson Falls so Shane could be one of my heroes. Shane's three siblings are showing strength in the school department as well – Stephen will graduate from Montana Tech in Butte, MT, soon; Matthew, 19, will start his second year at the University of Montana – Western – (Dillon, MT) in an attempt to be a teacher; and Aimee is a TFHS freshman.

Shane is a reader, which (hint hint parents) is a help to his ACT and SAT scores. His favorite books are the Redwall series. His reading ability, high GPA, and effort running illustrate that he is well-grounded. If he won $100,000,000, he would commit the money for tithes and offerings, a rubber track for TFHS, savings accounts and stocks, as well as a much deserved cruise and/or vacation.

Shane lists teaching and coaching as possibilities. Potential schools: U of Missoula, U of M – Western where his brother Matthew attends, Pacific, or even back to his parent's roots at the U of Arkansas.

His birth date of 3-30-90 shows an expected math ability. Shane Gregory Donaldson will use his blessings in the direction of college, living in a small town, and maybe even farming or ranching, as long as horses are involved.

His 5'6" size and 123 weight don't show it, but this kid can eat. At a Top Ten 2007 track meet, he annihilated the pound burger much quicker than the javelin thrower and pole vaulter. Shane's eating life shouldn't be ruined by knowing his metabolism might change in the future. He can continue to eat the way he does and stay small – as long as he starts running ultra marathons and triathlons by the age of 30. CC offers that *"when Shane eats lunch at school, it is probably the absolute grossest thing ever. He totally shoves food in his mouth."*

28

This theme is continued by Mariah: Shane *"eats a ton."* Jacob states Shane's nickname: *"Grease Bucket."* I can only conclude this is food related.

Delcie writes that *"this kid is a complete bottomless pit when it comes to food. Where does he put it all? It's gotta be scientifically impossible to put such a large amount into such a small body. I don't know how he does it! Obviously everything he eats is burned off to fuel his amazing running skills. Seriously, it wouldn't surprise me if he won State this fall."*

Monica's paper was too small, and ran out of ink several times writing about Shane. Here is some of her writing, *"Everyone probably recalls Shane as a 'porker,' not as in fat, but as 'you ate that whole chicken, and polished off the doughnuts?' Shane still astonishes me by the millions of pounds he eats, how little he stays, and how fast he is. I will always remember the bus rides when he jams out to his music and sings to himself! He is a great kid and an inspiration."*

Awe-inspiring proof exists that Shane knows how/when to carbo load.

Delcie adds something not related to food, *"Another good thing about Shane is he's never afraid to be himself!"*

Mariah says, Kids, stay off the sidewalks when Shane drives.

Shane is part of the crew that plays X-box & Halo. Bryant, Matt, RT, Jacob, and Ryan are also part of this Microsoft research project.

Mr. Gideon recalls running with Shane over the past three years. In 2005, Shane, Jacob, and Derek Naegeli (Jacob's brother, graduated TFHS in June 2006 and currently attending Pacific University) ran side-by-side. Last year, Shane made a move and commitment to being a front runner. In every day runs, he continually pushed the pace. This certainly improved his VO^2 max and was a sign that he wanted to lead and win; he gave his all. Looking back, I can see that his decision to push to the front has made a difference in his life and his running.

My favorite thing about Shane is his leg turnover. Shane is probably built for longer races as his leg turnover is tops on the team. He will push 190 plus (steps/minute) and he has leg turnover to make the Tasmanian Devil jealous.

I admire Shane for effort on and off the field – is he perfect – no – but he is a hero to me. I look forward to witnessing his success in the next 5-20 years.

Beca's words are good to end Shane's entry with: *"Shane is truly an inspiration to me. I think he has come a long way in his running and his character. He is a great friend and supportive of me & my running, always telling me how good he thinks I am or could be. He pushes me to do the best I can, and I really appreciate that."*

Beca Gunderson looks to follow in her father's footsteps – even if they wear different size shoes. Beca's father, Douglas Kirk Gunderson, put up some impressive State Track finishes "back in the day." Here's his list – two firsts (440 in 1974 and 880 in 1975), one second (440, 1975), one third (440 relay, 1975), two fourths (220, 1975 and mile relay, 1975), and one fifth (880 relay, 1974). He is also listed on the 1974 State Championship football trophy.

By Andrew Gideon

Beca has big shoes to fill (lame pun again), but goals such as breaking the 1600 meter school record (currently 5:29.34) show that her heart has thoughts of notoriety. Beca's best 1600 time is 5:39. However, she doesn't desire fame – conquering obstacles is the name of the game.

Her best 3200 is 12:48, while her best 3 mile XC time is 20:47. Beca, real name Rebeca Leigh Gunderson, is a weird duck. Most runners prefer cross country – she thinks running in circles on a track is more fun and challenging. This doesn't stop her from having a goal to beat 20:00 in a XC meet by her junior year and place in the top 10 in 07.

Rebeca's mother is Connie Dee Gunderson. Connie is proud to have such a goal oriented daughter. Beca's future possibilities include work in Physical Science, Engineering, and doing something positive for others. She would do this at Montana State University (Bozeman), Eastern Oregon U, or another smart college that would eventually add her to the graduated Dean's list.

Goals, goals, goals – it even filters into her advice for younger students and future runners. Here is her advice in list form:
set goals (reasonable but hard)
keep an open mind about how well you could do - you could surprise yourself.
Keep up with homework
Don't procrastinate on projects
Be friendly to everyone, and,
Most importantly, listen to your coaches; they know what they are talking about.

Beca's parents both graduated from TFHS. Our #1 runner will surely do the same, as well as her brother John. John is 12 years old, is a 7th grader, and competes on our cross country team.

If she were to win $100,000,000, she would buy the school a nice rubber track, just like Shane! Beca would also use her money for donations – to her parents for all land and vehicle payments, to the local 4-H clubs, and to herself for a nice new blue sports car. She would also help the wrestling team get a new room – which would keep them out of the gym so winter basketball practice could get over by 7:30 pm instead of 9:30. Beca is rational enough to realize that savings in a bank would be a smart use of her money as well.

Rebeca, born 1-20-1992, is an Aquarius, and she has a 4.0 GPA.

My vision of Beca always includes efficient form – her body moves smoothly. Her stride when she gets the baton in the 1600 relay is a beautiful thing to watch. Unfortunately, her turnover fades slightly on the back stretch – yet with strength and training, she should be the easiest chess piece to turn into a successful running machine.

Mariah writes, *"an over-achiever (just kidding), she broke her leg in third grade playing soccer, and she seems to be at my house a lot."*

Delcie adds comments on Beca's character and history, *"I've known this girl since I was little. Together we caught frogs and made fairy houses for hours while camping at Fishtrap Lake. From the beginning, Beca would always tire me out with all her running from place to place, while I tried (in vain) to keep up with her. I guess that will never change! We've drooled over cute Amish guys together, and I'm sure there will be plenty more good times in the future!"*

Monica writes, *"Becerrelli – 'Are you ready to run?' Beca– Meca– Shmeca–Deca–Leca...is one of my best friends, and is a great runner! All of the great memories of X-C with her will always make me laugh. Meeting Chip our first year...what a classic! Love ya girl!"*

Lest we think Beca, aka Super-Runner, is perfect, CC adds a final ominous warning, *"...super super grumpy @ night. DO NOT TOUCH HER WHEN SHE IS SLEEPING!"*

I dub her Beca the Kenyan.

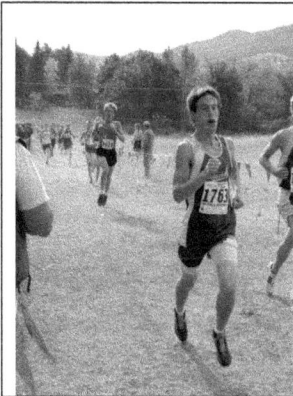

Shane Donaldson at Mtn. West 07   Beca Gunderson's Mtn. West Focus 07

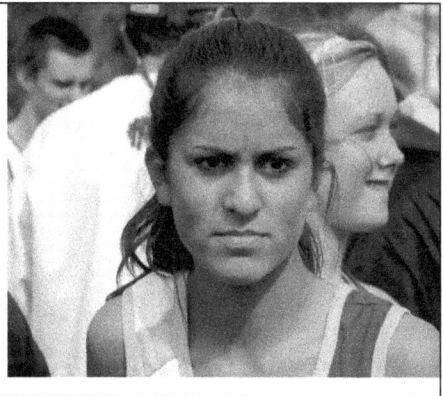

8-27-2007, Blue Monday (subtitled Monica hates pushup)

Team mileage today: 144   runners: 22   Avg. per runner: 6.5

Blue Monday – school started, and the runner's schedule has changed. Hopefully the change will be for the better in the long run (pun intended).

Students now attend classes 8:20-3:15 with a lunch from 11:45-12:20. Running occurs after school now (3:30-5:30) – yet another change from the 7:30 am, 5:00 pm, or 7:00 pm practice times we held the previous two weeks. This new schedule alters brain and stomach patterns. We are back to day one (8-13) and realize we are training the brain again. Each new change forces fine-tuning in thinking, feeling, and living patterns. With the strong student-athletes that we have, I have no fear that adjustments will be made in a positive direction.

When I ran today, eight miles total, I felt heavy and full – not to mention hot. Running at 3:30 is definitely different on the body patterns than running at 7:30 am. The temperature is different (heat); the body has different warmth on the inside also. Adjusting to every small change in life is actually solid preparation for adjusting to large changes in life.

"The journey of 1000 miles begins with one step." (Lao Tzu).

We need to make small step adjustments to our daily rhythms.

By Andrew Gideon

Monica stated today that she will not do another pushup after she graduates high school – unless she is forced. We cruel coaches at TFHS believe that pushups, sit-ups, crunches, and scissor kicks are chicken soup for the XC soul. A stronger core is required for running success. However, Monica smiles when she states that she hates pushups.

She also added, in completely random fashion, that Cindy is a nice name.

This is our Monica – who ran 7 miles today! Her Achilles injury from 2006 is so far so good, and she will be able to compete in our first race on Friday. Last year she hurt her Achilles during the second week of the season and was only able to run in the last three races in 2006.

We are thankful for her randomness, her push-up hating, and her health.

Subtotals exist for running mileage during the first two weeks. Please feel free to predict how these individuals will do at the State Meet in 54 days. Two week mileage totals are listed first, while summer mileage is listed in (parenthesis). These totals are updated through Sunday, August 26, 2007.

2007 Running Mileage   *The season started Monday, August 13, 2007.*

Girls	Rank	Boys
Delcie Peters (jr) 82 1st 2 weeks (124)	1	Jacob Naegeli (sr) 100 (205 summer)
Jeffreyanne Parker (so) 64 (15)	2	Shane Donaldson (sr) 100 (227)
Beca Gunderson (so) 62 (181)	3	Ryan Sol (sr) 99 (223)
Monica Conlin (so) 61 (130)	4	Matt Hojem (sr) 72 (70)
Lacey Wade (so) 58 (50)	5	RT Brown (sr) 72 (100ish)
Mariah Naegeli (fr) 44 (39)	6	Kyle Breithaupt (so) 62 (50)
Amanda Wood (sr) 39 (no idea)	7	Bryant Normandeau (sr) 61 (< 1 million)
CC Normandeau (jr) 22 (approx. 50)	8	Mike Morris (sr) 50 (0, hiking)
	9	Mike Barnett (so) 44 (ummmm…)
Coach Naegeli (age range 39-44) 3 (5)	10	Mike Kidwiler (jr) 38 (0, hiking)
	11	Bryce Miller (fr) 37 (0, hiking)
Coach Gideon (age 39) 126.5 (455)	12	Patrick Jamison (jr) 27 (16)
Coach Reall (age 69) 64 (180)	13	Cody White (so) 0 (77)

Tuesday, 8-28-2007, another Paper Article…and another

Team mileage today: 133   runners: 23   Avg. per runner: 5.8

Again, I have been enlisted by the *Sanders County Ledger*, to write the XC articles for the local paper. This piece felt like my 3rd preview article of the year. Next week, thankfully, I will be able to report times; we have our first meet on Friday, 8-31, in Libby, Montana.

Enjoy today's sermon!

The Weakest Link   *by Andrew Gideon*

There is an expression in the "real world" that things are only as strong as the weakest link. This can be applied in business, fencing, internet security, and cross country. If the "weakest" or "lowest" workers in a business steal, are lazy, or cause trouble, then the business will not be as successful as possible. If a fence has a hole or a weak link, then the fencing can fall apart or be broken into much easier. The internet – invented by Al Gore – needs virus scans, Spam killer, and firewalls to protect against weakness and work more effectively.

A reader may be asking how the phrase that a team is only as strong as its weakest link applies to cross country. Thank you for inquiring!

Last year at the State B Boy's Meet in Helena, Shane Donaldson (2), Jacob Naegeli (3), and Ryan Sol (17) ran the competition into the ground. The 22 points combined for those three harriers was better than any other school. However, cross country at the class B level scores a team's top five runners, with the sixth place member used as a tie breaker. The terrific trio was followed by Blue Hawk harriers Matt Hojem (50th), Mike Kidwiler (56th), and Bryant Normandeau (63rd). So, even though these three members ran the fastest race of their life, they were the "weakest links" and dropped Thompson Falls to a fourth place finish.

The team is working hard to shore up that scoring for the 2007 season. The six aforementioned runners return. They are joined by seniors Mike Morris and RT Brown, junior Patrick Jamison, sophomores Kyle Breithaupt, Mike Barnett and Cody White, and freshman Bryce Miller. The mileage totals this year indicate that hard work is being performed. The following are totals for the first two weeks of practice: Shane (100), Jacob (100), Ryan (99), Matt (72), RT (72), Kyle (62), Bryant (61), Mike M (50), Mike B (44), Mike K (38), Bryce M (37), and Patrick (27). The question of who will step up to the #4, #5, and #6 spot to complete the team scoring with Shane, Jacob, and Ryan will be the thorn in the team's side. For the season to bloom in full fashion, it needs to be answered in a positive manner.

The Thompson Falls girls are in the same predicament. To improve from 6th place as a team last year, the weakest runners need to improve as much or more than the top scorers. The girls have put in a lot of running as well with the following totals after two weeks: Delcie Peters (82), Jeffreyanne Parker (64), Beca Gunderson(62), Monica Conlin (61), Lacey Wade (58), Mariah Naegeli (44), Amanda Wood (39), and last, but certainly not least, CC Normandeau (22).

The nice thing about cross country is that each individual has to "gut it out" and perform on their own. However, with the team scoring rules, it is very wise indeed to be supportive of teammates, because the overall finish depends on more than one. The strong help pick up the weak, while the "weak" determine the total team fate.

Thompson Falls opens its season August 31 in Libby. Five members of the team will miss the meet due to involvement in 4-H and working at the Sanders County fair. This will obviously hurt the team scoring, but it will be a nice first race for those individuals able to race.

Another team in the Division, coached by my brother Steve Gideon, currently has eight high school athletes participating (4 boys, 4 girls). Plains has eight (5 boys, 3 girls). Therefore, we should feel great about the 21 athletes that we have out – great effort and participation from schools in the same classification.

I also wrote an article on our county rivals.

Plains Cross Country   *by Andrew Gideon*

Plains cross country will open the season August 31 in Libby. The team will be taking five high school boys, two high school girls, and seven junior high students. One other high school girl will be involved with 4-H in the Sanders County fair and will not compete this week. Coach Barb Steward is also hoping that another runner or three will come out for the team after the first day of school on Monday, August 27.

Having a full team of five is important for scoring purposes at State. Therefore Coach Steward says that the team is "focusing on staying healthy, putting in miles, and running hills for strength." Her main goal for the boys is to maintain health as a young team so that the team can compete well at State in Helena on October 20.

Results from the first meet for Plains will appear in next week's issue.

The Ledger (specifically John Hamilton, sports editor) felt that my first article (*The Weakest Link)* might "alienate" some athletes or parents because of the words "weakest link." I would not have trouble with it as a parent or a coach – but in this case, I took John's constructive criticism with a grain of salt and a drop of Tabasco sauce – and changed.

Kids can be great people, they can be great students, but in competition and comparison, even though we love you, you may not be as strong as the competition. Hello, this is a very cutthroat world! Therefore, in this respect, "the weakest link" fits. It doesn't mean love or respect for great efforts doesn't exist.

In the world of Thompson Falls, 1-14 in rank is determined on the running field. Throw that 1-14 in with the State of Montana and all the Class B runners, and our harriers do not remain 1-14 in the State rank! Again, this is not a lack of respect, it is the reality of competition.

So, my words were edited to be more "politically correct."

Thompson Falls Cross Country   *by Andrew Gideon*

Last year at the State B Boy's Meet in Helena, Shane Donaldson (2nd), Jacob Naegeli (3rd), and Ryan Sol (17th) ran the competition into the ground. The 22 points combined for those three harriers was better than any other school.

However, cross country at the class B level scores a team's top five runners, with the sixth place member used as a tie breaker. The terrific trio was followed by Blue Hawk harriers running the fastest races of their life: Matt Hojem (50th in 18:26), Mike Kidwiler (56th in 18:32), and Bryant Normandeau (63rd in 18:41). Champion Missoula Loyola, Colstrip, and Poplar all had four, five, and six runners place better. The final team scores were Loyola 93, Colstrip 97, Poplar 99, and Thompson Falls 128.

The Thompson Falls harriers have been running hard to shore up their #4, #5, and #6 scorers, and the mileage totals this year are evidence of that. The following are totals for the first two weeks of practice: Shane (100 miles), Jacob (100), Ryan (99), Matt (72), RT Brown (72), Kyle Breithaupt (62), Bryant (61), Mike Morris (50), Mike Barnett (44), Mike Kidwiler (38), Bryce Miller (37), and Patrick Jamison (27).

The question of who will step up to the #4, #5, and #6 spot to complete the team scoring with Shane, Jacob, and Ryan this year is exciting to watch. I am a coach writing this article and the competition within the team is fun to watch. There is a lot of respect and support for all of the runners on the team – from top to bottom.

The Thompson Falls girls look to improve from 6th place as a team last year. The girls have been putting in a lot of running as well to make that happen this year with the following totals after two weeks: Delcie Peters (82), Jeffreyanne Parker (64), Beca Gunderson(62), Monica Conlin (61), Lacey Wade (58), Mariah Naegeli (44), Amanda Wood (39), and last, but certainly not least, CC Normandeau (22).

The nice thing about cross country is that each individual has to "gut it out" and perform on their own. However, with the team scoring rules, it is very wise indeed to be supportive of teammates, because the overall finish depends on more than one.

Thompson Falls opens its season August 31 in Libby. Five members of the team will miss the meet due to involvement in 4-H and working at the Sanders County fair. This will obviously hurt the team scoring, but it will be a nice first race for those individuals able to race.

Is the article better the 2nd time? Is being politically correct the way to live life? Are rhetorical questions not worth answering?

Wednesday, 8-29-2007, 3 coaches and first results

Team mileage today: 97   runners: 18   Avg. per runner: 5.4

Three coaches exist for our Thompson Falls cross country team. Sarah Naegeli was the assistant in 1998 and has been the head coach 1999-present. Bob Reall has coached cross country for at least 35 years (Ohio), but hasn't been paid in his ten year TFHS XC coaching career. This author has run eight marathons, coached distance runners in track for five years at Seeley-Swan High School in Seeley Lake, MT, and coached XC in Thompson Falls for three years.

All three are quality coaches. All three have varied ideas and levels of workouts that are the "right" and "correct" way to practice each day, week, and season. For today, Coach Reall wants the top runners to go 7-9 miles, Coach Naegeli wants a relaxed 4-6 miles with some contest involved, and Coach Gideon wants the team to run 5-7 with rest breaks and a silly competition.

35

By Andrew Gideon

Can all three be correct - How will the choice be made - What is the ONLY right answer? Can you say, "too many cooks spoil the broth?" Don't look at me – I'm only writing down the recipe!

At the end of the day, some choice will have been made. The goals for all three coaches by the end of the year are the same: health, trophy, individual and team success, and, obviously, fame and glory.

Today's formula: the Hawk harriers ran between 6-9 miles on yet another 95 degree day. We didn't have a contest or competition.

Coach Naegeli is the master chef, sees the overall plan, and balances a running equation for each Hawk's health, strength, speed, and rest. She does an amazing job; I write this altruistically, hoping for a positive evaluation.

The last three days were HOT HOT HOT. Ouch for runners.

Coach Bob Reall   Mariah, Coach Sarah, and Jacob Naegeli

First results of cross country meets are in. At least two meets have been posted to the Montana Cross Country website (www.montanacrosscountry.com).

Again, there are four classifications in Montana: AA (largest), A, B, and C (smallest). AA has 15 schools, A 24, B 46, and C 98 (www.mhsa.org).

Several schools have already participated in two meets. Some schools have a more centralized location and don't have far to travel to attend meets; Thompson Falls is out in the sticks in more than one way and has a long way to travel – therefore, we cut out several meets for travel reasons to have quality workouts at home.

Here are some early times by Class B boys we are competing against. I give initials and the school: From an 8/28 Fairmont meet: DL Deer Lodge 17:49, JT Boulder 17:57, LS Whitehall 19:12. From an 8/25 meet in Boulder: CL Townsend 18:05, LS Whitehall 18:08, KS Manhattan Christian 18:16.

LS from Whitehall was named in both of those meets with times ranging from 18:08 to 19:12. It is tough to gauge anything from that because of 1 minute, 4 second difference – were the courses a full 3 miles – did one course have a ton of hills – was one course slippery and wet – did smoky skies exist in one city –

those are all questions that can't be answered just by judging times. However, we will keep track of each competitor as the season progresses.

We shall now compare to get a rough rough estimate. TFHS XC Hawk Harriers ran a timed four mile yesterday. So, each athlete ran 1 more mile hard than an actual race and our times for the boys compare quite favorably. These are all 3 mile times (first three miles) from our practice yesterday: Shane 16:02, Jacob 16:13, Ryan 17:20, Mike M 17:07, RT 17:55, Mike K 18:00, and Patrick 18:05. Wow! I didn't even mention two of our top six from last year who haven't worked into shape yet: Matt 19:15 and Bryant 20:11. Wow again, excitement – let's keep running, and let's see some times from some more teams.

Here are some early times from Class B girls (our competition). These times are from the 8/28 Fairmont meet: CP Whitehall 20:55 (2nd last year at State in 19:11), BJ Boulder 21:34, WG Boulder 21:57, RH Whitehall 23:12, KG Whitehall 23:16, and CW Whitehall 23:17. From the 8/25 meet in Boulder we have BJ Boulder 20:06, WG Boulder 20:17, KG Whitehall 21:10.

Again, these times had huge time swings: BJ ran 21:34 and 20:06, 1 min. 28 sec difference. KG ran 2:16 faster in the Boulder meet. Based on these two meets, I would definitely say that the Boulder course is slightly shorter or faster than the Fairmont course.

Our girls did the same as the boys yesterday – a hard 4 mile timing. The three mile split from that read Delcie 21:49, Jeffreyanne 23:04, Mariah 23:23, and CC 23:40. Okay to start, let's get on those courses and compete!

Thursday, 8-30-2007, not enough character analysis
Team mileage today: 128   runners: 23   Avg. per runner: 5.6

A weakness in my writing may be character analysis. How do I bring these kids, students, and athletes into a reader's brain and life? These Hawk Harriers are not static – they are dynamic. They lived, breathed, and struggled through three straight 95 degree practices. Our runners have sweated thoughts, had millions of feelings, and started another school year.

RT: He was probably 6' 4" tall on the first day of school with his bushy hair sticking straight up and out. RT is a class representative and looked like a wild man. Tuesday he came to school 6 inches shorter with a shaved head; his senior hair falling victim to his own razor. He has a nice quarter / half-dollar sized blister on his heel, so his workout today was barefoot running on a small 1/5 mile loop around the softball field.

Monica: She struggled severely on Monday and Tuesday's hot workouts, yet still managed to finish despite throwing up Monday on a 7 mile run, and wilting through Tuesday's timed four miles. On Wednesday, we (the coaches) wanted her to do an extremely easy workout on soft grass, yet she volunteered to run more. She lost a toenail; we were watching for a toenail on the other foot when a new volunteer shed its snaky enamel.

By Andrew Gideon

Beca: She missed three days last week driving to Oregon to attend a grandmother's funeral. Beca will miss Tuesday – Sunday this week due to 4-H and the fair (she will run on her own). In July she was only home for about five days because of a leadership conference in California and more 4-H in Bozeman. Yet I will go out on a limb and say she will maintain incredible potency to accomplish her running goals and continue her 4.0 GPA.

Mike B: He comes every day and works hard as a sophomore harrier. Mike rides the bike occasionally to take pressure off of his knees, but each day I watch him, he seems to get slightly more confident and is willing to push a little harder. (Next day – Mike would finish our first Libby meet with a bloody sock and big toe, losing half of a toe nail in the process.)

Matt had hip surgery as a child (right hip at ages 1 and 3), one leg is shorter than another (left), and not a day goes by where there is not some pain involved. His leg went dead on Monday. His knees take turns deciding which one will hurt worse. Ankles and shins beg to join the pain game also. Yet Matt works hard to improve himself and the team each day; he rarely complains.

Kyle: It is hard not to notice 6'3" Kyle, yet it is easy because he is so quiet. His strength between this year and last year is noticeable to the coaches. He does remain under the radar because his times do not meet with the incredible seniors we have this year. It will be interesting to see Kyle dig to improve times.

Cody: He just arrived back from summer vacation on Saturday. He ran on his own in Arkansas and gave two mile times as 19:13 (2 weeks ago), 16:44 (1 week ago), and 14:41 on Tuesday. He was literally willing to go the extra mile with Coach Gideon, MK, and Patrick on a cool down Tuesday – making a seven mile day his career long.

CC should not even be out for XC due to a bad back and having the threat of fusing two vertebrae together in her later life. After one week of working at Ace Hardware and missing her teammates and practice, she couldn't drop the sport. Her family received a doctor's okay, and we welcome her to the team. It is hard for coaches not to turn down a "*warrior*" (Coach Reall), but we do want CC healthy for life. We will have a different work structure set up for her. She went to school Tuesday, worked three hours at Ace, and came in with Coach Gideon for an extra practice at 6:15 pm – timing her three miles in 23:40.

A reader may wonder why I am spending hours typing a book on this team/season. It is because our Harrier Hawks are willing to go the extra mile and live life with the prospect that hard work will pay off in the future – with better times, better team results, or maybe better health. These student-athletes have personality, spunk, and character. Our society, our world, needs these people. I would love to bring them into your brain and life; we all need family like this.

Our Hawk Harriers are teenagers who struggle (and mostly succeed) with school, feelings, family, thoughts, and work (athletics). Yet, in 5-10-15 years I have no doubt that they will be thriving well in this big bad world. I look forward to their races this season, and their races in life.

8-31-2007, Friday, First Meet

On a first meet, other than injury, any result is a good starting point – especially if the Blue Hawks work hard. We (the coaches) pushed our harriers through tough workouts during the week – every day. 95 degree heat flamed their bodies Monday through Wednesday - after first days of school. (And we all know the mental strain that causes! Bulging eyes, migraines, and new excuses) Thursday morning was a long run. For the first meet, we wanted our runners to drive through the pain. We did not make life easy for them with our coaching (in the short term). Our strategy and focus is for better results later on (State), so an easy day Wednesday and a non-existent Thursday may have resulted in fresh legs, but for the long term, that would not do!

Yet, the Blue Hawks flew strong after a tough week and a meet in 90 degree plus heat.

Speaking as a runner myself, I ran 39 miles Monday-Thursday and would not have wanted to race today. The T Falls Hawk Harriers responded well with an impressive start.

The Blue Hawks and county rivals Plains arrived together for the Libby meet at 10:15. A cooler morning with good cloud cover greeted those who stepped off the bus after a 90 minute trip. A new course turned out to be mostly asphalt; a good route for an adult road race, but for high school runners who want to wear spikes and are used to grass…time to adjust and pound those shins!

Our course walk through took 45 minutes for the three miles. Overall it is a pretty course with a bridge over the Kootenai River and a trail through a wild bird sanctuary. However, Monica did become slightly dizzy (Monica slightly dizzy – is this possible?) running over the bridge, and Coach Gideon had to run like the mad man he is to get to the mile mark for times. It is not really a fan friendly course, but for a first race, running on hot coals or a mine field should make our Kenyan Hawks happy. The Harrier Hawks did not race with scissors.

Cody and Patrick did not have enough practices to compete, so we had them run the three mile course as a practice. *"What a great idea coach,"* surely coursed through their brains.

Austin K was our lone junior high runner. His race started at 12:30, and Austin completed the 1.62 mile meet in 12:24.

Mike M, in his first year with us, needed his scissors to cut the tape and win the JV boys meet in 18:14. His time in last year's state meet would have saved us 9 points – already closing the gap from first place (first place scored 93, we had 128. Mike's time would have lowered our score to 119). It might not sound like much, but to me, "one small step for a man, one giant leap for mankind." (Thank you Neil Armstrong!) If you could see my smile as I type this, you would know the significance of this time: It's HUGE.

Bryce, a freshman in his first meet, ran 19:41. Looking at this number compared to last year, Matt ran 21:19 at Libby in 2006 (1st meet) and improved to 18:26 for State. MK also made a huge jump in 2006 from start to finish (19:42

By Andrew Gideon

to 18:42). Bryce's 19:41 ➔ Our future is so bright, I've got to wear shades (thank you 80's song lyric).

Today, Kyle ran 21:38 and Mike B pushed to a 25:24 with a bloody toenail (reminiscent of Curt Schilling for the Boston Red Sox in the 2004 baseball playoffs).

Amanda struggled at the 2 mile mark, but figured out a way to have a faster third mile than second mile (11:06 mile 2, 10:24 mile 3) and finished with a 30:35 in her first race. I am very happy she is out for the team – and she beat five other girls too!

I'm sorry to go off topic here, but this is interesting. I am typing at school (9:30 am Sunday) with the door open. Two birds flew into my room, turned and slammed into windows. One is staring out the window like a high school prisoner in the classroom. I am pretty sure the other one is injured badly as his body is twitching. I will go pick him up gently and set him outside – no, I am not giving a bird CPR.

The verdict: broken wing = cat food. I set the bird outside. It took several minutes to corral the other one – he is okay. My thoughts consist of why there are no bird or mice flavored cat foods.

Back to serious running business….and the Varsity boys race.

Thirteen teams fielded athletes in this race, including Flathead (AA team with 2537 students in their Nov 2006 enrollment – this is now split between Flathead and Glacier (the new school)), Glacier, Whitefish (with 705 enrollment), host Libby (565), and two Idaho schools.

At 2:22 pm. MST and four hours into the sunny, now 85 degree plus day, Shane burst out of the gates into his customary first place position. He would eventually finish second in this race in 16:09 (16:43 in first race last year) and beat a competitor from Polson for the first time in five years. Logan (Polson rival) had bested Shane in track, cross country, and road races for five years. Today, Shane had the better time by twelve seconds. That's got to feel good.

A thought related to Shane's beating Logan: I had a life goal to qualify for the Boston Marathon. In 1993, I was 25 and ran my first 26.214 mile race in 3:14:48. However, I needed 3:10 to qualify for the prestigious Boston Marathon. So, I "failed" in May of 1993 – and November of 1994 (Seattle Marathon 3:12:38) – and January 1995 (Tacoma Marathon 3:46). Then I didn't try again until May of 1998, five years after my first attempt. I still needed a 3:10 to qualify, and this time, my 3 hour, 8 minute, 38 second time indicated "success."

Similarities: It took Shane five years to beat Logan – it took me five years to beat a qualifying standard. Both of us ran a lot of miles and experienced "failure" in one respect. In a more important respect, we had health to run, we beat a lot of other people (including everyone who didn't try), and we worked our tails off. And yes, we were "successful."

This should give hope to the Harrier Hawks that goals and times can be obtained. It should also send a message that perseverance leads to positive results and breakthroughs.

Today, Shane, our fearless leader, was followed by Ryan (17:59), MK (18:41), RT (19:22), and Matt (19:46). RT was kept out of double sessions and used a bike for occasional training during the first two weeks of practice to help prevent the week 3 injuries he sustained the previous two years. Between mile one (in 6:09) and mile two (in 6:32), his stride changed. His third mile was 6:41, and he was icing his hip at the end of the day. Ice bath and RT, please make acquaintances, I am sure you will be need to be life-long friends.

The varsity boys lost only to Flathead (AA), Glacier (AA), and Whitefish (A). Flathead (aka Kalispell) has won 7 of the last 9 AA titles! They are the standard for Montana boys cross country – soon to be replaced by Thompson Falls. Please remember, we had two boys with not enough practices, and two boys at the Sanders County Fair (including our #2 runner Jacob).

The varsity girls started in 90 degree heat roughly 4 ½ hours after getting off the bus. Delcie would later say that she felt hot, "sticky and a little more tired than usual" before a race.

Dear reader, drift back to day one and "train the brain." Delcie, Mike M, and Ryan received a post race "lecture" on training the brain to pace the body through the long wait before a race. It is tough to sit, stand, walk, talk, laugh, and warm-up properly for 4-5 hours before a race and be primed for a peak performance. As each meet goes by, the brain and body will slowly adapt to the time schedule. This will be important as the boys B state contest will be the 6th race of the day on October 20th, while the girls will be the 8th and final event.

Taking a long hot day into consideration with a brutal week of practice, our runners did a great job of working hard after a tough week.

The varsity girls: Delcie was our top girl in 32nd place in 22:36. This discouraged her to the point of asking if our practice mile loop was short since she ran 21:49 on Tuesday. She was reminded about the brutality of our workouts during the week, the 4.5 hour wait in sunshine before her race, and the phrase, "stay positive." She did great. Monica ran 24:52 and mentioned becoming disoriented running across the 100 meter bridge twice during the race. Combined with the heat, this is a condition coaches keep an eye on. Lacey was our third and final girl in this race with a 26:11. Lacey ran 26:50 in her first race last year.

We missed four 4-H girls at the County Fair, including #1 runner Beca.

We waited 45 minutes after the race for results. Our TFalls runners sat in the Libby Rosauer's parking lot as the store's power went out due to a storm; we waited, bonding like gorilla glue. Okay, I'm not sure we bonded, but it sure sounds like that means our team is coming together, showing respect for each other, and becoming a group that is stronger than the sum of each individual. Don't step in that fun, deep, and psychologically complex sentence!

By Andrew Gideon

Our bus stopped at approximately mile marker 19 between Libby and Troy due to a downed Power Line. At least eight Spruce trees littered the road from a storm that dumped .44 inches of rain in less than a half hour – the first significant rain in that area since June. The power line helped us enjoy each other's company for another 45 minutes. Either that or we became grouchy because we were getting home later!

Our day, like this sentence – load the bus at 8:30 am (Plains left at 8:00) – get home at 7:15 pm (Plains by 8:00 pm) – run 5 separate races – and exhaustion from a tough first week of school – was long. TGIF.

Just to be fair that other sports exist at TFHS, lesser sports of course, it can be reported that the football team won 35-6 today. The gridiron game began at 7 pm, so when our bus arrived at 7:15, our team was already ahead 7-0. The game was cut short because the same storm we had in Libby knocked out the field lights at the end of the 3rd quarter.

The storm was exciting to watch – lightning, etc.

It must be reported that the football team is a "revenue" sport. Therefore, if cuts have to be made, then cross country, a sport that doesn't bring in much money, would be the first to go. Yeah, cut the sport that stresses and maintains high standards for GPA, the future leaders of our country, and the finest students to walk the halls. That's all I will say on this topic (for now).

September, a new month is upon us, 9-1-07

A new day, a new month, a new start – the possibilities at the start of this month gives us hope. A Bob Feller quote fits here: *"Every day is a new opportunity. You can build on yesterday's success or put its failures behind and start over again. That's the way life is, with a new game every day, and that's the way baseball is."* This month continues our hope for each individual and our team for a successful season.

Thompson Falls Cross Country - Top 11 List

	Girls	Boys
1	**20:13 Kellyn Gross (2000)**	**15:51 Adam Oswald (2001)**
2	20:18 Holly Conlin (2001)	15:57 Shane Donaldson (2006)
3	20:28 Ciara Normandeau (2005)	16:12 Nathan Block (2001)
4	20:47 Beca Gunderson (2006)	16:14 Spencer Bird (2001)
5	20:51 Dwy Simpson (2002)	16:20 Derek Naegeli (2003)
6	20:57 Delcie Peters (2005)	16:37 Jacob Naegeli (2005, 2006)
7	20:58 Sara Merriman (2002)	16:53 Stryker Clark (2002)
8	21:35 Jamie Kuzma (2000)	17:15 Ryan Sol (2006)
9	21:43 Erica Soderlind (1998)	17:27 Seth Lambrecht (2001)
10	21:52 Leah Clark (2000)	17:34 Phil Culbertson (2001)
11	21:54 Monica Conlin (2006)	17:36 Luke Chambers (2000)

With that in mind, I decided to enter some information from our school's website: www.thompsonfalls.net. We hope the top 11 can add new runners and improve the current athletes on the list now. We currently have seven runners active on this list (highlighted in school colors – unless of course, this is copied in black and white). CC, Beca, Delcie, Monica, Shane, Jacob, and Ryan – I hope and pray you can move up this list this year!

The All-State list: the cream of the Class B crop each year rises to the top. Shane and Jacob will hopefully be joined by others this season. A genius reader can see that Shane and Jacob are a solid basis for a team. All-State status is given to any runner who finishes in the Top 15 overall finishers at a State XC meet in Montana.

The following individuals earned All-State status during careers at TFHS from the Montana High School Association.

Boys
Adam Oswald – 2000-01 – Junior and Senior
Nathan Block – 2001 - Senior
Spencer Bird – 2001 – Senior
Stryker Clark – 2003 – Senior
Derek Naegeli – 2004 – Junior
Shane Donaldson – 2004-06, Freshman-Junior
Jacob Naegeli – 2005-06, Sophomore-Junior

Girls
Kellyn Gross – 2000 – senior
Holly Conlin – 2001 – Freshman
Ciara Normandeau – 2005 - Freshman

9-02-07, Sunday, Ice Cream chaos

Don Kardong (1976 US Olympic marathoner) said, "Without ice cream, there would be darkness and chaos."

This quote is on the back of shirts for the Sundae Run in the middle of July in Missoula, MT. That's a big reason my wife wanted to enter this race – for the t-shirt (and the free ice cream from Dairy Queen). All runners know the shirt cannot be worn without the race being run. She now proudly sports this quote on her shirt.

This is the introduction to two more real-life heroes: Our # 2 runners are Delcie Peters and Jacob Naegeli. Delcie and Jacob have things in common: they are beautiful people with curly multi-colored hair, they serve ice cream slowly, and they are a little off-center.

The <u>fact</u> is that our entire team is an attractive bunch of personalities and appearances. Beauty is in the eye of the Bee Holder, but I don't need a second opinion of an apiologist to strengthen this attitude. Nor do I need to be an apologist in this politically correct society when I write that a boy or a girl is a beautiful person. However, it sounds like I just did!

By Andrew Gideon

The Little Bear Ice Cream shop in TFalls is world famous – at least in our small town Montana minds! Drive here, taste, and you will come back.

A sign that sits just outside the Little Bear shop on Main Street, Thompson Falls, reads, "Attention customers. This is not a fast food restaurant. Please be patient. We know you will find our food and ice cream to be well worth your wait."

Attention readers. Delcie and Jacob are not abusing the fast lane of life (except on the track). Please be patient. We know you will find their personality, skills, and attitude to be well worth your wait.

My words will not do justice to Delcie's personality and style. If a picture is worth a 1000 words, stick to a portrait and her amazing writing ability as opposed to my organized chaotic text.

Her future plans include being a free spirit and a hippie. If she were given a $100,000,000 ("woa, that's a lot of cold hard cash"), then she would buy a hot air balloon and travel the world.

As a junior, she currently has "no idea" about her future, but she is sure it doesn't include "plumbing or (being) an executioner."

Free spirit – hippie – no idea: it sounds as though Delcie has loose change or rocks for brains - maybe even a bit of blonde hair. Wrong!! First of all, her hair is extremely frizzy (did she stick a fork in a light socket before she school?), but it is actually a combination of tie-dyed and plaid. Really, she just wants to "accept my curly afro hair."

Secondly, thirdly, and finally, Delcie's GPA of 3.8, her magnificent writing style, and her effort in sports indicate that she is in control of her destiny.

Described as severely shy by some when she was younger, her personality and strength slowly builds each year – just as her strength in running and life grows. Life is a slow process that goes too fast, but shouldn't each repetition of daily existence grow the soul's muscle? Her self-portrait surely reflects these changes. Delcie's self-portrait would have changed drastically from $5^{th} – 7^{th} – 9^{th} – 11^{th}$ grade, although all pictures would include freckles.

Her parents come from different areas of the country. Mom (Chris Magdalene) is from Anaconda – known as a tough Montana town. Dad (Dale Peters) hales from Wittenburg, Wisconsin. Delcie Josephine Peters ("Delc") was born 11-18-90.

The Wisconsin connection and her dad led to a tremendous experience this summer. Delcie spent 5-7 days in Northern Minnesota kayaking, canoeing, and portaging various lakes. Not being around mountains bothered her, and she didn't see much animal life. After Minnesota, her family traveled to Glacier Park. She camped, saw wildlife and mountains, and was much more at home. Fittingly, her favorite hobby is "anything crazy & outdoors."

Being at home in the mountains is her only deciding point for college right now. It doesn't matter which school – mountains do matter. Delcie wants to travel to Greece, known for its interior mountains and vast history (Greece information plagiarized from some source).

Her future plans are to *"find something I love to do."*

Her advice to younger runners is *"do your best, it's okay if you're not Super Kenyan woman or something. There's a good feeling when you know you've given all you've got."*

A school pole vault record (which she will break in spring '08) is on her resume (she is tied with 4 other girls). Her best times include a 2:32 (800), 6:00 (1600 meters), and 20:57 XC three mile.

A track incident from 2006 gives insight into runner Delcie: Shane recalls her words, "Do these spikes make my ankles look fat?" Jacob, Shane, Ryan, and Beca heard that comment and will not let her live this one down! At 5'5" and 125, the only spikes that might make her ankles look fat exist in Kenya.

Since this manuscript is about putting one foot in front of the other, thoughts on her running exist: she would rather run in the woods with bear, deer, and elk – than with people on a race course. She has a little twisting motion we are working on to straighten out, and when she gets really tired on a long run her right arm swings and flips violently. I love to give advice to runners, sometimes during hard timings; Delcie would rather have me shut up and push her by pacing 5-10 strides in front. I can't even clam up when I'm typing, how could I shut up when I want her to have growth as a runner! Maybe if I clammed up, my writing would produce a pearl of a thought to improve her times.

She enjoys track more than cross country because of the variety of events. The spring sport also has pole vault, but she really dislikes the 8-lap 3200 meter. Talking with her on the bus on the way home from Libby, she stated that, in terms of running, she "has to do it – I don't know why." She knows it is a good thing to "push and work harder," but it is a mental obstacle or challenge to compete that she can't quite put into words. Therefore I will follow suit and up mess words my; I can't why explain that did I.

Last spring she missed ten school days and track, because her cornea was being eaten away; she literally couldn't see for a week. If Delcie were eternally blinded, her hazelnut lattee colored eyes might have become decaffeinated - a true loss to any espresso fan. Her window to the soul (eyes) would have become a one way mirror, yet certainly would not completely block the view to a superb personality and style.

Despite the ten day set back, she got stronger each meet. She placed 6th in three events (top 5 go to the State Meet) and 8th in another at Divisionals – bringing tears to several people's eyes – especially Beca. Beca had already qualified for State (3200) and really wanted Delcie to follow suit. Delc lowered her time by ten seconds in two weeks in the 800 and came within a second of making it in the 1600. In the last race of the Divisional meet, the 1600 relay, Beca ran a personal best 400 in her anchor leg attempting to get Delcie to state –

yet finished the dreaded 6th by a second. Beca broke down in tears, hugging Delcie's sister Hannah. Side note: Hannah writes that *"Delcie doesn't do hugs."*

If it weren't so poignant (missing state by a second, twice), I would be inspired by the love and effort of Beca. Okay, I am anyway.

Favorites include <u>Practical Magic</u> (movie), *Sisterhood of Traveling Pants* (book), and nectarine (food). She would rather be in Art or PE than any other class, yet her preferred educator is a Math teacher, Mr. Thompson.

Somehow I have bribed her enough with enough compliments to earn a distinction as favorite coach, *"especially for pole vault."*

Matt must have an insider story about a rope swing. His only comment toward Delcie is *"let go."* How many insider stories for more personality and description could be written on each athlete and person? Enough to fill a book!!!

Jessica Moritz was an exchange student from Germany during last school year. She lived with the Naegeli family and Delcie befriended her. She even threw a going away party for Jessica - complete with water, pizza, and good honest fun. A party for this XC team isn't the stereotypical high school bash. I thought about editing out this paragraph, but these words indicate that the Naegeli family has repeatedly had exchange students (Japan also), as well as choice of friends for Delcie. Side note: Jessica, an exchange student, had the best grammar of any student I have taught in eleven years.

Beca's words end another entry: *"Delcie always pushes me to run faster even if she doesn't believe me when I say that. She also is an amazingly fast runner, even if she doesn't believe that either. As she said about me, we have many great memories going way back, and I love this girl to death. She is also absolutely beautiful for readers who don't know, and I love her curly hair."*

Delcie in Kalispell 07   Jacob at State 07

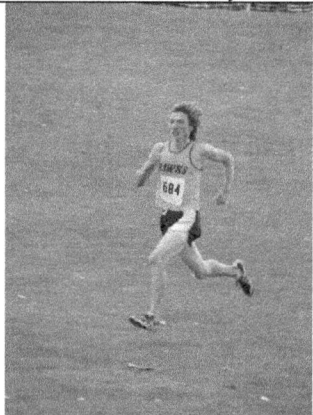

Jacob Naegeli is as cool, calm, and collected as James Bond.

Jacob Naegeli also merited a Beca essay, *"Jacob and I have some amazing memories. We have had some long discussions on runs when it is just the two of us. He is like an older brother, <u>always</u> teasing me about one thing or* *another, but also has served as a 'bodyguard' a few times. And Jake, you really should have done that amazing bunny hop across the finish line in track!* ☺"

Monica's words: *"Nope. No. Uh-uh. Ugly. Heavy. Yes! Check. Jake is a funny kid I would have to say. Definitely enjoyed all the card games I never got on bus trips, & the time he took to explain them to me. Much appreciated! I also think that I couldn't name a guy who dyes their hair so much. Impressive!"*

On Saturday, July 15, 2006, Jacob, Derek (Jacob's brother), Ryan, Shane, and I kayaked on the Blackfoot River northwest of Missoula. In the morning we ran the 4-mile Sundae Run in Greenough Park (Missoula), so the afternoon was reserved for fun and sun.

I own two kayaks; thus the five of us took turns - every mile or so down the river, we switched floaters. At one spot, two girls on tubes, two hilarious girls on tubes, commented on Jake's hair by calling him a blue raspberry smurf. This backs up Monica's claim of dying hair.

What color is Jacob's hair - the same color as Delcie's – a combination of tie-dyed and plaid! Both have curly hair.

Jacob's goals/future plans are to *"live forever, so far so good....finish college...have a successful & fun job...keep running."*

His advice to younger students is "Don't procrastinate!" This is humorous, because it took him two weeks to get his answers turned into me so I could write up his profile. Practice what you preach young man!

His advice for future runners is that *"it's all mental."* I won't go there!

Jacob's life has been forged from the imaginative fires of his parents: Sarah Scherzer, from outside Cleveland, Ohio, and William (Bill) Naegeli, a Thompson Falls native. Yes, forged because, as Matt, Mike B, and Delcie point out, Jacob welds, makes swords, and knows how to use fire in a positive manner. Smokey the bear would be proud.

Just as Smokey is proud of Jacob for his safe and effective use of red hot heat, Bill and Sarah are proud of his running and his 4.0 GPA. His grades tie him for top honors in the senior class with his current girlfriend, Katie. They will be co-Valedictorian at graduation if they maintain their 4.0 GPA's this year. It could be because he is often seen with a book in his hands.

Katie, Jacob, and Ryan traveled to Europe for ten days in June 2007. He could not produce any pictures of a leaning Eiffel Tower, and insisted he had fun despite taking a break from running.

Jacob is 5'9" and weighs 125 pounds. Shane weighs 123 pounds. Derek, Jake's brother, weighs 130. The reason I coach cross country is that I am not afraid of heights, but I am afraid of widths (source: Steven Wright humor).

Mike B says Jacob's hobby is *"making swords & other weapons."* Matt H writes that Jacob is a *"crazy welder, insane pool digger."* These comments help us understand possible college majors of Landscape Architecture and Art.

Jacob's family consists of 19 year old Derek, currently a Pacific Boxer in Oregon, frosh Mariah, and 5th grader Logan. Logan doesn't like being low man on the Naegeli totem pole; he gets a lot of the small house jobs that Derek used to have, then Jacob, then Mariah....

This family is an amazingly beautiful family. Jacob fits right in.

The family is solid because of Grandma Naegeli. Her life has been positive for not only the Naegeli's, but for the cross country kids, the community, and anyone who meets her. Grandma Naegeli is *"one of the greatest people alive"* according to Jacob.

All Naegeli's are good runners, maybe they are part Kenyan – the part that stands on the sidelines and claps! Okay, so Derek and Jacob crush me. Soon Mariah will be doing that, and when Logan beats me, I am retiring.

Jacob Naegeli has a 1600 meter PR of 4:39, 3200 meter of 10:37, and the 3 mile cross country of 16:37. His goals are to break 4:30 in the mile, get low 16's in the 3 mile. Matt describes him as a *"fricken awesome runner."*

Jacob is currently wearing his "without ice-cream there would be choas (misspelled) and darkness" (red 2005 Sundae Run shirt). He is my student-aide 6th period (1:13-2:05), he is correcting tests as I get to type and play with the keyboard, and he just told me the story of the shirt. Apparently the race directors did not know the shirt had a spelling error – Shane alerted them – yes, teaching spelling does matter! So he has a limited addition, spelling-error shirt.

Jacob's favorite movie is <u>Muppets from Space</u>. He loves welding, Pottery II class, XC (cross country), and "The Wheel of Time" book series. Mr. Gideon and Mr. Nelson tie (if you call 51% to 49% a tie) for favorite teacher, while he loves his mom as a coach.

Give Jacob his bacon; it is his favorite "other." How this factors into winning $100,000,000, only a reader can dig that deep, but he would *"put it all in a single bank account. Even with a tiny interest of 3%, I would make $3,000,000 a year. This would easily pay for any college I want and a new track for TFHS."*

Shane comments, *"Not just one, but 2 decks of cards. Who is up for a game?"*

My recall of Jacob as a runner: a deer-like prancing gait, slightly oblong, and this causes him to spend a little more time in the air than is ideal for a runner. His turnover is good, but can be improved – think light and move forward, not up. Running with Jacob is always an adventure; he crushes me on fast days and is a good person to converse with on a slow run. Humor, food, and good serious topics of interest to our world are always options to discuss.

Another item that sticks in my brain happened July 4, 2007. Approximately 10 Hawk runners traveled 35 miles together to run the 4th of July Noxon three mile race. The finish was pure Hawk: Shane first, followed by Derek, Jacob, Coach Gideon, and Ryan. Bryant finished in about 42 minutes and learned a valuable lesson about eating before a race. We drove back to the Naegeli ranch as a group. As several members ate, hooked up video games, and otherwise prepared to have a lazy 4th of July, Jacob trudged out in his boots, work clothes, and went out to hay and drive tractor all day. It is a good image of how hard Jacob works at life: run a hard race and work all day. That's why he will probably be All-State for the third straight year, as well as Valedictorian.

Delcie's comments are a Jacob's final reminder of our beloved Jacob: *"comes from a fine family of runners. He does crazy things like 4-H, welding, digging his own pool, community service…geez, such a bad egg. Just kidding. After I tasted his bread, I thought he should open his own bakery! But most bakers are fat, right? Could you imagine a chubby Jacob? Nah..... ☺"*

9-3-2007, Monday, Labor Day, Jeremiah 29:11

Team mileage today: 123.5   runners: 23   Avg. per runner: 5.4

Jeremiah 29:11 ➜ *'For I know the plans I have for you,' declares the Lord, 'plans to prosper you and not to harm you, plans to give you hope and a future.'*

Another bible quote by a public school teacher/coach (gasp)! Realize this is how my brain works. Realize Jeremiah 29:11 sounds like a coach preaching to athletes! Or maybe a father to his kids – listen up Jaxon and Kaden!

We have hope and a future, running ten miles will not harm us. Timed mile repeats, terrible Tuesdays, and exercising in 100 degrees is healthy (he, he, heeeee). The pain is only temporary, we hope!

Labor Day – a day of labor or rest?!?!?!

The Hawks had three times and two diverse places as running options.

Zero people showed up at the cool temperature time of 8:30 am at the high school to run with me. I did not take it personally. Wouldn't it be nice to be able to sleep this long.

At 7 pm, I ran with four people at the high school: Delcie and Cody ran five miles with me, while junior high twins Austin and Dakotta ran 2.25.

At 7 pm at the Naegeli ranch, the majority of the others ran a workout in different terrain with a home-made pool to ice in. Shane really wanted that icing opportunity – this leads my brain to believe his knees and shins bother him a little more than he reports to the coaching staff.

The 4-H kids had to clean up stalls at the fair – concluding an exhausting week of fair work. Today that ends, yet the catch-up to sleep and scheduling will most likely haunt their bodies for a week.

Tuesday, 9-4-2007, 26 Letters in the Alphabet

Team mileage today: 138.5   runners: 24   Avg. per runner: 5.8

Letters in the alphabet = 26 ➜ an amazing coincidence to 26 miles in a marathon. These letters can be arranged in unique combinations to soothe our pathos, just as workouts and running can be arranged in unique combinations for superior Hawk Harrier performances. Letters become words, steps become miles, words become pages, and workouts make a season and a book.

Just as the letters and words are being mixed and matched in this book, the coaches are constantly arranging harriers, workouts, and knowledge. It will be a unique coincidence if I arrange this excess of information into a successful book, and we arrange our workouts and overload of running into a triumphant cross country season. My words and letters will overload and train your brain, yet you cannot cut our workouts with scissors, because our athlete's brains are trained too well. Please don't cut this book up with scissors.

Whatever!

On Wednesday 8-29, I commented on three coaches and three different ideas of what workout to do on one particular day. This is an on-going concept that applies to every day and every runner. How does one arrange all the legs and arms and letters and words into the swiftest race and the next bestseller? There needs to be an overall outline for success, rather than just random thoughts each day. Oh, trust this there is profound thought and planning in both.

Today: Bob wants to pound our harriers with a timed 3, 2, and 1 mile. Sarah wants less, while Gideon desires something completely different.

All of us have a goal for success for the individual and the team. We plan together for the ideal training regimen.

Coach Naegeli has the toughest responsibility to put all the puzzle pieces together. She has paper work responsibility (insurance, parent forms), planning (times for meets, itineraries, practices), and the final pressure of the end result. She also gets to deal with the parents!

We have injuries to keep an eye on: RT (hip), Monica (Achilles), Shane (shin splints, knees, although he isn't quite admitting it), and Mike B (knee, toe). Those aren't all the injuries – we haven't touched on the mental ones yet!! Ouch!

Mental – Jacob, Mariah, Rebeca, JP (Jeffreyanne), CC, and Bryant all worked at the fair (4-H, cows, bread, quilts, etc). Their days were 6 am to 10 pm – maybe not strict hours, but long days. Coach Naegeli emphasizes that the 4-H kitchen gave our harriers good meals.

Yet the kids put a lot of effort into different projects, continued to run on their own, and now come back to the "school schedule" and 3:30, 95 degree running temperatures.

Terrible Tuesdays have been the normal practice for years. Dare we disturb the universe? I say yes, especially for the girls. I say NO for the boys, they are at a spot where they believe in who they are as runners and how they will place at State. Boys – don't mess with success; girls - start a dynasty!

Looking at the All-State chart (9-01) and looking back on the past three seasons, my brain is more and more convinced that our efforts with girls do not do them justice. I am also certain there is more room for error in coaching boy runners than girl runners. A coach must be better / more exact coaching girl runners vs. coaching boys.

What do I mean by that? I mean that any hard workout will improve boys, but there must be more perfection in choosing workouts for the girls. What do I know!?!?!

50

In the end, I hope the journey is good, and the destination receives a peak performance. And the book becomes a best seller.

Today, all athletes ran a timed mile to start.

The girls then left the school grounds in two cars to the State Park four miles away. Timings of .4 miles and .2 miles on tricky trails were a fun break from longer intervals. This was very close to the ideal workout needed for the girls today – as four girls had spent much time at the fair working last week. Shorter was better – the scenery was more relaxing – and the trails forced the eyes to focus on each step instead of other painful running thoughts.

Plus the girls "iced" in the river together after the workout as coach Gideon left them alone to bond as he ran three more miles.

The boys ran intervals between two and four miles at the school. The longer 2 x 2 mile intervals were a source of strength literally and figuratively for the boys. Some athletes with injuries did slightly less.

Coach Naegeli did want to watch how some boys would work without the girls present.

Clicky-top Twins

Running near Beca and RT, one will surely hear the incessant clicky-top pen sounds reverberating with every step. Ankles: Beca's right and RT's left both click with every stride. Just as an annoying high school student clicks his clicky-top pen to irritate the teacher and class, causing unlimited chaos, Beca and RT's ankle cause me unlimited concern.

Should I even hear these little sounds that can turn the business world upside down (do we order clicky-top pens or twisties?). (Please don't laugh, I worked at First Security Bank in Helena, and this question caused internal chaos for months. Simple solution: order both kinds! No, the boss only ordered her favorites – clicky-tops; True story from an American business). Dilbert would have been thrilled. To emphasize this point on successful American business thinking even further, here is a personal anecdote. I put a quote on my business card by Benjamin Franklin, "remember that time is money." Big mistake – nobody else in the bank had a quote, so why should I have one? Because I'm special!

Back on track to the clicky-top twins, RT seems to be an accident waiting to happen. Hips, ankles, toes, brain, and newly shaved head are probably all subject to injury – if the wind blows the wrong way. The coaches worry about sending him out on a run, wondering if he will come back in one piece or several. It is not as if he has a kamikaze nature, although he does. Just as dust of ancient civilizations finds Pig Pen (Peanuts), accidents find RT.

RT was injured in week three for the third straight season. The first two might have been from overload and double sessions, so we kept him away from overuse injuries this season. Still, his right hip pained him during the Libby Meet on Friday (four days ago).

Therefore, RT's ankle, which he has injured before, may be due to a past injury. His tendons, ligaments, and joints just may be warning him to "take it easy, big guy, we want to stay in one piece." Small cries from the foot must be ignored during races and workouts, yet listened to for long-term health.

Beca's right ankle may be due to running track laps in counter-clockwise direction. Track workouts don't have to be run the same way as track meets, but a runner gets used to curves and straight-aways at certain interval points. Disrupting this routine is plain wrong! Yet, the left leg running constantly on the inside will surely endure a slightly different effect on the corners as the right.

That's my theory on why Beca's right ankle clicks and I'm sticking to it.

I could be wrong. It wouldn't be the first time.

(footforum.info/archives/2426.html) offers: *"When an ankle is sprained, a peroneal ligament can be torn. Over time it can flop out of position, causing a clicking sound, often when the ankle is flexed, as when going up or down stairs. Usually patients can reproduce the sound on request, and sometimes you can see the tendon pop around the ankle joint. If it isn't painful and doesn't bother you, you don't need to do anything about it, but if it becomes painful you should look into it before the tendon becomes irritated or even degenerates. Surgery can put it back in its place."*

Another website states, *"If the clicking sound is your only symptom, then you probably have nothing to worry about. This is a fairly common occurrence in young, healthy individuals and is considered normal. The clicks are usually due to flicking of the ligament from one position to another. These clicks can also occur in the knee, hip or even fingers. Clicking is also common in the jaw, especially in people with temporomandibular joint syndrome (TMJ)."* (www.drdonnica.com/faqs/00009108.htm)

For my third and final study of the ankle clicking, I logged on to WebMD and learned, *"There are 28 bones and over 30 joints in the foot. Tough bands of tissue, called ligaments, hold the bones and joints in place."*

Did we learn anything? Probably not, but the clicky-top ankle twins are forever in our hearts and minds.

RT – avoid injury, and Beca – run circle the other direction occasionally.

Wednesday, 9-5-2007, It's the Journey, not the destination

Team mileage today: 122   runners: 24   Avg. per runner: 5.1

Father Alfred D'Souza: *"Happiness is a journey, not a destination."*

This week did not pound the phrase "State Champions" into the TFHS coaches' hearts.

Poplar HS, our chief competition, had three athletes race under 18 minutes last weekend.

From the Billings Invitational on 8/31: Colstrip (a possible top 3 team)— Blythe, 18th, 17:16; T. Blythe, 20th, 17:20; Shaw, 33rd, 17:43; Martine, 49th, 18:10; Oxford, 57th, 18:32.

Our goal = State Championship; I am not shy about saying it or typing it.

However, another real goal is to have the Blue Hawk harriers get stronger as runners, as people, and as a team. They have respect for each other, and I do emphasize to them continually to appreciate the fact that they are healthy enough to run – a blessing in itself.

If by some tragedy we do not win state, the journey will still be gold that stays in our hearts. This I am convinced of – Appreciating the journey is the gold medal; earlier in my life I would have been crushed if it didn't happen (for example, coaching the 1992 Libby Loggers Legion baseball team, a 4th place finish at State was devastating at the time).

The journey is a blessing and the running miles are logged into the memory. We shall see the destination on October 20th, 2007, and beyond.

Today's workout was at the Mule Pasture (a.k.a. Forest Service Trails).

JP reported heavy tree logs for legs, Delcie didn't want to go the "extra mile" during the run because of a tiredness (yet she did run an extra cool down mile with Lacey at the end), and Cody turned back early.

Running easy with the leaders did not produce much conversation despite a slower pace. We had some tired Hawks today. The team made a trip after practice to Wild Goose Landing. A ten minute "ice" session energized some spirits, yet sluggishness definitely existed today.

There was a 5:30 pm potluck and required "rules" and "forms" meeting. Parents sign papers and learn team rules, practice schedules, and make sure insurance forms are filled out, etc. This is the day I'm glad I'm not a head coach.

Personally I felt like the tired Hawk harriers when I got home after 7 pm; I could not move I was so exhausted. (Fortunately I felt incredible the next morning and put some extra miles on the bike before school.)

Thursday, 9-6-2007, No Fair!
Team mileage today: 169.5   runners: 24   Avg. per runner: 7.1

"Life is not fair," said one student, and only one student/person in the history of mankind. Life was fair – last weekend – for seven of our runners. Here are some "fair" numbers:

Mariah $2.75/lb on an 1185 lb steer
Jacob $2.50/lb on a 1055 lb steer
Bryant $2.00/lb on a 1215 lb steer
Beca $5/lb on a 110 lb sheep
JP $3.00/lb on a 217 lb swine
CC: approximately $400 swine

Beca says that a person earns every penny taking care of sheep.

A net profit is something businesses (and farmers/ranchers) need. It is also something cross country coaches want; net profit is a time improvement from the start of the year until the end. Mariah netted $3000, Jacob $2500,

By Andrew Gideon

Bryant $2200, Beca $450, JP $500, and CC $300. Each person is only allowed one market animal at the Sanders County Fair.

An interesting note to the reader: CC had a steer step on her right toe during cross country season (at the fair) two years ago. This year Mariah had it happen to her. So, the 4-H steers like to break our runners' toes. They are steering us in a broken direction (ha, ha).

It will always be the right toe that is broken because a person shows the steer on their right side at an auction. CC went on to All-State status two years ago, so maybe we should break her toe again! She already has a bad back, so maybe that is her "good luck" for this year. Mariah, you are in good company with that broken toe.

Here are some more, life is not "fair" facts (source Coach Naegeli): Jacob had the best of show exhibit for his bread in open class, and best of show and grand champion for his bread in 4H. Mariah had best of show and grand champion for her shirt in sewing and a best of show in open class for her flower arrangement. Beca received a grand champion ribbon in leadership projects for her notebook. Bryant received a grand champion ribbon (People's Choice Award) for his car (rebuilt 1948). Logan Naegeli made sushi and octopus pie. (We still have one octopus pie frozen, to try at a later date). Jacob also received the Little Chief award, basically an award for a senior 4H-er for leadership and community service.

Today's workouts: Boys: start at Power Park along river to State Park (3 miles), 4 x ¾ mile loop (easy, medium, easy, hard), 3 miles back – 10 miles on a lovely and "cool" 83 degrees.

Girls: with Coach Naegeli – Thompson River road, 3 groups out easy (25 min, 20, or 15) and back hard (tempo run), then icing in a chilling Montana stream, the little Thompson River.

Monica did 10 pushups today.

Delcie stated to Mike M, "It seems like we just ran yesterday." Mike's response was YEAH obviously. Delcie was probably trying to say something deeper. Hmm. It seems like I just ate yesterday, I just took some breaths yesterday. I just wrote in this book yesterday. YEAH.

CC worked all summer at Ace Hardware so that she could buy a laptop and an IPOD. She put in 40 hour weeks and accomplished her goals. Yesterday I read that Ace hardware has a $154 million shortfall, but I'm pretty sure it has nothing to do with CC and her purchasing expensive electronic equipment.

Bryant took three years to rebuild a car. It was a 1948 Dodge. Total cost of the rebuild was $3000, and his dad helped him quite a bit. The car looks good in the parking lot – I'm sure it is a source of pride – great work Bryant.

September 6, 07 *Sanders County Ledger*, front page: by John Hamilton (graduation speaker May 31, 2008). *"The Chippy Creek beast is finally on a short leash...The fire-breathing, forest-eating, smoke-billowing monster called the Chippy Creek fire, one of the largest and most costly Montana wildfires of a very busy 2007 season, finally appears to be on its way out of existence...Finally, thanks to the hard work of hundreds of firefighters over the past five weeks, the battle with the 99,090 acre Chippy Creek fire, widely recognized as one of the largest fires to ever burn in this area, looks like it has been won...The Sanders County portion of the Chippy Creek fire most affected by the blaze includes the drainages of Big Rock Creek, Chippy Creek, Bear Creek, Little Rock Creek, and the Little Thompson River, plus portions of other drainages."*

Thompson Falls is the county seat of Sanders County.

Friday, 9-7-2007, Easy day – NOT!

Team mileage today: 120   runners: 24   Avg. per runner: 5.0

Beca was excited today during our warm-up mile. She was singing a little song about today being easy because it was the day before a race.

I asked her if she wanted Coach Naegeli or Coach Gideon to burst her bubble. What??!?!

A longer day on the day before a meet – cruel coaches strike again. Yes, it is for your own good in the long term (he ehe hehehee!).

The Hawk Harriers ran long; we are running through the first two meets.

Life lesson: make the self uncomfortable at times so that goals can be obtained; then enjoy a comfortable feeling. This means work hard now so that the future (State) will be good.

I see too many students daily who take the easy way out and are comfortable now. Those people set themselves up later for an uncomfortable life.

The XC Catch-22: To be comfortable, one must make himself or herself uncomfortable. Make yourself comfortable and the future is uncomfortable.

Sorry Beca to burst your bubble. A songbird sang and exploded (Shrek!)

Ho Hum, our money-making sport traveled to Florence and won 38-0.

We have a quality football program; however, there is a respect issue between running and football. Our runners actually understand football players work hard, yet I don't believe the same respect is returned. I've played both sports and running dominates my brain as to which sport teaches more lasting life fundamentals in a positive manner.

There are thoughts to nail down on the football issue: Michael Vick? 350 pound lineman? Testosterone? Success on and off the field of competition? Stay tuned for something on this thought pattern!

Saturday, 9-8-2007, Meet # 2, Kalispell

13 September 07 article in the *Sanders County Ledger*.

Red-Lining the Harrier Hawks   *by Andrew Gideon*

"It was the best we've ever run in Kalispell," said assistant coach Bob Reall of the Thompson Falls Bluehawks.

The Kalispell meet that coach Reall referred to was on Saturday, September 8, and the Hawk Harriers have left engine exhaust on this course

By Andrew Gideon

yearly since 2002. 13 current team members of Thompson Falls raced on this speedway in 2006. 10 of those runners improved their efficiency: Kyle Breithaupt, sophomore, was better by 4 minutes and 23 seconds. The other improvements were as follows: Mike Barnett, sophomore, by 1:52, junior Mike Kidwiler by 1:38, senior RT Brown by 1:28, senior Matt Hojem by 1:06, junior Delcie Peters by 56 seconds, sophomore Beca Gunderson by 51 seconds, senior Jacob Naegeli by 28 seconds, and senior Shane Donaldson by 26 seconds. In the junior high division, Austin Kinser bettered last year's time by 7 minutes!

That list doesn't even include the first time racing qualifiers: Dakotta Kinser and John Gunderson made their junior high debuts with respectable times. Freshman Mariah Naegeli, sophomore Cody White and junior Patrick Jamison revved their engines and did not take the scenic route in their first high school pursuit.

The Bluehawk boy harriers were the top B school in the 22 team varsity division. Thompson bested rivals Loyola, Plains, Cut Bank, and Eureka. In the girls division, 23 teams had athletes, and Thompson Falls placed 15th. However, the only class B team to beat the Hawks was Cut Bank in 13th place.

Should the Montana High School Association (MHSA) mail a trophy to the Hawks now?

"Absolutely NOT," said assistant coach Andrew Gideon, "We need to continue red-lining our workouts to strengthen our running machines, while maintaining a superior quality of oil and perfecting our tire pressure."

Without proper rest and nutrition, the Hawk running machines may lose viscosity, which would result in more friction and amplify problems. Current engine problems reside in sophomore Monica Conlin and RT Brown (cracked belts, i.e. hip problems), Mariah and Mike B (piston malfunction, a.k.a. knees), and sophomore Ciara Normandeau (rolling chassis, a backbone problem). Despite these machinery troubles, good gas mileage (times) have still been produced by these five.

If the lifters (legs) have wear – there is a chance of valve failure – and thus catastrophic breakdown. Attention Hawks: Eat and sleep well!

Overall though, despite a tremendous amount of tread wear on the tires in the first four weeks of the season, the Hawks have had solid fuel efficiency. Shane "I am speed" (Lightning McQueen) ran an impressive race again – Mike K and Beca G complimented the skid marks he left on the Kalispell surface. Jacob said Mariah and Mike K should be mentioned for their good engine combustion. Head Coach Sarah Naegeli declared that Delcie, Kyle, and Bryce Miller deserved respect for their gas mileage. Mike Morris complimented Patrick Jamison's carburetor performance, while Coach Gideon stated that Mike M, JP (Jeffreyanne Parker) and CC (Ciara N) must have electric engines because they ran so professionally.

Coach Reall was "amazed at the amount of work we did and coming out of the fair, and doing such an awesome job."

An awesome engine indeed is the Hawk running machine right now, so the team should keep tuning up, red-lining workouts, and focusing on the checkered flag.

Thompson Falls will next compete in Ronan on Thursday, September 13th.

Varsity boys:

Thompson Falls - Shane Donaldson (16:38, 5th), Jacob Naegeli (17:11, 16th), Ryan Sol (18:14, 48th), Mike Morris (18:30, 57th), Bryce Miller (18:59, 79th), Matt Hojem (19:43, 100th), RT Brown (21:09, 113th)

Plains: Justin Allison (18:31, 58th), Valin Heward (18:51, 71st), Jared Sine (19:07, 82nd), Thad LeClair (20:39, 110th), Kenneth Beech (21:20, 114th)

Loyola: Mike Evans (17:39, 25th), Erik Kappelman (18:12, 46th), Conner Collins (19:02, 81st), Daniel Evans (19:25, 93rd), Erik Dale (19:33, 95th), Dan Cloninger (19:35, 97th),

Eureka: Matteus Hartley (19:53, 103rd), Corey Graham (21:44, 118th), Lucas Hofstee (23:02, 122nd), James Mepham (26:00, 129th)

Varsity Girls:

Thompson Falls - Beca Gunderson (22:21, 51st), Delcie Peters (22:25, 55th), Jeffreyanne Parker (23:24, 77th), Monica Conlin (25:16, 103rd), Lacey Wade (27:10, 110th)

Plains - Rio Crismore (24:01, 95th), Kara Bates (25:28, 104th), Zoe Banovich (25:44, 106th)

Loyola - Jordan Scolatti (22:09, 45th), Emilie Loran (23:26, 80th)

Eureka - Catherine Hall (21:54, 38th), Bailey Malecha (22:39, 62nd), Nora Hodsdon (25:52, 107th), Annesse Burris (32:08, 113rd)

JV Boys:

Thompson Falls - Mike Kidwiler (18:44, 7th), Patrick Jamison (19:03, 10th), Bryant Normandeau (20:55, 63rd), Kyle Breithaupt (21:17, 73rd), Cody White (24:26, 122nd), Mike Barnett (25:33, 131st)

Loyola - Chirag Patel (19:49, 29th), Steve Rehbein (20:29, 48th), Erik Ramone (21:02, 66th), Charlie Pritchard (23:56, 115th)

JV Girls

Thompson Falls – Ciara Normandeau (23:07, 15th), Mariah Naegeli (23:43, 28th), Amanda Wood (29:34, 110th).

Loyola – Alex Scolatti (22:39, 9th)

PS – thanks to Bill Naegeli for the car terminology for this article.

Coaches Naegeli, Reall, and Gideon have left the first two meets feeling incredible. The effort of all the athletes this year has been tremendous.

What a great feeling to be part of this group. Keep on motoring!

Are we doing well? Does a bear !@#$ in the woods? (red neck for yes.)

Here are some pieces edited out of the article: Some of these pieces are similar to the article, yet phrased different, so I include them.

By Andrew Gideon

Jacob said Mariah and MK should be mentioned for their running effort in Kalispell on September 8. Coach Naegeli said Delcie, Kyle, and Bryce deserved honor for their exertion. Mike M complimented Patrick's contribution, while Beca was impressed by JP and Shane.

This writer was equally impressed with the entire team. The coaching staff commented that the team really doesn't get an easy day until the fifth week, and then it will only be one day.

All five days were hard this week for the harriers: Eight miles Monday, timed miles and intervals on Tuesday, seven miles on Wednesday, 10 miles (including three miles of 1200 meter intervals or a tempo run) on Thursday, and a not-race friendly seven miles on Friday. The entire team netted 169.5 for 24 runners on Thursday = 7.1 miles/Hawk – wow! That recipe makes for a difficult week. Wait, all that, and they had to run a race - what are the coaches thinking?

Beca answered that feisty question, "*We worked hard all week - for the long haul, not immediate gains.*" Yet immediate gains still occurred. Jacob understands the work is making the team "*better prepared for State.*" Mike M has a goal of making All-State (top 15 at the State B meet) and helping the boy's team improve its 2006 4th place finish.

The team is "*bonding well,*" according to Beca, sophomore. She also mentioned the good "*camaraderie.*" All the athletes I talked to mentioned positive efforts of various teammates.

Teams we beat in our division were Plains, Loyola, and Eureka.

Notice Beca used good MT red neck wordage - "camaraderie" - Nice!

Some things I learned on this bus trip from various interviews.

I need a lap top on the bus so I don't have to retype later!

Beca likes to run with the boys because it pushes her in practice (heart rate increase for a longer time than her female teammates). She does not like to hear someone yell "almost done, only a mile left." Yelling instructions during a race is good, as long as the words are short. Letting Beca know that a rival is immediately behind her can serve as proper motivation. She likes XC for the feeling of success and the diversity of running routes.

Jacob needs a few more days recovery from the fair, especially with a no shade Kalispell course. He knows summer miles have made him better prepared for state, which is good because the Helena course is his favorite. "Tuesday's suck, but are best for specific training knowledge," says our #2 man Jacob.

Mike M is a former surfing legend in his own mind. Seriously, he was on a surf team in Del Mar, CA in 7th-9th grade. He wanted to run XC despite the fact he had never run competitively until he arrived in TFalls (2005). Mike ran with the track team in the spring and did well; yet he did not finish the season due to discipline reasons. His goals are to reach the top 15 at state to achieve all-state status, and in the process of this, he will improve the team. Snowmobiling is Mike's favorite winter activity. He has size 11 shoes and used an M-10 rat boy board in his former legendary surfing days. Shane and Jacob, TFalls veteran runners, label Terrible Tuesdays as their least favorite, despite admitting how it helps. Mike lists Terrible Tuesdays as his favorite workout.

Two different focal points existed for our harriers before today's race.

The first group had a discussion of heart and lungs. The obvious reason for warming up would seem to be for the muscles, joints, and tendons. However, one huge focus for pick-ups or accelerations, as well as jogging, is to get the heart and lungs ready to accept what is next. There can be no shock to the system if one is to perform at a high standard. The heart rate when the gun goes off must be near the same rate as during the race. The lungs must have opened and worked to a similar level of what will be experienced during the three mile jaunt. Muscles will adapt if cold, but the heart and lungs need to be eased closer to what will be experienced during a race. Shane, Jacob, and Ryan are all experienced racers; my talk with them was to help train the inexperienced teammates to learn this information during the season.

The second group, runners who have raced before, tried to learn about hills. Kalispell has a good set of up and down hills; going down hills actually hurts racers more than the ups! In Thompson Falls, no matter where we run, we get up and down hills, so we are building strength, especially for the up part. The down hill strategy: don't raise the heart rate going down; it is okay to use momentum from the hill to advance faster down the hill, but the runners who turn this into a 100 meter dash pay for it for the next quarter to third of a mile.

CC was picture-perfect coming down the hill today. JP did a fantastic job and came up after the race to tell me that she listened and it helped. They did great; there were probably 25 athletes from other teams who sprinted down the hill, crashed their systems for the next 400 meters, and paid for it.

Going up hill: Coach Bob says take 6 strides (12 steps) hard after the crest, Coach Naegeli believes in three hard strides (6 steps), while Coach Gideon believes that one should keep driving past the crest "until the legs sense an feeling of ease," then the breathing and stride should be readjusted to the terrain.

Sunday, 9-9-2007

This morning, at 7:08 am, 56 minutes into my 21.5 mile jaunt, I came within five feet of a bear. I was on a trail that Ryan showed me two years ago - a great training route. It connects Harlow Road to Blue Slide Road and is two miles long; the Blue Hawks used this to train on for a double session run on 8-20.

The bear: I was five feet from the claws of nature. If the bear would have moved to the trail, one step, I would have run into it. However, it scrambled 20-25 feet up a tree. I stopped and glanced up. About a foot long string of drool was dripping from the bear's mouth; the drool dropped softly to a splash about three inches away from me and my thought was "is that for me; I am a mouth-watering piece of meat!" Nice! Yet, I wasn't scared because I felt the bear was thinking that he needed to climb further up and away from me.

By Andrew Gideon

What a fine morning, 7:08, health to run, and a drooling bear staring me in the eye about one mile away from the nearest residence. The bear could have devoured me and no one would have heard my screams, yet the animal seemed much more afraid. On a scale of 1-5 with 5 being the largest, this bear was a 2.

That is my introduction to another athlete, Ryan Sol, who deserves mention this Sunday. Thanks for showing me the trail Ryan.

Ryan Sol asked for a letter of recommendation to attend the Coast Guard or the Air Force. We talked about this on our Friday, 9-7, run. Here is the letter.
"To: Senator Max Baucus / Silver Bow Center / Butte, MT 59701
RE: Ryan Sol / Sunday, September 9, 2007,

I have known Ryan since August 2005. In that time, I have grown to appreciate and respect him. His work ethic, quiet attitude, and drive to improve are three areas and traits that make Ryan into the quality individual that he is.

We have worked together in English 2, cross country, and track.

In the past two years he has improved from 45th (2005) to 17th (2006) in the State B cross country meet. This year he put in some serious summer running mileage (including the Missoula 1/2 marathon, 28th place in 1 hr 32 min) in an attempt to get to All-State status at this year's meet in Helena on October 20th. However, I don't believe Ryan's motivation is simply so that he can be awarded some merit of achievement. His sacrifice and effort is so that the team can improve from its 2006 4th place finish. Ryan wants to help the team win state or at least get a top three team trophy this season.

Ryan works hard in the classroom and is near the top in the class standing. I enjoyed teaching him in English 2 when he was a sophomore. His writing was always appreciated, and he was willing to accept constructive criticism and improve. I would welcome more students like Ryan into my classroom.

I look forward to seeing the success that Ryan will have in the next six weeks of cross country season this fall. I look forward to his success in the next five, ten, and twenty years as well.

I highly recommend Ryan for scholarships, good jobs, and other interests he may pursue.

Thank you for your time, / Andrew Gideon / English Teacher and Cross Country Coach / Thompson Falls High School"

Ryan Scott Sol was born June 4, 1990. On his next birthday he will have graduated this fine establishment. His decision between the Air Force Academy, the Coast Guard, the ROTC program at Central Washington University, or another lucky school will have been made. Whether he is a pilot for 10 years, a journalist, an Aeronautical engineer, or a computer science geek, Ryan's future will be a high-flying one.

Despite being a high flying Hawk, Ryan's family helps him stay well-grounded. Ryan's parents are Scott and Julie Sol. Both are Montana natives.

Brother Joe is 18, graduated from TFHS in 2007, and is currently a freshman at the University of Montana in Missoula. The family operates Birdland Bay RV Park on the western outskirts of our little metropolis of 1500 people. Scott works for Energy Partners making sure people have their gas.

Ryan is not full of hot air when he states his GPA of 3.6. Therefore his advice to younger students should be listened to: *"work hard and learn a lot but also use this time to make lasting friendships & to try as many things as possible. Find out what you like & who you want to be!"*

Attention TFalls residents 3rd-8th grade: listen to Ryan's advice to future runners: *"Start young! Don't wait until high school to start running, those who run in Junior High have a jump start & usually become much faster! Most of all, know that your running career doesn't have to end when you graduate, running is a great lifelong hobby that will keep you healthy & happy!"*

Happy is a good transition word from last paragraph to this one. Goals for Ryan include success and happiness. A fulfilling job and a wonderful family are also part of the life for the man with the plan, our Mr. Ryan.

Favorites: movie (Stealth), food (pizza), hobby (reading), book (Harry Potter series), class (Media Arts), and sport (watch – basketball, play – golf).

His favorite teacher and coach are both, *"Mr. Gideon, of course! Who else would spend countless hours running with the rowdy, obnoxious bunch known as T-Falls cross country?"*

I am thankful for Ryan's words. I have a ton of respect for Ryan, and for Delcie, for what I label "delayed success." Let's explain "delayed success." Ryan is a little slow-footed and doesn't have pure speed. His size isn't pure Kenyan (5'10" 145 lbs). He didn't blaze a five minute mile as a freshman. Delcie's best 1600 time is 6:00 with a 2:32 800. Breaking certain barriers makes one a "success." However, some people take more time. Delcie will beat 6:00 and 2:32 in spring 2008 as a junior. Ryan, a junior at Divisional Track May 19, 2007, finally broke the 5 minute obstacle. During that race, Jacob (2nd place) and Shane (3rd) did well and made State, but I only timed Ryan. I approached him after the race with the 4:57 showing on my watch. Did Ryan make State? No. Did Delcie make State? No. Neither of them, despite hard work, prayer, and healthy habits made it to the "promised land" of the State Meet.

Another explanation: Ryan and Delcie will improve 0.5 seconds (in a 3 mile race) for every 10 miles and 1 mile hard they run. Others will improve one second with the same training. Wow, that's a great example Mr. Author / Coach.

Delayed success, and sometimes no success have been a theme in my life; I love to run and have worked hard for 14 years, but I have yet to break the 1 hour 30 minute half-marathon; my best time is an agonizing 1:30:01. Yes, one second – ouch! So why did I love to see Ryan break the 5 minute mark as a junior? Why will I love to see Delcie break the 6 minute mark as a junior? One second can make a difference for a team at State, and one second can make a difference in life. I pray for the "one second" – the small thing we can do right to

61

help Ryan win a State Championship in cross country, and I pray for the "one second" for each individual that will make the difference in their life.

Getting back to writing a pure profile without the scenic route, Ryan's best times are 4:57 (1600), 3200 (10:55, at the same Divisional Meet that he broke the 5 minute mile), and 17:15 (XC 3 mile). His goals for running expand beyond high school – *"run a marathon someday, maybe a mini-triathlon if I'm feeling crazy."* His least favorite workouts are timed two miles conducted in 90 heat and above. There is a sentiment of an emotional and difficult journey in his words about a favorite workout, *"All of the relaxed tempo runs the week before state, no longer have to work hard, just hang out for one more week."*

Recall that Ryan and Jake traveled to Europe last summer.

Matt knows first hand that Ryan is not good with bikes on cliffs. The scar on Ryan's shin proves that, RT's video recording saved it for posterity. Matt, with more insider information, writes, *"ahhh my face."* Maybe that remark deals with Pine Sol or jumping off 60 foot cliffs: I don't have all the answers.

Teammate Jacob writes, *"Don't worry. Ryan is a very calm guy. He never gets in trouble, and he's only broken one table. And one arm."*

Monica, Beca, and Delcie all have similar thoughts on his personality, but quoting them exactly is better than paraphrasing.

Monica lets readers know that *"You would think Ryan is a quiet guy, but once you get to know him, he is a hilarious person! I also really love his car…it looks so cute! Especially the horn! Haha. X-C this year was great with Ryan!"*

Beca preserves her thoughts forever by penning (in pencil), *"Ryan is awesome! A quiet kid before you know him, he actually has a great sense of humor that I only first saw starting in track last spring. I suppose he is probably the most 'normal' of us all, but we are trying to convert him. Judging by the large scar on his shin, I'd say we have been pretty successful."*

Delcie writes, *"The time has come to write about Ryan. Ha Ha. He's a super nice guy, probably one of the nicest you'll meet. You might not hear as much out of him as some others on the team, but he's pretty funny. I bet there's a side of him we don't see (and it may be evil ☺) that he will let out someday and surprise us all. Even when Shane and Jake are getting all the attention for their running, Ryan's always there, steadily improving and pulling his weight for the team. He's on his way to All-State!"*

Hopefully Delcie is right, and he is on his way to All-State status this season; I pray his time is "one second" better. Seeing a shy smile on his face may partly come from a Top 15 finish, but he will enjoy hoisting the Championship team trophy even more.

Monday, 9-10-2007, Charting your Course

Team mileage today: 144   runners: 24   Avg. per runner: 6.0

Confucius said, *"If you shoot for the stars and hit the moon, it's OK. But you've got to shoot for something. A lot of people don't even shoot."*

TFHS has had a video production company (Camfel productions) give a presentation each year. A motivational video of about thirty minutes is watched by the entire student body in the gym. This year, the 6th-8th graders were bussed over from the middle school ¾ mile away.

The theme of the motivational video was "Charting Your Course."

Charting your course: goals! What a great topic for an entry in a cross country book!

The American Heritage Dictionary defines goals as "1. The purpose toward which an endeavor is directed; objective. 2. The finish line of a race." Maybe it is a solid definition, but it lacks depth of the runner's soul. It lacks the motivation to get there and the challenge that one must overcome to make something happen. Goals need to push one to the limit.

Or cross country team now needsto establish time targets. All three coaches are very goal-oriented individuals with a team attitude. I follows that our coaching emphasizes goals.

We don't write our goals immediately at the season's start. We literally let the kids get their feet wet with ice and cold water for awhile before we want them to aim at a mark.

Now is the time for all good goals to be written down.

In December 2006, we had a team meeting to discuss XC 2007. My three personal goals were (1) trophy for the cross country team: boys and girls, 1st place preferred, (2) run the 7-15-07 Missoula Marathon, and (3) run the most miles ever in a year for me (1518 previous best) and/or run every day of the year.

Goal (1) is a work in progress. (2) Check – done – 3:14:20 time, 11th overall, 1st age group 35-39. This goal may have helped motivate three current members (Shane, Jacob, Ryan) and one former (Derek Naegeli, 2006 TFHS graduate) to run the Missoula ½ marathon. (3) 1392.7 is my current mileage. 1518 is only 125.3 miles away. Since I plan to run a 50 mile race on October 13th, and a 26.2 mile Seattle Marathon Thanksgiving Sunday, I just might make it. In fact, I now have 2000 imprinted on my brain. Can I train my brain to achieve this successfully?

After school, as a start-up for this week in XC, the Hawk Harriers wrote down goals.

Goals: Here are samples of our Hawk Harrier goals.

Amanda: *run a race in 25 min. or better, run at least one varsity race, and get straight A's. (Remember, she will take only three years to graduate high school. She jumped 7th grade earlier and will graduate at 16.)*

CC: *team – push each other and do well at State. Personal – be careful, stay healthy and contribute to the team as much as possible, TRY my BEST!*

Patrick: *academic 3.5 GPA, run an 18 flat or under, run at State; team – win State.*

Ryan: *Team – 1st at State; Individual – top 10 at State, 16:43.*

Bryce: *team – win state; personal – break 18:30, go to State.*

RT: *self – recover from injuries to run at State; academic – a 3.3 GPA.*

Mariah: *hit low 23's, end up 4th on team; team – place top 3 at State.*

Cody: *self – run a 3 mile less than 19:30; team – win State.*

Kyle: *personal – better time and place; all – work to do better together.*

Monica: *find out what's wrong w/ me so I can run better. My time is horrible, & I at least need to keep up with Delcie. Under 21 min.; team goals - take a higher place at state.*

JP: *get within 45 seconds of Beca at the end of a race or 30-40 seconds behind Delcie. And keep a 3.0-3.5 GPA or higher all X-C season. Team – get at least 4th or 5th at State this year.*

Jacob: *team – win state; Jacob – 1st or 2nd at State, stay 4.0 GPA*

Shane: *personal – win TF meet; break 15:30, win state; team #1 @ State.*

Lacey: *get 15 seconds better than last year, which I still have yet to achieve by 3 minutes. Team - everyone to achieve a personal best and improve.*

Mike B: *self – get 20's or under for a 3 mile time; team – have great memories and for everyone to do great and have an awesome season.*

Mike M: *easy break 18, medium mid 17's, hard low 17's; team – place higher from 4th place at State. To help others or the team improve by encouragement and or running with them or trying to push them.*

Delcie: *individual – get my 3 mile time into the 21 minute range again; team – never have the girls team be last again this year.*

Matt: *team – win state; me break 18; academics: 4.0*

Bryant: *go to State, stay above 3.0; team – win state.*

Beca: *place in top 10 (State), improve PR by <= 30 seconds, push harder, give 110% at every workout, take initiative to improve each day, improve competitive mindset; break down barriers in mind; team – place 3rd at State, have at least 2 in top 15 @ State, stay healthy.*

Goals, goals, Goals…Grades, team concepts, improving… NICE!

Our top runners ran 8 miles today (3 boys (Jacob, Shane, Ryan), 2 girls (Beca, Delcie)) as the heat soared above 90 yet again. Only two people (Cody, Lacey) got "lost" on our slightly shaded route (Mule Pasture).

Since I ran 21.5 yesterday, I was not in the mood to travel with the "Big Boys." I ran with Matt, CC, Patrick, Mariah, and Mike M. CC dominated 90% of the conversation; Patrick was next with 8%. Matt, Mike M, and Coach Gideon added 1%. Yes, this adds up to 101%, but Mariah actually contributed negative 1%, so it now adds up to 100!!!!! CC's current fave word is "intense."

Everything is "intense." Raise the intensity Hawks!

Tuesday, 9-11-2007, Favorite coach??

Team mileage today: 171   runners: 25   Avg. per runner: 6.9

Coach Naegeli sprang an interesting writing query to each member of the team: tell why each coach is your favorite coach.

Wait, all three can't be our favorite coach?!?!?!

When I questioned her impetus for the inquiry, she replied that we all need positive reinforcement at times.

In general, coach Naegeli was noted most for being a good planner and pusher. She is also obviously known for being Mariah and Jacob's mother. This is an advantage so that food and video games can be played after practice with a family within a family.

Specific comments for Coach Naegeli include *"...lets us all be crazy and laughs with us...really tough, knows what is best...makes me run farther than I want cause it will make me better...Halo...easy going...video games & food...striped socks...she comes up with practices that will challenge us and help us out for state and our races...laughs at everything... amazing...not searas (obviously Bryant)...always supportive...friend...she rocks!...nicest coach ever...she knows about coaching"*

Of course, Jacob actually listed his mom as his favorite coach. Time will tell if Mariah follows suit when she is a senior. One athlete wrote that coach Naegeli is the favorite because she is "Mariah's mom," while another wrote it because she is "Jacob's mom."

"Running with the team" and "motivational" are probably the top two responses for Coach Gideon. His third charm may be his dry sense of humor and comic relief. Tact is for people too dumb to be sarcastic.

Specific comments for coach Gideon contain words such as *"...shorter timed intervals at the State Park...just gives lots of energy...jokes and articles...funniest teacher I've met so far...pushes us to go faster and better...cool...an all-around great coach, runs with us, writing a book, encourages everybody...the cat came back the very next day (a video I showed last year to emphasize the meanings of stubborn and tenacious)...runs TOO much...random tips ☺ that work...always remembers everything we plan for ourselves...the smiley face! (shaved into my head last May) & has two kick-a@@ kids...puts in the time and effort...gets to know all of us one on one...offers good advice...is absolutely obsessive about running (and life)"*

The #1 response for Coach Bob Reall was "...back in Ohio." Our people / kids love Bob's stories. The Hawks also love his organization and meticulously kept stats.

Specific comments for Bob are as follows: *"...makes us stand still while icing...good stories and reminds me to use my arms...gives advice...funny, great ice bath maker....I love the 'back in the day' coaching or running story's – as well as the effort that is put in to our time and results...I **LOVE** Bob's Ohio stories...impressive...all stats are extremely accurate and very informative...awesome...modavashimal (Bryant)...encouraging...has Fords...tells me what he believes I can do, and coming from him I know it's true – always make me feel better about my running...wicked-awesome flip-up sun*

By Andrew Gideon

glasses – 'Arms – Arms – Arms!!'...<u>hilarious</u>!...we ran 13 miles a day, on our hands...helps me understand my limits"

Bob was lab partners with John Havlicek and Bob Knight in a college class at Ohio State in the early 60's. Impressive company! Coach Knight is one of my heroes. According to Coach Reall, Coach Knight would negotiate on what he would do with each assignment.

Another Terrible Tuesday – and the heat rises above 95 – nice!

Really, not nice, it was too hot, but our warriors, I mean harriers, pushed through. The top runners did 10 miles with timed mile sets of 2, 1, and 1. With mile easy loops between timings, it was indeed a Terrible Tuesday.

Nine boys completed the entire workout, while three girls finished. The finishers include Shane, Jacob, Ryan, Patrick, Bryce, Matt, Kyle, Bryant, Cody, Beca, Delcie, and JP.

We also had a new addition to the girl's team today: Jessie had her first practice. Welcome to 95 degree heat and Terrible Tuesdays!

Wednesday, 9-12-2007, the competition heats up

Team mileage today: 87   runners: 25   Avg. per runner: 3.5

Not only is the temperature rising, but the state's competition is getting fast and furious.

My brother coaches Darby and they have four top quality harriers that could give the Tigers a trophy. However, their frustration is a #5 runner. Since five runners score, having a #5 at 26:00 for boys just doesn't cut the tape – no matter how sharp or long the scissors are.

Colstrip and Poplar are tough. There are no state rankings for cross country in Montana; my rankings right now would be Colstrip first, Poplar 2nd, and T Falls 3rd.

Here are some tough competitor times from Class B teams.

From Frenchtown meet 9/11 - Abrahamson, Darby, 16:03, Lombardi, Deer Lodge, 17:11; MEvans, LoyolaSacredHeart, 17:15; Garbett, Dar, 17:16, Stuart, Dar, 17:51; Kappolman, LSH, 17:55; Allison, Plains, 17:58.

From Glasgow Invitational 9/8 - Azure, Poplar, 16:18; Knowlton, Pop, 17:03; Fourstar, Wolf Point, 17:27; Loewen, Glasgow, 17:36; Riediger, Pop, 17:58; Wilson, Glas, 18:12; Hopkins, Glas, 18:20; Alvernaz, Glas, 18:31; Archdale, WP, 18:38; Hoods, Harlem, 18:44.

Our Harrier Hawks need to be strengthening their wings from now until October 20th.

We had an easy workout today. Four miles was the top mileage for any person – and that included a fifteen minute stretch break after one mile and a ten minute ice/water break at 3 miles. 3.5 miles per runner for the day; an easy day for us is a hard day for the average overweight American high school student.

Jacob – *"I can't remember the last time I only ran four miles!"*

Some lost energy returned to the systems.

A Buffalo Bill NFL football player was hurt in the spinal cord on Sunday. A treatment was used on the player called the "Miami Project." Apparently his body was iced with a catheter down to 93.8 degrees as soon as possible. Doctors kept him this way during back surgery in what was called a catastrophic injury. His original diagnosis was that he would probably not walk again. Yesterday (Tuesday) he moved his hands and legs, so hope is restored. This story is chronicled in the book <u>Standing Tall: The Kevin Everett story</u>.

Does this further our belief in icing?!?!?! Oh yeah.

The majority of Hawk Harriers received scissors on the 1st day of practice. To complete team bonding, fresh scissors (old & dull) were handed out to those who missed day one. Welcome to the team BM (stabbed his stomach slightly, so Bob confiscated his scissors), JP, Patrick, MK, Mike M, Cody, and Jessie. Today was their day to run with scissors. This will certainly help harriers understand about being a little crazy to be part of our team. Hopefully no injuries occur, no insurance has to be used, and no coaches get fired!

Thursday, 9-13-2007, Ronan Invitational

Is the best thing about today's meet the fact that we miss school 4th-7th periods???

No, the best thing is we gave the runner an easy day yesterday; the Harrier Hawks will fly high on the Ronan course.

Lacey's goal (given to her by me this morning) is to get rid of the term "sophomore slump." Mr. Gideon told her that he is in a permanent "I'm getting older slump."

Today turned out to be a phenomenal day. An article is below.

Our top eight boys ran under 19 minutes. Last year at this time, only three had achieved this status. The boys won the meet today, besting all the bigger Class A teams, as well as three conference B opponents. If we plug our times from today into last year's State B Meet, WE ARE THE CHAMPIONS. This is the part where I pray, "Please Lord, let this happen."

Coach Reall – *"We had people out there doing things that were fantastic."*

Our wings apparently liked our first easy practice on Wednesday.

Notes from today's bus ride home and interviews:

JP wears size 8 shoes – Brooks for practice, Nike spikes for Terrible Tuesdays and meets. Last year she wore Adidas.

Her dad watched two meets last year and came to today's meet. The family of 11, yes 11 (9 kids, 1 mom, and 1 dad) are farmers and ranchers. The oldest child is 33 years of age, while the youngest is 2!!!

JP has to travel from her farm/ranch/house 15 miles to school on Highway 200, 30 mile round trip daily. She takes the bus to school, and gets a ride home from the parental units.

By Andrew Gideon

She was talked into cross country during 4-H, on the phone, and at the fair by Coach Naegeli. Keep on recruiting those 4-H kids coach! JP's initial thoughts about cross country include *"This is crazy."* Let's run with scissors.

After finishing and finding out her time, JP was *"almost in tears."* Last year was JP's first career race and she won the JV event. This year she moved into the Top-11 All-Time; her words obviously reflect something about this Ronan course, *"I love it – my favorite course by far."* Since her favorite course was today's, is life all downhill for this harrier? Yes and No, her 2nd favorite course is Missoula – we run there next Saturday and on October 10th.

JP's favorite thing about XC is that she gets to *"laugh & have fun, being together with team, while still getting done what needs to get done (accomplishing goals)."*

Goals – we wrote them Monday and JP accomplished them today. She wanted to get within one minute of Beca and/or 30 seconds of Delcie. She hit both – while Beca and Delcie ran great races! Her next goal is under 21:30.

JP has a comment about the team – the "team bonds well." She admires CC because she is injured (bad back), but still does well – in fact, 2 seconds better than JP today. JP also complimented Shane's running.

About the current book she is reading in English 2, <u>When the Legends Die</u>, she originally *"thought it would be dumb, but it's actually not too bad."*

I also interviewed Patrick on the bus ride home.

He is currently wearing spikes size 10 ½. These Asics are a bit too tight, and he would like a ½ size bigger. In practice he wears Adidas, size 11.

XC bus rides are good for interviews. Patrick, however, fell over three people, the trash, and dropped his sunglasses in an attempt to make his way to the front of the bus. This is the same runner who has messed up twice understanding the courses. In Ronan, he probably cost himself ten seconds taking an incorrect turn and returning to the spot where he went wrong. In Kalispell, he lost track of a loop and mentally lost 20 yards on a far turn. This is the same Patrick who hiked in the mountains all summer and knows how to use a compass.

Patrick complimented harriers Delcie, CC, and Bryce for today's effort.

XC is favored over track because of the size of the teams and the fact that cross country is minus the "lame people." The team "fits together well." We have a nice 25 piece jigsaw puzzle.

Patrick, like JP, has a 30 mile round trip each day. In the morning he rides the bus; in the evening, his home manager picks him up. Patrick lives in a "program" for kids who have been sent to small town Montana to get away from big city pressures. Most, all, have made bad decisions in their life, and are here to get back to the basics of life.

His parents divorced three months ago; mom runs an MRI station in California, while his dad produces ads for radio. His mom went hiking with him for five days in Montana in August.

Animal Farm by George Orwell is a favorite book. Patrick is a good writer and won a student-of-the-quarter award in English 2 once last school year.

The funniest kid on the team: *"That is hard. We are equally funny, depending on the day and the mood."*

His first thought after finishing today was not the same as JP's *"almost in tears."* Patrick's first thought was *"Crap, I didn't beat 18."*

I am thankful Patrick is a Hawk; his personality is a plus for our harriers.

Dakotta (junior high) really really really really wanted to be interviewed today. He likes longer runs because he can *"hold my breath for a really long time."* Dakotta, we need to talk!

Dakotta was born two minutes before brother Austin. Dakotta, yes 2 t's, has scars on his stomach, left arm, and right pectoral. The stomach is a pretty wicked looking beast, but will be a big hit with the ladies someday.

Our 8th grader was "tricked" into joining XC by his brother, because it would *"help improve his wrestling."* (It works for Matt!) They seldom stop this boyish wrestling activity. Yet, Mr. Kinser knows XC is *"good for me in a way."*

He can *"control his anger"* and *"hates losing"* so if he can rechannel this energy, then we will be good for it – as a team and as a society!

An article for the 20 September, 2007, *Sanders County Ledger*.

Racing Well in Ronan   *by Andrew Gideon*

On Thursday, September 15, the Thompson Falls Blue Hawks traveled to Ronan for a cross country meet. Coach Sarah Naegeli stated, "We were working toward this race to have fast times and the kids succeeded."

The harriers were given their first easy practice of the five week season the day before. This must have worked wonders for energy levels as the boys took first place against nine other A, B, and C schools. The girls placed third, but the Lady Hawks were first among all B teams entered.

The girls were a solid team in Ronan. Four Lady Hawks finished consecutively in 13th - 16th place in the three mile race. Beca Gunderson's 21:14 clocking gave strength to the next harrier, Delcie Peters, who timed in at 21:30; Ciara Normandeau (21:32) and Jeffreyanne Parker (21:34) used Peter's momentum and were the next two racers to cross the line. Mariah Naegeli rounded out the Hawk scoring with an impressive 22:44 freshman time and 25th place.

Coach Bob Reall, with a smile on his face, chastised the girls for "coming in too fast" for him to write down times. Coach Gideon smiled as well, as the prospect of improving last year's 6th place State finish vaulted into his mind.

JP (Parker) was "almost in tears" after finding out her time from teammates. Operating as a group worked well as JP's time vaulted her to the 8th best time ever for a Hawk female runner. For more information on the Top 11 all-time and other cross country news, please see the website at www.thompsonfalls.net and go to the cross country page. Parker won the JV girls race at Ronan last year and had a phenomenal showing today. She describes the Ronan meet, *"I love it; it is my favorite course by far."*

She was certainly not the only Hawk to enjoy this course. Shane Donaldson improved his career best time to 15:54, moving within three seconds of the school record in the process. Jacob Naegeli bettered his Personal Record (PR) by 17 seconds; Naegeli also tied his brother Derek (2006 graduate of TFHS) with a PR of 16:20, 5th place on the all-time Hawk running list.

Donaldson and Naegeli finished 2nd and 4th overall. Rounding out the scoring was Ryan Sol (17:27, 11th), Mike Morris (17:38, 13th), and Patrick Jamison (18:06, 16th). The top three teams scored in at Thompson Falls 46, Whitefish 56, and host Ronan 109.

While the Hawks were flying high after this meet, work still needs to get done.

There is not an official ranking for cross country in Montana, but Coach Gideon currently ranks the State B Boys as follows based on meet times: Colstrip 1st, Poplar 2nd, and T Falls 3rd.

As far as the State B Girls, Coach Reall ranks the Red Lodge girls 2nd, behind powerful Glasgow. However, all three coaches were impressed with how well the T Falls girls competed in Ronan. There just might be a hint of a state trophy in the Lady Hawks' future.

Other Hawks running the three miles today were as follows: Bryce Miller (18:13), Mike Kidwiler (18:37), Matt Hojem (18:51), RT Brown (19:01), Bryant Normandeau (19:51), Kyle Breithaupt (21:16), Mike Barnett (23:03), and Cody White (23:24).

For the Lady Hawks, three other runners competed: Monica Conlin (25:15), Lacey Wade (26:06), and Amanda Wood (29:42).

In the junior high division, a two mile run, three competitors entered for Thompson Falls. Dakotta Kinser may have been born two minutes before his brother on 3-8-94, but Austin came out ahead today by 2 minutes and 15 seconds. The times were Austin Kinser 15:53, John Gunderson 15:57, and Dakotta Kinser 18:08.

The next meet for the Hawks is the prestigious Mountain West Classic on Saturday, September 22, in Missoula. This is one of the biggest competitions in the Northwest.

Friday, 9-14-2007, Relationships

Team mileage today: 146   runners: 25   Avg. per runner: 5.8

Why does a coach make himself a lattee and get to school by 4:30 AM to work on the cross country website and type on a book on the Hawk Harriers?

"Relationships" is my quality answer.

I have a wife and two kids sleeping now. I have another family in the cross country team as well. Balancing the time between both is important.

The 1979 Pittsburgh Pirates (Major League Baseball) theme was "We are Family." Pittsburgh won the World Series, and the idea of family was cemented into my 11 year old brain.

This team is a good second family.

What a blessing to end each school day with this group.

However, the type of relationships I am writing on today includes those of the male-female variety. What is a high school book without discussing hormones. On my 8-13 entry, I used the term "hormonally challenged."

Out of the loop is a great term for my ability to see their relationships.

It's hard to fathom how 22 high school kids could exist without some thoughts of the opposite sex. In the words of The Princess Bride, it is "inconceivable."

Last spring Ryan may have been dating Beca. He will be taking Monica to Homecoming in two weeks. Jacob has been dating a Katie for quite a while. RT dated a girl this last spring, but his shaved head probably indicates he is back on the market. CC says she loves men, but on her run, her comments are about movie stars and a 19 year old Coast Guard cadet she met once.

That's all I see.

Today our current # 7 harrier, who is "twitterpated" by a girl, may have skipped practice for this reason. (Author note: twitterpated is jargon. The American Heritage Dictionary defines twitter as "A state of agitation or excitement," while pate means "the brains, intellect." Put the two together – agitation/excitement in the brain. I.E. hormonally challenged.) Our # 7 talked with Coach Bob and Coach Naegeli and didn't make the workout. Several other "family" members revealed he has a "thing" for a girl and had plans to go to another student's house to meet her. We shall see how this plays out.

#7 harrier – Listen please: you have no better family to show respect to than this cross country team. Give them your strength, energy, and respect, and it will be returned 100 fold.

Maybe having the majority of our athletes without "significant others" is good for our team. Sometimes having the carrot in front of the rabbit makes the chase faster. Greyhounds chase rabbits, and fast runners chase stopwatches. Suppose performing as a runner to impress someone is on someone's brain. Maybe a person will work a little harder to catch the attention of someone's eye. Infer that there are attractions out there, but they are below the surface. What happens below the surface is the human battle of all-time.

Relationships bring out hidden qualities with time. Time is a battle for all – dealing with parents, kids, peers, co-workers, lovers, prospective dates, slight acquaintances, and the politically correct "significant other." Bit by bit strength is built into a runner and drawn out on race day (hopefully!), and bit by bit our thoughts are made known by words or deeds in terms of relationships.

There must be more to write on relationships, but I'm not a nosy coach or maybe I am just not observant in this manner. Again, there has to be some emotions, thoughts, stress, and teenage angst involved in our runner's minds. Maybe this is information needed for a perfect coach, but I fail in that respect.

Is this a perfect family? No, is there such a thing?

Our family did extra push-ups, sit-ups, and abs because we had several potty-mouthed individuals yesterday. Beca and Shane were overheard swearing by Coach Gideon = bad leaders. Coach Reall calls this *"toilet tooth,"* and says it doesn't belong on our team. We don't want to take any chances that an official at State disqualifies a swearing athlete.

Shane also was grounded by Coach Naegeli for driving poorly on the way home from practice. We drove seven miles to the Thompson River road for an LSD day. After running, we iced in cold river. Shane drove too fast and passed us in what we felt was an unsafe manner. Overprotective maybe, but we love our family; better safe than sorry.

I love ending my school day with the Hawk Harriers and coaches. Each day I wake up with hope for their future and improved times.

Families should work together for the good of all, and we do that.

Relationships….a deep subject, yet justice to the idea was probably not done as well as it could have been.

Some information on Hawk mating habits: *The mating and breeding habits of these birds include aerial displays meant to advertise their readiness for breeding.* (www.wild-bird-watching.com/Red-tailed-Hawk.html).

Another site (http://desertusa.com/aug96/du_hawk.html) states: *Mating and nest building begin in early spring, usually in March and continue through May. This is accompanied by spectacular aerial displays by both males and females. Circling and soaring to great heights, they fold their wings and plummet to treetop level, repeating this display as much as five or six times.*

We are safe – this is the fall, so our Hawk Harriers won't be mating anytime soon. However, they do have "aerial displays" to catch other's attention.

Delcie brought silly nylons for the girls today. Her pair had flowers, while others were plain, colored, or black. That strange addition to practice was appreciated. If laughter is the best medicine, this team will cure a lot of diseases.

Girls, Nylons before the Thompson River Run   Boys and Icing after the run

Saturday, 9-15-2007, Half-way Home

Is the cup half-empty or half-full?

The season is five weeks over with five weeks left. Exertion, toil, and strain, Listen to the Wizard of Oz, "Exertion, toil, and strain, oh my! Lions, Tigers, and Bears." We have worked tremendously hard, and the harriers can mostly be described as "able to play well with others."

The Hawks flew under the radar today with 4-6 miles for each harrier "on his/her own." Several were told not to run to rest slight injuries, while Beca was told to add a hard 100 meter surge per mile.

Our progress has been phenomenal. We have worked hard for five weeks (half full); it remains to be seen how we will fill the cup the next five weeks (half empty).

Let's fill that cup with the right lattee: Hazelnut Venti, double shot, please and thank you. A little taste of heaven on earth.

"Two roads diverged in a yellow wood and sorry I could not travel both And be one traveler, long I stood and looked down one as far as I could to where it bent in the undergrowth;	And both that morning equally lay in leaves no feet had trodden black. Oh, I kept the first for another day! Yet knowing how way leads on to way, I doubted if I should ever come back.
Then took the other, as just as fair, and having perhaps the better claim because it was grassy and wanted wear; though as for that, the passing there had worn them really about the same,	I shall be telling this with a sigh Somewhere ages and ages hence: Two roads diverged in a wood, and I -- I took the one less traveled by, and that has made all the difference."

Robert Frost wrote "The Road Not Taken." My English 2 classes have to memorize this so that their 3.5 pound blood-soaked sponges of brains will have it permanently imprinted in the neural pathways. It is a good time to recall this as we are half-way through the season.

We, the High-flying Harrier Hawks, have made a decision. We, the Thompson Falls runners, have taken the road less traveled to make the difference. Actually, most of our paths and routes are extremely well traveled by us at least.

Will we continue on the narrow path for the next 5 weeks? Yes, yes, yes, yes, yes, yes, yes, yes, yes (9 yes answers for the top 7 boys who will run at State and the 2 alternates). Yes, yes, yes, yes, yes, yes, yes, yes, yes – for the other sex and Title 9 equality so I don't get sued.

Thank you Mr. Frost, I recall your poem for the readers. It is reprinted without your permission, for you died in 1963. Frost wrote this before he died.

Today I ran with Jessie, so she could get another required practice (the first ten practices by MHSA (Montana High School Association) rules must be with a coach present. Other than not knowing how to breathe, having foot issues and back problems, and chanting, "I hope this gets easier," Jessie is an

73

experienced runner. She tried to understand breathing patterns, and she has track familiarity at shorter distances, so she will come around.

I had to cut a tree on campus so Shane wouldn't hurt himself. The tree was obstructing half of our route. It could easily be avoided, but Shane continually ventured over and jumped on the smaller limbs to break them off. Future injuries splatter my mind.

If coaches have to haul Shane off to the hospital because a tree falls on him, then great. If Shane hurts himself on a fallen tree, then not so great.

My experience as a lumberjack helped immensely: "I'm a lumberjack and I'm okay, I sleep all night and I work all day." Thank you Monte Python.

Shane, we coaches worry about you at times.

I am sure Shane worries about the author too.

Sunday, 9-16-2007, Happy 3rd Birthday Jaxon

My oldest child, Jaxon, turned three years old today. This brings me to an age, peak, and performance thoughts.

What does one do when the sport loved has reached a peak? I basically cried after my 3:14:20 marathon on July 15, because I only achieved one of four goals. One – break three hours, my dream goal; two – 3:03 and under 7 minute miles; three – PR of better than 3 hr 8 min 37 seconds; and four – 3 hr 20 min to qualify for the Boston Marathon. If the heat wouldn't have been 80 plus degrees for the last ten miles, all times that day would have been better. I had trained as hard as I could while still finding time for job, family, and other responsibilities; in fact, for one three week period, I averaged a half-marathon a day.

As I told my wife after the run – if I couldn't set a PR today, I never will - sad; my peak is over, it's all downhill and not in the faster sense! Anguish!!! My second thought was that I wasn't worthy to coach the kids because my times just aren't top quality. I was overjoyed with the half-marathon efforts of Shane (1:22:29), Derek (1:22:45), Jacob (1:26:13), and Ryan (1:32:03), but wish I could have been more of an inspiration by accomplishing more than one goal of four.

When all is said and done, I am blessed with health to run my 8th marathon of my life, in a decent time, and I almost have 1400 miles this year. To be thankful for health is important.

To be thankful for Jaxon turning three is important. Pizza for dinner!

With thoughts of peaking, my thoughts drift to Monica, who has a fear that she will never beat her previous best times. Monica loves cross country, but this year is proving to be a struggle for her, so this issue needs to be addressed in a positive way. Some girls just don't improve from freshman-senior years like the boys do. Boys generally make a steady progression, but running improvement can be more of an unpredictable battle for some girls.

On Thursday, Monica dropped out of the Top 11 in TFalls school history. She had been 11th, but JP's PR (Personal Record) of 21:34 to move into 8th place all-time. This forced a shift of position, dropping Monica to 12th place.

My fear is the same as Monica's – she may not ever get to a 21:54 again. Does it matter that she is intelligent, attractive, positive, and well-liked? Does it matter that her future is unlimited, except maybe not as a USA Olympic distance runner? Does it matter that she is a leader influencing others to become better people? At Ronan's meet, where her time was 25 minutes for the third straight race after last year's 21:54 PR, then all those things don't matter – at least in her mind. Thoughts get focused on the negative running times and performance.

I love running, and maybe I've reached a peak; we can look at Monica and know life will have so many positive blessings for her. However, she still is feeling as dejected right now as a 39 year old man felt with a 3:14 marathon and a dream of 3 hours pounding like shoeless feet on the pavement of emotions.

Thank you for being part of our team Monica. Maybe your hip will improve, maybe your migraines and medicine are affecting your running, maybe, maybe, and maybe....maybe there will be other routes to race in life. There is some anguish in life, but life is a miracle, so taking the good with the bad is something we all must adjust to.

My son Jaxon has been mostly healthy, but there are times when raising a child is frustrating. When he gets sick and cries, anguish fills my heart. When a yellow jacket stings my boy and pain fills his brain, then too much empathy filters into my own emotions. I want only good and not bad for my son, but life happens. Excrement hits the fan; hopefully with prayer and blessings, the positive will outweigh the negative. I will teach him to count his blessings, even if he doesn't become a professional baseball player or a Kenyan.

Can we teach Monica to count her blessings, even if she never drops her time below 25 minutes again? Prayer will hopefully move her to a new PR this year and next; we can hope.

This Wednesday the top 11 All-time athletes are being treated to a 15 minute professional massage. Since Monica dropped to # 12, does that make Monica's pain worse?

My introduction to Monica Conlin seems a bit melancholic. Sorry. Her personality is anything but melancholic, as we Hawk Harriers know.

Beca writes: *"Monica is one of my best friends. She is also gorgeous (despite those red shorts...no; jk!!) Even last season when she was hurt, she told me that now she was my biggest fan, which meant a lot to me. Her and I also go way back. She has a quirky sense of humor and can almost always cheer me up. We support each other in all areas of life, always."*

Beca's words back up my view of a beautiful set of people. She called Delcie *"beautiful"* and Monica *"gorgeous."* Beca did not say the same words about the boys so far – Shane, Jacob, and Ryan, but I will go out on a limb and say they are an attractive team, like bananas to a monkey. Beauty is more than physical – the mental and spiritual are strong in these kids.

Monica was born 3-9-1992 as Monica Laine Conlin. I'm not really into astrology, but let's take a look to see what traditional Pisces traits are

75

"imaginative and sensitive, compassionate and kind, selfless and unworldly, intuitive and sympathetic....on the dark side.... Escapist and idealistic, secretive and vague, weak-willed and easily led." (astrology-online.com/pisces.htm)

Wow, I learned nothing and added little insight to Monica's personality. Maybe we can read her words and look back to see if any of them fit.

Miss Conlin just won $100,000,000. She would put most of it toward college, give to several organizations, including breast cancer, save some, and buy several pairs of Brooks and lots & lots & lots & lots of high heels. She would also take trips around the world, get a Great Dane, and a tea cup Chihuahua. Okay, maybe this paragraph didn't really support the idea of physical, mental, and spiritual beauty, but a reader will just have to keep reading.

Future plans consist of *"Get outta here! Move to San Diego with Holly (sister), work & community college for 2 yrs, then go to Australia, become a chef or go into international aviation."* Goals for life: *"get to see the world & not be stuck in a little town like this. Make lots of money. Be happy! ☺"*

Offering advice to future runners and younger students can be tough. Yet, Monica had some stellar words, *"Be yourself & don't be fake! Work hard at everything you do. Try your hardest. Never give up on your goals."*

So that leads us to find out what Monica will never give up on – a 20:00 time in high school, becoming a chef or international pilot, finding her way to San Diego Community College for 2 years, and then possibly the Sydney Culinary Arts School in Australia. Honestly, in 11 years of teaching, that is the first time someone has mentioned the Sydney Culinary Arts School in Australia.

She probably gets her individuality from a large family. Dad Jim Conlin lives in TFalls, while Mom lives in Ekalaka, Montana. One sister (Holly, 20 years old) also ran XC for the Blue Hawks (#2 all-time). 4 step-brothers (13, 13, 16, 18) and 2 step sisters (10, 21) certainly add energy and/or confusion to her life. Maybe that is why she wants to escape, I mean, travel to Australia.

She is currently in my English 2 class, has a solid GPA, and is a good writer. If she writes as fast as she talks, we will surely have some fun reading. The Hawk Harriers enjoy listening to her randomness and she is a team favorite.

Monica's 5'6" 130 pound frame has PR's of a 5:48 mile, and 21:54 three mile. Running goals: *"get under 20:00 min in high school career."* Please do!

Monica's list of favorites: movie (*anything w/ Will Pharell*), food (*Crazy foods! Like Thai or from exotic countries...I'm up to anything...except Mexican!*), book (5 people you meet in Heaven), class (any kind of History/Chemistry), sport (X-C), Teacher (*Is this a trick question?*), and coach (*even though she's tough, my mom*).

Matt says Monica *"dislikes puking....Dumb!...Constantly has blisters."* Do we know if it is dumb to dislike puking or does Matt think Monica is dumb? Answers: who does like to puke? And, don't be dissing Monica!

Jacob was laughing as he wrote his words: *"Monica reminds me of a female version of Shane. Minus the massive amounts of food consumed by Shane and a few hair style and physical traits differences, they're almost identical."* Except for several style issues, some horror, some gruesome deaths, and many bestsellers, my writing is identical to Stephen King and James Patterson.

Save us, Delcie, from the boy's text! Delcie writes, *"If there was one thing I could steal from Monica Conlin, it would be her radiating self-confidence. She doesn't hesitate to ask her boyfriend to smell her armpit. She's not shy, she'll burp in your face or chat up any guy. Oh ya, she has incredible fashion sense, and many long tales to tell. (I love her stories!) On top of it all, she's a very aggressive and phenomenal runner with every reason to believe in herself!"*

I already had a long discussion of Monica's running. She was much smoother last year, but she was recently taking some medication for migraines; she finished that up on Friday. We are hoping that will spring some energy into her, because she has seemed a little sluggish.

Her favorite sport is XC; I pray for her running and her future.

Ryan Sol in Ronan 2006   Monica Conlin, Thompson River, 2007

Monday, 9-17-2007, Girl Power in the 21st century

Team mileage today: 143   runners: 25   AvG. per runner: 5.7

This letter to the editor appeared in the *Sanders County Ledger* (9/13).

"Editor: / I attended the Thompson Falls High School Alumni reunion on Aug. 11 and 12. I have never missed one and saw several persons that I have not seen in almost 50 years. I was impressed with the casual demeanor of the football coach, Chad Laws, who spoke and made a good impression on me. Coach Laws seems to be proud of being coach of his winning team, and I am sure that he has left a positive image on the young men that he coaches.

My sister Ilene Shoemaker, who had her 77th birthday on Aug. 11, and her husband Maurice, who is 82, are avid and enthusiastic fans of the Blue Hawks. They keep me informed during the year of their progress. While I was there, I heard that in spite of the fact that the team is inspiring and successful, there is not a cheer lead squad to support the dynamic efforts of the young men. These young men are proud enough of their efforts to become champions, so therefore why don't the young women feel the same sense of pride and obligation to become cheerleaders?

By Andrew Gideon

Mr. Pauli's goal is to build character as well as educate our young people. Therefore he should make every effort to fund this program. I sincerely hope that this letter is not my swan song as I am 78 years old and this could have been my last reunion. So I hope that as a past alumni my request is given consideration and granted.   Eugene Risbon   Salmon, Idaho"

What was I thinking coaching girls to run? Our lady Hawks don't feel "pride and obligation"? They can't become "champions"? They are not supporting the "dynamic efforts of the young men" in our community? Obviously I should quit now because I have failed Beca, Delcie, CC, JP, Mariah, Monica, Lacey, Amanda, and Jessie.

Please listen to Coach Naegeli's response:

Editor, / I feel that a reply is needed for Mr. Risbon's letter to the editor of last week. I have the privilege of working with nine talented young women at Thompson Falls High School. These young ladies are members of the Bluehawk cross-country team and are fine athletes in their own right. Not only that, but 2/3 of these girls are on the honor roll and several of these ladies are representatives on student council. When they compete they want to do well for themselves and for the Thompson Falls' Bluehawks. These nine young women are hard-working athletes in their own right and to imply that they have no sense of pride or obligation to their high-school does them a huge disservice. I daresay that any of the coaches who are lucky enough to work with the Lady hawk athletes would agree that our female athletes have a tremendous amount of pride in their school, and enjoy representing Thompson Falls.

I believe that we should be thanking the Thompson Falls' school system for giving our young ladies the many opportunities to represent their school in their own right, as an athlete. And thank you Ladyhawks for making us proud of Thompson Falls High School.   Sarah Naegeli

----

Long slow distance (LSD) day: ten miles of conversational paced jogging greeted our harriers.

Jacob, Patrick, and Ryan, and I led the group and discussed "Iraq," - *"good serious topics of interest to our nation and world"* (9-02 entry). I'm guessing the football locker room had seriously intelligent conversation too. No brachiating in the locker room please.

Two runners, Beca and Ryan, luckily received a "competitive" workout after their LSD. These two recorded ten miles with some hard track intervals. Not wanting to be outdone, Shane and Jacob ran an extra cool down so they could maintain a total mileage lead over Ryan.

After five weeks Shane and Jacob have 235 miles. Ryan, at 230, is next, while Delcie's 189 leads the girls. Beca's 155 miles is 2nd for the Lady Hawks.

Six athletes used bikes as an alternate workout. Shins, knees, hips, and brains have had some wear and tear and need tender loving bicycle care.

Tuesday, 9-18-2007, To compare or not to compare, that is the question
Team mileage today: 159   runners: 24   Avg. per runner: 6.6

A great reader can recall that Coach Bob Reall was in Lancaster, Ohio, for at least thirty years as a teacher and coach. It is important to note that Coach Reall's main influence for a coaching approach would be Arthur Lydiard. The Lydiard method is a lot of mileage, in other words, an emphasis on endurance.

The Lancaster Purple Horde (Back in Ohio!!!!) was ranked #1 in the nation in 1967 and 1979. The boys won State Championships in 1979 and 1990. A third place finish is also to their credit in 1980. League championships occurred in 1964, 1965, 1967, 1968, 1977, 1978, 1979, 1980, 1981, 1982, 1983, 1984, 1985, 1987, 1989, and 1990.

Girls were league champions in 1982, 1983, 1984, 1985, and 1991.

Four individuals won state titles – Debbie Crist 1965, Bill Beaty 1968 and 1969, John Zishka 1978 and 1979, and Clark Haley 1980.

The top 11 times for Lancaster Boys for 5K times are John Ziska (1979) 14:16, Clark Haley (1980) 14:34, Bill Beaty (1969) 14:43, Doug Conroy (1983) 14:56, BJ Holland (1990) 14:58, Tom Stickel (1980) 15:01, Dave Agosta (1978) 15:03, Carl DeVault (1980) 15:10, Gary Dille (1991) 15:11, Todd Walker (1990) 15:12, and Gary Graf (1968) 15:16.

The top 11 times for Lancaster Girls for 5K are Cathy Dye (1984) 18:00, Angie Dille (1985) 18:03, Susan Wohlfarth (1981) 18:26, Missy Dittmar (1980) 18:51, Marianne Valentine (1981) 18:52, Helen Clark (1982) 19:11, **Jenny Reall** (1981) 19:17, Jenni Blind (1981) 19:25, Sharon Wood (1981) 19:27, Stacey Owens (1982) 19:46, Pam Hamilton (1986) 19:49, and Michele Lynch (1983) 19:49.   ---------------------------------------

Jenny Reall is Coach Bob's daughter. Here is some information that I noted from Bob about Jenny. Her freshman-junior years were good. As a senior, she would cross the line and collapse; apparently she had some health problems.

Troubled health didn't stop her from competing in college however. Jenny started at Bowling Green and won her first race. However, circumstances caused Jenny to red-shirt and she didn't run again for them; she transferred to the College of Southern Idaho for the next two years. After CSI (not the TV show, the school), she graduated from Idaho State. Jenny ran two years for CSI, but because of her health, she stopped competing after that.

A master's degree from Mankato, now Minnesota State, would follow. Jenny has degrees in business and marketing.

Jenny would give Bob a grandson, his only grandchild; Jack was born on 12-26-2001.

Did Bob coach Jenny or was there another girls coach? Good inquiry! Bob coached his daughter for three years of high school. It would have been four years, but freshman at the time could not compete on a varsity team; therefore, Jenny had a separate team and coach. Currently Coach Naegeli coaches Jacob and Mariah. Derek has already graduated, while Logan can "officially" join the team next year as a 7th grader. Basically she will coach each kid for six years from 7th grade through senior year.

Shall we compare our times to the Lancaster teams?

Bob started coaching Lancaster in 1963. These times are a collection of 30 years of running. TFalls XC began ten years ago. JP vaulted into the top 11 all-time, lowering the 11th best time by two seconds. It doesn't sound like much, but slow and steady progress will help the Hawk harrier catch the rabbit. Let's see how the TFalls times stack up in 20 years.

Lancaster had an average graduating class of 650. TFalls has an average of 50. Therefore in 30 years, 19,500 people had potential to run for Lancaster. In the last ten years TFalls had 500. So for every year of Lancaster times, we should get 13 years of running to get our top 11 all time chart to an equivalent shape. Therefore check our chart in 260 years and compare the two teams!

Shall we compare our times to Colstrip, Poplar, Glasgow, and Red Lodge? Yes and No; we should challenge the self individually and the Hawk Harriers collectively to see how we stack up against others. That is part of the challenge and competition that exists in the world for sports, jobs, relationships, and general living.

However, each individual should strive to deal with life's challenges in a healthy manner; the competition to be the best person one can be is maybe the major part of life. Repeat after me: Obstacles, adversity, breakthroughs, successes, and failures! Our harriers have done an amazing job with these words so far this season – and in their life: Success being the governing word.

We, the mighty Hawks, solemnly swear that the battle we are fighting is with our individual self. The nice thing about this struggle is our many supporters: teammates, coaches, parents, and most certainly, a Hawk mascot.

We will run and not grow weary; we will run and not get caught by opponents. Our times will improve; our lives will go in a positive direction. We will run…

If, by chance, we do stumble in our efforts, then we will laugh. We will first laugh at ourselves, and if we can't do that, then we will make fun of others. Stumbling, bumbling, tripping, and falling, we will get back up and wipe off our dirt-stained faces to bravely stand before the mirror and say, "I tried."

A quote to consider: *"We may run, walk, stumble, drive, or fly, but let us never lose sight of the reason for the journey, or miss a chance to see a rainbow on the way"* (Gloria Gaither).

"Veni, vidi, vici." Translation (Julius Caesar): *"I came, I saw, I conquered."*

An army slogan is "Be all you can be."

This bunch of student-athletes has me so excited that I can only drink one lattee per day, because the adrenaline from each practice and meet replaces the java junkies caffeine hit.

As light as my fingers dance on the keyboards, our runners shall tred lightly and dance with scissors across the XC course of life.

Maybe we can use this phrase instead, "Veni, Vidi, Cerebros consumpsi."

Translation: "I came, I saw, I ate his brain."

Like a worm threading through my veins, like a computer virus destroying a C-drive, the java devours my neural pathways.

Okay, okay, I am not a caffeine addict. However, my point is that sometimes blood is not the only thing flowing through our veins.

This is probably why I wanted to analyze relationships (9-21 entry). How many of our athletes are hinging on hearing someone say hello to them, or losing patience or memory space due to some important person looking at them wrong. Love might be flowing through veins.
Love for friends, family, team, or significant other is a daily deliberation.

Sometimes the only thing flowing through veins might be endorphins. "Run, run, run, as fast as you can," says the Endorphin-filled Gingerbread man. I run because I can, I run because pain is weakness leaving the body, and I run because of the runner's high. (Actually this "runner's high" doesn't come as often as the aching shins or muscles, but it sure sounds good.)

Sometimes the only thing flowing veins might be dreams. Currently I am enjoying the journey on the dream road to a State Championship. This trophy ending flows through my veins.

The point is that blood is good, but to have a reason to go forward in life and have this reason flow through the veins is important. Championships, relationships, dreams, endorphins, love, and, of course, caffeine are vital life ingredients. I am obviously speaking of positive flow of life.

Healthy levels of the above – some say moderation in all things. However, I am a believer in overdoing something to see where the line is. If you never cross the line, then you either don't take chances or you are in too much of a comfort zone. Runners learn to push the limit and sometimes always seem on the verge of injury. Runners who toe the line by constantly pushing are the ones to stretch records and goals, while pushing teams to a new better level.

Here is a serious caffeine story: My son Kaden was born 6-9-06, three months premature. His brain did not communicate with his lungs with the message "breathe." So, from June 09, 2006, until late October (4 ½ months), Kaden was given caffeine to stimulate his body and lungs to do what seems obvious – breathe. One of Kaden's major problems was taking life for granted; breathing was not in his vocabulary, so caffeine had to flow through his tiny veins. He needed to understand breathing is not optional. Every breath is a gift.

Reader: breathe and let some things flow through your veins along with blood: championship dreams, love, family, and endorphins.

Coach Bob often comments on his former top runners. However, one of his favorite all-time harriers was Mike Toay, a 1985 Lancaster graduate. As a freshman, he timed a 25:30. Three weeks after his senior season ended, he clocked an 18:38. At college Mike went to SMU (Southern Methodist U.) and received a Student Filmmaking Collegiate Oscar; only four of these are awarded each year. He went to California and worked as a filmmaker. His wife recently received a new media job in Oregon, so that is where he lives now. Mike isn't on the top 11 all-time for Lancaster, but he is fondly remembered by Coach Bob.

Today, Terrible Tuesday # 6 of the year, we had timed mile repeats of 2 x 1 x 1. With warm-ups and cool downs, our top runners would have a second consecutive ten mile day!

Eight boys and four girls completed the workout. Six of those twelve had their fastest mile of the day on the last mile.

On the first two mile timing, I, Coach Gideon, was breathing down Patrick's neck The jerk wouldn't let me beat him, but he had to run 15-20 seconds faster than he would have without the old man haunting him! Six runners beat me on that two mile, including MK and his strong second mile. Strength for the later miles; this is a good thing!

I paced Beca under 7 minutes on the third mile and Monica to under an 8 on the 4th one. Monica's 7:37 might not seem impressive for her 4th hard timed mile of the day, but the smile of progress on her face was well worth the pain of a tough workout.

When I run with the team, I don't get an overall perspective. Coaches Bob and Naegeli see all the runners. Coach Naegeli was impressed with the aforementioned "six" who showed tremendous heart at the end of a hard day: Shane, Ryan, Patrick, Matt, MK, and Monica.

Ryan and Beca did a tremendous job today pushing through yesterday's extra intervals. Beca, on Thursday, September 13, had asked Coach Gideon to make her more competitive. So, on Monday, Ryan and Beca did some extra track work after the long slow distance. Muscle memory, speed, and quicker strides after an extended day; they did great. That made today a little harder, but will make State a little better. Thanks for making your legs uncomfortable now so that you could be comfortable with a time on October 20th.

This was a long Terrible Tuesday entry – as long and terrible as our workout. Ouch! My fingers and brain are as heated and worn out as the Hawks after running today. The workout will pay off in the future. The writing will too!

Wednesday, 9-19-2007, Glow sticks and Dixie cups = Massage!!!

Team mileage today: 83   runners: 20   Avg. per runner: 4.2

Team practice – in the dark at 6:45 am. Not completely in dark mind you, never could we accuse our team of that atrocious type of mind set. Some brought glow sticks, the coaches brought food, drinks, and Dixie cups.

Today's title is attributed to Patrick – glow sticks and Dixie cups. He made this comment jogging this morning.

Practicing in the morning is a great way to recover. It is hard to get up at first, but then run and be done. The body will have a full day and a half to recover until Thursday after school. The mind will be tired, but comfortable with the thought that there is no practice after school.

We had a good attitude, even RT who has never, in his life, seen 6:45 am. Thanks for running Hawks and for waking up the town.

The reason we ran early was to set up a "double session" for the Top 11 All-Time runners for Thompson Falls HS. We currently have seven: Beca, CC, Delcie, JP, Shane, Jacob, and Ryan. These harriers were given the words of dread and double session. Mr. Gideon even sang a little ditty, "Double sessions, oh yeah, double sessions, not much fun for the students, but oh, much much fun for Mr. Gideeeeeoooooonnnn."

Yes, the fear of a fifteen minute speed session was in their brain. Trepidation crept stealthily into those seven young minds as they were aware of a separate 15 minute "workout."

Think positive!

A professional massage therapist was brought to TFHS. Yes, a masseuse, not a masseur. It is a very important distinction for lawyers and parents. A woman giving a massage is acceptable to high school students. A man would probably be a big No-No and get a coach fired.

Let's get rid of male nurses too! (I'm joking.)

CC was the first to receive a massage – she gave the woman (my wife's cousin) a big hug afterward. At least six harriers described this as "relaxing," and I did see some HUGE smiles on faces. Again, the runners may have thought a workout, speed session, or something worse, was coming. However, think positive, today was a good afternoon to be a Hawk runner in the Top 11 all-time.

Another nice bonus was that I spent some time conversing with these runners as they waited their turn. We were able to view pictures and see examples of some habits talked about on runs. Communication was opened, which means even the ears of the coach listened to comments of runners. I learned several thoughts of our Hawks which could help us design better workouts and stronger athletes.

Shane and Beca had the tightest backs, with the therapist mentioning to Beca that she could use a full 1 ½ hour massage. Delcie was the shyest upon entering the room where we had the massage table set up. Shane was "stumbling like a drunk" after his 20 minute session.

We may just have to do this again. The original thought was to let the Top 11 All-time have a second massage, sometime soon, before state; there would be no objectors for that idea among the seven!

However, the second thought would be to include the group that will complete the top seven at State. Boys #4-7 and girls #5-7 would be the

83

beneficiaries to this second idea. The first seven would agree to this, because a strong plan of **team** is in their brain. The top three boys, Jacob & Shane & Ryan, know all too well how important the next scorers are for the team.

Three stages to watch out for: pain after a run, pain during a run, and changing stride (Coach Naegeli). Our changing stride people to keep an eye on are RT, Matt, and Monica. Monica was leaning so far to the right last Thursday at Ronan, that if the race were another mile, she would have fallen over.

We are hopeful for RT, for the third consecutive year. We keep hoping for Monica; she had some smooth running and a breakthrough mile time on Tuesday; A 7:37 mile isn't earth shattering, but it was a level start to improvement and time/form of 2006. Matt looked horrible (yet he ran through it for progress on a bad day) on Tuesday, even after a Coach Gideon pep talk.

Thursday, 9-20-2007, Homecoming Kings?
Team mileage today: 116   runners: 23   Avg. per runner: 5.0

Rain, rain came today, and soaked us in our clothes. The top runners ran seven miles in drizzling rain with two push miles in a team competition.

Delcie stated that she "tweaked" her back Tuesday. Wednesday morning it bothered her, but halleluiah, the massage on Wednesday after school took it away. Thank you massage therapist for that!

Jacob and RT are two of the four possible homecoming kings.

Coach Naegeli asked our student-athletes to write a snippet on why RT and Jacob deserved to be homecoming king.

Shane's pure envy cried, *"what if they don't deserve to be kings?"*

Others were less hurt and more co-operative.

RT (the following are direct written remarks) – *he's an okay guy; he's bald and bold! Maybe the crown will keep his head warm; he is goofy; he promised to wear his orange jump suit to prom; because he's RT; he is hilarious; he's funny! He'd be the first to wear the crown with a bald head; he'll give me something to laugh about and be in shock about; he's bald, so the crown will cover it; he has supersweet bass; he is friends with everyone; he's a runner; he would wear the yellow short shorts and the retro jersey; he needs a headwarmer.*

Jacob (again, direct written statements) – *XC runners rock, He needs to be embarrassed, He is smart!? (I guess), He is the best cook on earth!, He has school spirit, blue hair and body, cuz he's gonna have corn rows, He needs something to cover his head, face, and hair; He makes awesome bread, he's my brother, he's an alright guy, good student, he needs something to cover his hair; he works very hard at running.*

Friday, 9-21-2007, Recruitment
Team mileage today: 113.5   runners: 25   Avg. per runner: 4.54

The following letter is one of four similar letters I sent out this week.

What is a Hawk Harrier to do after high school? It is a time for decisions and more decisions. I'm glad I never have choices now in my adult world.

Friday, September 21, 2007,/ Coach,

Thank you for your recent letter requesting information on our athletes.

Our teams (boys and girls) have been improving each year; the boys are in a position to win the State B boys title this year, while the girls are in a position to receive a trophy (top three at State).

We currently have four junior and senior athletes that I would like for you to consider for your program. They are solid athletes, but more importantly, they are successful students who create a positive atmosphere for those around them. These are kids you want in your school and in your program.

Shane Donaldson *is a senior with a GPA above 3.9. Last year he placed 2nd at cross country state. He also ran a half-marathon this summer in Missoula, MT, and placed 4th overall in 1 hr 22 min. He has a goal for individual reasons, but he places it second to the team title we WILL win on October 20th in Helena.*

Jacob Naegeli *comes from a wonderful family of runners. His brother ran last year for the Pacific Boxers, but had to stop this year; he currently wears a heart monitor. Jacob placed 3rd overall at the State B meet last year and works hard on and off the cross country field; he is involved in 4-H, student council, a state champion Envirothon team, and sometimes paints his body blue during homecoming for school spirit. If he comes to your school, get him to cook or bake some food for you - you won't let him leave.*

Shane is currently the senior class Treasurer, while Jacob is the President.

Mike Morris *is a huge piece for our State Championship. He solidifies our top five for scoring purposes at State. This is his first year in the program, and, as a senior, he is making tremendous progress for our Blue Hawks. I have enjoyed getting to run with Mike this fall; he has tremendous potential.*

These three have the following best times for three miles so far this cross country season: Shane 15:54, 3 seconds off the school record; Jacob 16:20, tied for 5th all-time on our list; and Mike 17:38, 12th place on the All-time list.

Delcie Peters *is a junior harrier for our Lady Hawks. She is an amazingly gifted writer with a tremendous personality. Delcie is shy and modest, and these characteristics sometimes seem to limit her running potential; she doesn't quite believe how good she can be. Delcie has started to learn pole vault in track and is currently tied for the school record. Her best three mile time ever is 20:57, and she ran a nice 21:30 last week. Delcie is a tremendous worker and person; evidence for this is the fact that after five weeks, she is 39 miles ahead of the next girl in our program. Any college would do well to have her as a student; a future Dean's list will include her name.*

I am the assistant coach for Thompson Falls; Sarah Naegeli is Jacob's mother and is the programs' head coach. She requested I respond to you.

By Andrew Gideon

These four kids are amazing to be around. You would do well to recruit them for your track and cross country programs./ Thank you for your time, Andrew Gideon / Thompson Falls HS / English Teacher, Cross Country Coach

I would have included Ryan, but his decisions don't include Dakota Wesleyan. I would have included Beca, but most coaches only request juniors and seniors. CC's name was sent out last year to several schools, but because of her back, she was not included as a potential college runner for this letter.

I talked with Mike M for 15-20 minutes this evening. It was probably the longest stretch we talked consecutively, and at the right time too. The letter above included him; we discussed college, running, and thoughts of the future.

Mike M currently has a cumulative 2.4 GPA because of poor decisions at the start of his high school career. That is why he was shipped from over-populated and over-cultured California to Red Neck Heaven, Thompson Falls, Montana. We can straighten lives out!

He says he "wishes he could have started running earlier." "Do you think I can run in college Coach," he asked me. Yes I do, see the letter above.

Dear readers (young or old, but mostly someone who thankfully bought this book), recall Ryan's advice (9-9 entry): *"Start young! Don't wait until high school to start running, those who run in Junior High have a jump start & usually become much faster! Most of all, know that your running career doesn't have to end when you graduate, running is a great lifelong hobby that will keep you healthy & happy!"*

Keep running Mike M, keep on running.

Coach Naegeli reminded people not to eat fruit off the Oswald's trees. On one of our routes, some runners pick fruit from the Oswald's trees. Bad fruit eaters! Adam Oswald is the # 1 All-time runner for Thompson Falls. Matt stated that he "almost feels bad" for eating the Oswald's fruit. If it tasted worse, he might feel bad. Everything is relative.

Today was a spaghetti feed at Monica's house. Thank you Ryan and Shane for the great shoe Easter egg hunt. Everybody took off shoes at the door of Monica's house. Big mistake – Ryan and Shane hid them like Easter Eggs in the yard: in trees, bushes, hornet's nests.

New uniforms! We will debut our new asymmetrical jerseys tomorrow. They look sharp on some quick looking scissor-bearing runners.

John (junior high) was happy/proud/excited to tell me he kept up with Bryant all the way back from Town Pump. Our 7th grade wonder-runner put in three miles of nice work. His energy is good; he is putting it in a good direction.

Bryant is a good kid for John to look up to. It's kind of like Bart Simpson looking up to Homer; without role models like this, how could American society go on! Doooh!

We had a stray Hawk who rejoined our team after two missed practices. He won't participate in tomorrow's meet, but he is welcome back to our family.

This student-athlete wrote two apology letters – one to the team and a separate one to the coaches. These are some of the words written to the coaches: *"I want to apologize for my lack of effort and dishonesty I showed to you last week. I didn't try at my speed work-out last Tuesday and skipped practice to hang out with a girl. I'm sorry for my lack of effort and honesty. It won't happen again. I will do whatever I need to to make up for my mistakes."*

The team's letter is similar, *"As you probably already know that I skipped practices to hang out with a girl and some of you might not know, but I have been given a really bad effort in my practices the last week. I've had a negative attitude and have snapped at some people because of my attitude. I'm sorry for letting you down and not give my best effort in my running. It won't happen again."*

Each Hawk should realize this is a very loyal family. We need to help each other make right choices and support each other in times of bad choices.

I got carried away with lines today. I almost feel bad for that.

Saturday, 9-22-2007, Mountain West!

(September 27 article for the *Sanders County Ledger* says it all~!)
Inspirational Donaldson leads Hawks   *By Andrew Gideon*

Franz Stampfl: "The coach's job is 20 percent technical and 80 percent inspirational."

The coaching staff for the Thompson Falls Blue Hawk cross country team has a new formula now thanks to Shane Donaldson. Their job apparently will be 100 percent technical since he has inspired the boys' team, the girls' team, and the coaches. This inspiration came without any cheerleaders too!

On Saturday, September 22, at the Mountain West Classic in Missoula, Donaldson set a new school record. His clocking of 15:45 in the three mile cross country race broke Adam Oswald's 2001 record of 15:51. Donaldson's previous best had been 15:54 (set last week in Ronan).

Donaldson's inspirational time led a furious charge of Blue Hawk harriers at Montana's biggest cross country event of the season. These Hawk harriers placed first among all B teams, while the Lady Hawks placed second only to Manhattan.

"Woo Hoooooo!" shouted a normally quiet coach Bob Reall. His exclamation point on the day told an inspiring story despite this writer not being able to spell his excitable quote perfectly.

Jacob Naegeli, with a 16:11, moved into third place all-time for Thompson Falls (sorry Brother Derek, 2006 TFHS graduate, you now drop to sixth). Mike Morris added himself to the prestigious list with a 17:10 timing, good for 8th place in the school's history. Donaldson, Naegeli, and Morris were the first three Hawk harriers to cross the line. Ryan Sol, already on the top 11 list, ran a swell 17:23, while freshman Bryce Miller added a stellar 17:58. Patrick Jamison's 6th place time of 18:13 is not shabby, considering it beat the

87

By Andrew Gideon

#1 runners from other class B teams Valley Christian, Manhattan Christian, and Eureka. Jamison's time also beat the #2 runners from other Class B schools Cut Bank, Lame Deer, and Plains.

Head Coach Sarah Naegeli had only this to say about the performance of the boys' team, "Far better than expected since we were working through the meet."

"Working through the meet" means something like this: Ryan Sol, a senior Blue Hawk, ran 10 miles Monday with several hard 200 and 300 meter intervals at the end of the day. Sol ran 10 miles with four of those timed hard on Tuesday. Thursday, in pouring rain, the coaching staff had Sol (and others) run 7 miles (with 2 hard miles and six surges of at least 100 meters).

Coach Naegeli's comment wasn't only directed at the boys' team. Beca Gunderson, sophomore, did the exact same workouts as Ryan. All she produced after this hard week was another personal record (PR) of 20:46.

Gunderson wasn't the only girl to set a PR – Jeffreyanne Parker (21:32) and Mariah Naegeli (22:23) also eclipsed previous best times. CC Normandeau (21:20) and Delcie Peters (21:44) rounded out the Lady Hawk varsity's performance.

Twelve Hawk harriers, out of 21, had their best time ever. Seven have already been mentioned. Other Hawk PR's included Kyle Breithaupt's 20:56, Mike Barnett's 22:18, Cody White's 22:39, freshman Jessie Drake's 29:02, and Amanda Wood's 29:05.

Also competing for Thompson Falls today were the following athletes: Matt Hojem 18:45, Bryant Normandeau 19:21, RT Brown 20:35, Monica Conlin 23:27, and Lacey Wade 25:40

A junior high race of 1.3 miles followed the three miles high school races. John Gunderson led the way for T Falls with a 9:34. The Kinser brothers pursued Gunderson; Austin ran 9:34, while Dakotta clocked an 11:14.

Coach Reall summed up the day with his earlier quote, but he did add that the team needs to "keep working, but stay healthy."

Shane Donaldson, thanks for your inspirational effort. Donaldson's and other Hawk efforts will hopefully motivate some fans to venture out to the local golf course on Thursday, September 27th, for the homecoming meet.

I include the article for the Plains team as well.

Plains runs well in Missoula   *By Andrew Gideon*

The Plains Horsemen placed 35th overall, and 5th against all B teams, in the Mountain West Classic in Missoula on Saturday, September 22. Justin Allison's 17:24 paced the team. The other four Horsemen were Thad LeClair 18:33, Valin Heward 18:52, Jared Sine 19:16, and Kenneth Beech 19:18. Three of the five Plains harriers had their best time of the year: Allison (improved from 17:53), LeClair (19:33), and Beech (20:22).

Coach Barb Steward complimented LeClair's effort today and noted that his time moved him from #4 runner on the team to #2.

Justin Allison has "potential to be in the Top 15" in State B, according to Coach Steward. The top 15 at the State meet earn All-State status. 15th place last year was 17:01.

The Plains Trotters had three girls compete in Montana's biggest race. The times were as follows: Rio Crismore 22:17, Kara Bates 23:46, and Zoe Banovich 24:11. All three of these Trotters had their best times of the season.

"Rio Crismore is a hard worker and never complains," commented coach Steward. This work ethic is paying off with an improvement of 1:10 over her previous best of 23:27. Banovich improved 49 seconds, while Bates made a tremendous gain, shattering her earlier mark this season of 25:28.

Coach Steward has done an excellent job with the team – six of the eight runners (75%) had their best time of the year on a difficult course. The weather was amazing as far as running was concerned; a day later and the athletes would have been performing in a swamp as Missoula received 1.16 inches of rain on Sunday.

As far as practicing in the rain, Coach Steward stated that her team will practice the same "rain or shine."

Two junior high harriers were entered in Missoula's 1.3 mile race. Karlena Heward produced a 10:46 time, while Robert Earhart placed 15th out of 101 boys with a time of 8:00.

The next meet for Plains is in Thompson Falls on Thursday, September 20.

Bus interviews were conducted with rookies (frosh): Mariah and Bryce

Mariah – size 9.5 Brooks, yet she wears 9.5 Adidas spikes. Once again, another person with different brand names on different pairs of shoes. Kids these days just don't understand it when they sign their names to endorsement contracts. On top of that, her socks were Nike. These socks were colorful, yet when her shoes are on, the fancy color isn't visible! A waste of flamboyancy!

She thinks Bryant and Shane are witty, while Monica is the most side-splitting female. Considering Mariah's favorite tree is a quaking aspen, we can't take her opinion seriously.

Miss Naegeli, the third child of four, would like to praise RT's effort today for finishing the race with a bad hip. She also gives a shout out to JP, not because she likes people with initials as names, but because JP ran a good race and accomplished a goal by beating Delcie.

Why are you out for XC Mariah? She replied, *"Running is awesome, fun, and a good place to get rid of anger."* Really, I wasn't aware that anger was a big issue with the Naegeli family. A good reporter uncovers the true issues of our society. Anger management by running, we know the Naegeli cure now!

Mariah had early goals of lows 24's and then 23's. She has already shattered those times thanks to (1) good coaching, (2) great teammates, and (3) no effort of her own. Her re-evaluated goals now include 21's and low 21's at that!!!!! It is nice to see Mariah do well; she has worked hard for over a year with knee exercises, taken slow but steady steps for rehabilitation, and generally has enjoyed good health. Her mileage is a little lower than others for knee reasons. The knee bone is connected to the... brain bone, which is connected to the Naegeli anger management bone....

Mariah, being the nosy freshman she is, asked the coaches why we coach. Coach Bob has always been a runner (133 pounds as a college graduate), he loves to *"take scrawny guys & make runners out of them."* Coach Naegeli (Mom) comments that it is nice to *"do something to share with kids and make progress, while making her own personal kids life miserable"* in the process. She did say that with a smile on her face. Coach Gideon mentions, *"Endorphins!"* He added, *"Running helps with the battle of self and success in life."*

Bryce finally comes through for us. The rookie has it together – at least in terms of shoes – his training shoes are Nike, and so are his spikes! Thanks for being the first harrier to have both spikes and shoes be the same brand name! Thank you for employing slave labor in third world countries. I'm joking Nike company, you have sound business practices, don't sue me – you have better lawyers than I can afford.

Bryce ran under 18:00 today, the second fastest frosh all-time behind Shane. Speaking of fast, it is all relative, Mike M deserves a compliment for beating Ryan today, while Jessie earns one for a finish in her first career race.

Monica and Shane are the funniest harriers; they are *"goofy,"* says Bryce. A weeping willow is a favorite tree, while he is out for X-C because he likes running. Nice!

Bryce grew up in south Texas; in Kindergarten he was the only white in an entirely Hispanic / Mexican area. He moved to Northeast Texas in grade school to a district equivalent to a Montana A high school (350-700 students).

In summer of 06, Bryce ran a marathon conducted by his program in approximately 5 hours. The next summer he made it in 4:30 approximately. Five more summers at that improvement pace and he may set a world record.

Both Mariah and Bryce, rookies, list Ronan as a favorite course. An original 18:30 goal by Bryce has been decimated' he adds a new goal to 17:30. Bryce believes Mike M, Ryan, Shane, and Jacob can make top 15 at State. Four on the podium out of 15 would be nice. He "thinks we can" win state. Talk to the train going uphill, I think I can, I think I can.

Endurance is a favorite running movie. Coincidentally, I just showed that to my English 2 classes in our cultural study on Africa.

Bryce really wanted to know why I wear mis-matched socks (one black, one white, unless I'm dressing up for school, then I do have incompatible dress socks). My essay answer bored Bryce, as he just wanted to sneak back to his friends on the bus and avoid further contact with the coaches. This fits into my answer # 1 - the black and white socks are like Yin and Yang, a balance to life, a reminder to not take myself too seriously. Just like this crazy book. Here I am, slaving away, writing word after paragraph after page, for what reason? I believe what I'm doing, and that our lives are important, but somehow, somewhere, there are crazy people with scissors who might not think this is important. Answer # 2 - I wear different colored socks because my feet only care about thickness. # 3 - I wear them because I can. I wear them Sam I am, because I do like Mis-Matched Sock I am. My fashion changed in 1998 from any mismatch to only black and white; this emphasized my own personal running style. Oh no! Black and white sock guy is ahead of me.

Please reader, drift backwards on the fashion runway to the spring of 1994 in Jamestown, ND. I was giving a lecture to 7th graders (teaching!) about life, the universe, and everything; if these young, innocent, ready to be molded minds would only listen for 20 minutes, then life would be easy. Secrets to success in life were being shared. A shy girl raised her hand and asked a question; a girl who never talked in class – Wow, Ka Ching! I was really teaching that day - oh glorious education! Then the girl busted my silly thought bubble, exploded it with her words, *"your socks don't match your shirt."*

Socks are supposed to match shirts??? – I'm a guy! The next morning as I put on socks, her words smacked me – I haven't matched socks again; I would show her and all other kids that not only do socks not have to match shirts, but socks don't even have to match. So, if one is taking the self too seriously, remember others are far away. Hey, wake up, wake up! I'm making a point here.

I'm sorry, where were we on Bryce – we are done with his silly questions. Get to the back of the bus and concern yourself with teenage angst, gossip, and successful XC bonding!

A joke by John, 7th grade: The blonde heard that 99% of accidents occur in the home. So she moved!!!!!

How excited was this coach after today's meet?

After arriving home, I ran 18 miles Saturday evening 7:15-9:45. I thought of running until Midnight; however, I was hungry and cold. My excitement for our harriers today was amazing.

I am training for the 50 Le Grizz Ultra-Marathon on October 13. The Hawk Harrier efforts today motivated me to a great endeavor.

(Sunday morning I would run 17 miles 7 am-9 am. My legs were sore and tired, but if I want to run 50, I had better learn to run and push through sore, tired, complaining legs. The run, once again, was fueled by thoughts of the amazing efforts of our XC team. Thank you for helping with my training.)

Sunday, 9-23-2007, Rain, rain, and rain!

Around 9:15 this morning it started to rain, and it dumped buckets all day. Yesterday's results would surely have been altered if harriers had to slog through a swamp. After several races on a wet XC course, life can become an adventure. It would have been fun to see how our harriers would have competed, but for motivational reasons, it was nice to have a sunny day.

Is all we have left in this book relationship is to talk about the weather?

By Andrew Gideon

Let's talk about two more runners: Mike M and JP. They are currently our #4 runners.

Ladies first, so here is our entry on Jeffreyanne Parker, JP.

JP is another of our 30 mile per day round trip athletes. At least 9 out of 25 harriers travel 30 miles or more per day to/from school. All of them discover a way to do well, despite travel time, and that certainly includes Miss Parker. The variation in the commute is cars / traffic (big city) vs. cows / trees (our MT red neck of the woods).

Jeffreyanne Marie Parker was born March 29, 1992, to Michael Marie Parker and Carl Parker. A large family greets her every day; she has eight brothers and sisters. She is a tough 5'2" and 110 pound sophomore. Siblings she has had to contend with at the dinner table are as follows: Carl 32 is the oldest, Bonnie 28 is next, and the rest are Sherry 26, Kendall 21, Talan 19, Hannah 12, Elliot 9, and Garth 2. That would make her the sixth kid out of nine, and we all know about the sixth kid out of nine, especially an Aries. What, someone doesn't have that 6th kid Aries personality already pegged and deciphered? Well, let's find out more….

A Walk to Remember and Facing the Giants are her favorite movies, while chocolate ice cream gets the food nomination. A Child called It was her recent book report in English 2 and serves as the category leader. PE is her favorite class, while Mr. Laws, teacher, and Mrs. Burky, coach, land votes in their respective categories. Mrs. Burky was JP's basketball coach last year, and the orange round ball is her favorite sport – soon to be replaced by cross country.

Finding out what one wants to do when she grows up is essential. I'm still hoping to figure something out despite 11 years of teaching, four years of banking, 41 seasons of coaching, 2.25 years of UPS (United Parcel Service), and other various jobs. JP's future plans include being a *"p.e. or elementary teacher and have a happy life. With a big ranch and family."* Her possible majors at the U of Montana include PE teacher, elementary teacher, and/or athletic director. Her 3.3 GPA, athletic ability, and positive focus are a good start.

She also lists the Air Force for several years as an option.

Solid advice is easy to come by, but hard to follow. JP practices her own advice for youngsters: *"live life to the fullest and have no regrets."* She goes all out running, works well in the classroom, and somehow does family, 4-H, and other responsibilities. She has a full plate, even if her brothers steal her food.

Let's move to the serious business of running. Her best times are mile (6:19) and 3 mile (21:33). Actually, as of yesterday, that 3 mile time is now 21:32. Her goals will fall quickly; her last one only lasted three days, her re-evaluated ones lasted nine days, and the ones she wrote for this expose will be met: *"to get somewhere in the 21 minute range again or under!"*

As far as running is concerned, having her on the team is a tremendous blessing. Her attitude, effort, and personality all help others.

Running: her style is somewhat like CC's. That is a definite compliment because CC is a strong runner and a work horse. Delcie's writing fits in well here, *"JP is really improving as a runner! I'm scared now, she was right on my butt when we raced in Ronan!"* Delcie wrote that early last week before yesterday's race: repeating times - JP 21:32, Delcie 21:44. She may only weigh 110 pounds, but her strength outweighs a diminutive frame.

I see tremendous improvement in both JP and Delcie in the near future, although JP seems more confident when it comes to running. Her advice to younger runners to "always try hard and think positive thoughts" is certainly listened to by her own brain. Maybe she can create a wave of optimism for our hottie harriers all the way to a team trophy on October 20th.

Being a 4-H kid has its advantages for strength – it seems to work for Jacob, Mariah, JP, CC, Bryant, Beca, and John. Chasing steer, cattle, and hay seems to make for good runners, so let's recruit more (4-H-ers, not more bull).

She lives the 3-R's of a true Montana education: reading, ranching, and running. JP dislikes Terrible Tuesdays; she loves an easy four miles Sandy Beach run.

Her aim: *"do my best, mess up the least amount possible, and have fun!"*

If she won $100,000,000, then she would *"give at least 15 million to charity a lot to the church. Get a nice house. Help my mom pay off her bills and support a child in another country."*

JP has several positive comments from teammates. Delcie added, *"I don't think I've ever heard her say something mean to anybody."*

Ryan wrote, "kinda quiet but cool (& fast)."

Beca pens some nice words about her teammate, *"This girl is amazing! Besides improving so much this year and being an awesome runner, JP is one of my best friends. We're both in 4-H and all the same sports. JP is really sweet, and has an infectious laugh, and is as motivated as I am to get better at running which helps me a lot. She pushes me.* ☺*"*

| Mike Morris winning in Libby 07 | JP, Mountain West, 07 |

Michael Kiri Morris stands 5'11" and weighs 158 pounds. He is a strong and good-looking dark-skinned kid of Cambodian descent who is with us for the first year. Mike is a senior who had a late start to his running career. Better late than never for the Blue Hawks! He is a solid #4 runner, who recently passed Ryan to become #3.

Coach Bob looked over Mike's information sheet and stated that *"he doesn't realize how much potential he has."*

His best times include a 4:50 mile, an 11:10 3200m, and a 16:58 3 mile (practice). Mike's goals are *"just be able to not let myself slow down from lifting weights, and to break 17 min. and place top 15 at State."* In 2006, 15th place was 17:01, so Mike, I hope you get under that 17:00 and you get All-State status.

Mike recently passed Ryan for the # 3 status. Ryan has worked hard all summer and for several years now. Ryan wants Top 15 status as well, so I hope we can crown at least 4 in that category. It does tell how far Mike can go when he advances so quickly. His weight of 158 doesn't put him in Shane's 123, Jacob's 125, or even Ryan's 143 range, but it does help him with strength.

Mike likes to push himself fast & hard. Terrible Tuesdays fit in well for him – along with the bench press. He doesn't like the long slow distances as much, but it does benefit stamina. The current list of mileage after six weeks reads: Shane and Jacob 280, Ryan 276, Matt 217, and Mike M 198 (5th on the team). His distances have been curtailed and he has ridden a bike due to shin splints and bribes to the coaches.

Does Mr. Morris practice what he preaches in advice to future runners? He writes, *"Run hard, don't doubt yourself, and ICE if you're injured. Listen to THE COACHES!"* Yes, he runs hard, believes in himself, ices like a Montana road in January, and listens to our wise coaching advice. Listening to the coaches has probably saved him three minutes (1 minute per coach).

Mike has lived in Anaconda, Montana, and Little Beaver Creek Road, Montana in the past three years. He has at least a 30 mile round trip daily.

Mike Morris is in what is called a "program." Programs are designed to get kids back on the "right track." He hiked 4-10 miles daily in the summer, wrote in a journal daily, and lived a more primitive life for three months in an effort to figure out who he really is.

Our Montana secret: inner demons can be driven out by running, by camping in the woods of Montana, and by having people help move a person in the right direction. However, be very afraid of the bears, red necks, and vultures. There, I tried to get a reader excited about Montana, but not too excited to actually move here and invade our space.

Twenty Peaks is the name of the program where Mike resides. Three other harriers join him out there: MK, Patrick, and BM.

It is a solid family unit at "20 Peaks." The XC team is a solid family. Most kids at programs like this have had family trouble, addictions, or other problems. Lives were falling apart and a new direction needed to be taken.

Mike was snatched from Del Mar, California, for poor life choices. Anaconda was a first stop; 20 Peaks is his current location. This program has done well with a lot of kids I have worked with in three years at TFHS.

If you are like me, I never heard of a "program" before coming to TFalls in 2005. TFHS has about 10-12% of its high school population from programs.

So, if your kid is into gangs, violence, drugs, or just getting a D- in English class and he/she can run, then send them to Montana. We will shape them up literally and figuratively. We also accept Kenyan transfers!

These kids also attend the same church I do – the Thompson Falls Christian Church. Shaping up comes in all forms: physical, mental, and spiritual. Last December, another 20 Peak program student chose to be baptized – in winter – in icy water - in Montana – in the Thompson Falls Reservoir. That student transferred back to Florida for this school year.

Mike seems to have a solid grip on life – although he was removed from from the track team last May. We all fight a daily battle, but I have great respect and admiration for Mike in the past six weeks of cross country. He may have been born 3-5-90, but he is getting a second birth here in Thompson Falls.

Cambo's (nickname) plans indicate a good direction: college as a drafter or mechanical engineer (CAD) at Montana Tech, Missoula, Northern (Havre, MT), or maybe some school that will let him run. Mike writes, "*My goals for life are to graduate from college with a drafting education and start my own architect business in California as well as to keep running for as long as I can.*"

Advice to younger students begs to be listened to: "keep working hard in school and plan for graduation as well as life after that." Four years ago, would Mike have listened to that? If he had, he wouldn't be in Montana with us!

Mike, jr. has parents: Mike Morris, sr. in California is now re-married to a Shirley Morris. He doesn't really talk about his real mother.

Mike would like to work for the forest service in the summer! He will be a great worker and is on the road to success.

Mike just won $100,000,000. ¾ of it goes to charity, while he would use the rest to buy his friends "the one thing that they want the most." He obviously doesn't do well in Math; he believes there will be leftover cash for himself.

Mike, starting with that for the 4th straight paragraph, has no favorite movie or food (although RT lets us know Mike M eats eight waffles every morning with extra syrup). A male with no favorite food: isn't the way to a man' heart through his stomach? He also has no favorite book. Maybe Harrier Hawks Fly High will be his #1 soon. He loves snowmobiling, CAD, and the sports of baseball and football. He adds, "I like to build and work on off road trucks. (I like driving them after they're done the most)." Yes, he did use the wrong their; it should be "THEY'RE." Ack. No, I never had him in an English class!

95

By Andrew Gideon

No name writes, *"He's not quite black and not quite white – we dub him 'Gray.'"* Delcie adds, *"Funny kid. He has so much energy to channel into running. Unbelievable."*

Ryan tops it off the way we will top off the season, *"Combo – the newest recruit to the fab five that are going to win state."* Is that good grammar Ryan? I did have Ryan in class, but that was as a sophomore. His junior teacher for language must have messed up his verb use.

Monday, 9-24-2007, Homecoming week
Team mileage today: 144   runners: 25   Avg. per runner: 5.8

Memories imprint on the brain. Life forms before our eyes. Depth of living creates in us a feeling of soul satisfaction. Precisely the amount of wisdom obligatory in a book on high school life!

Memories - Homecoming week: No school on today created an opportunity for an early morning 7:30 run on the golf course where our home meet will be Thursday. "Parent's night" for seniors will also occur that evening; families will be honored before a volleyball match.

All but one athlete attended practice this morning. Kyle did not communicate with us BEFORE the practice, bad Kyle. We will try to recover from this lack of student / teenage communication.

Teachers did have meetings in the school all day. During a break, JP, Jacob, Beca, Mariah, and Jessie were spotted with paint on their feet and footprints scattered over paper on the school's hallway ground. Homecoming signs were being created; from this we find that Jessie has really flat feet.

A discussion on different style shoes for diverse feet could occur here (high, middle, or low arch - key word "pronator" or not – different shoes for different feet help injury prevention), but won't – other than the running a mile in someone else's shoes may give proper perspective, running more than that could lead to injuries. Find a proper fitting shoe (corporate (not!) sponsor plug – check with *The Runner's Edge*, Missoula's local running store for proper footwear).

Memories: footprints on yellow butcher paper, footprints on our life. Wow, it's getting deep! Blue and white footprints cascade across yellow with "TFXC" lettered on them. Each individual's sheet will fit on a locker and have space for various written comments.

Monica was yanked (politely requested) from study hall for a secret mission – collect top comments from each of the lockers. There are 211 lockers in TFHS; our harriers use 22 of them. Here are the results: the writer's remain anonymous, while the locker occupant is listed. (No, I have no idea what these mean either. I am not in the loop, although I have been considered loopy. These are high school kids forming relationships, a spirit of team, and memories.)

Beca – run faster, it's the solution to everything! I'll have to get physical! CC – I have a secret, keep throwing some D's on it! sprite. Delcie – You're the frog in my pond. You are my rock. Lacey – Hey (grufly) Yaargh

Matey! <u>Monica</u> – Glad you're not running lopsided anymore! Monica, No!
<u>Patrick</u> – Patty …Cakes optional, you're the fat fish in my pond. <u>RT</u> – did
shaving your head make you faster? <u>Matt</u> – You rock the crib! I think you could
run a little faster. <u>Mike M</u> – you smell like a girl, keep your guns in check. <u>Jacob</u>
– running faster is <u>not</u> the solution to everything. Don't OD on candy. <u>Ryan</u> –
drown them in the bathtub, you dropped your socks. <u>Shane</u> – grease bucket,
you're one crazy kid. <u>Bryant</u> – if we put any food in front of this locker, it would
be gone immediately! <u>Amanda</u> – you're too smart, you're junior in your heart.
<u>Mike B</u> – I got the silly string, trip & break a leg. <u>JP</u> – Rawr, cuteness does not
guarantee a fantastic steer! <u>Kyle</u> – you are super duper. Give up the cell phone.
<u>Cody</u> – I think it's cause I'm too fat, ummm... two days later... Hmmm. <u>Bryce</u> –
Bryce-a-roni! Rice cakes! <u>Mariah</u> – share your Triscuits, Holy Buckets… this is
my sister! <u>Jess</u> – UR the woman! I'm calling you flat foot. <u>MK</u> didn't play the
same game as the team and had his locker decoration on the inside.

Life forms before our eyes: In the following paragraphs in this section,
several names will be mentioned. Don't worry about the names – the ideas
behind the stories are what is important – relationships, and life in general.

In the mail this week I received a CD from two former students at
Seeley-Swan High School (Seeley Lake, MT). I taught there 1995-2000. Last
year these two hallowed SSHS alumni requested $25 in advance to work on a
musical album. They have some CD's out already, have toured small venues
over the United States, and played music for ten plus years. Finally, the CD
arrived. David Boone and James Wasem, thanks for the music.

James was a 4.0 GPA high school student who had a full ride scholarship
for engineering at Montana State University. He attended one semester and then
dropped out to pursue music, drumming, and electrical wiring. A picture of him
hangs on my school wall, behind my desk: James is wearing a fireman's outfit
and holding a sign which reads, "Will Drum for Food."

Here's what James had to say about life since high school graduation: *"I
had an Air Force ROTC scholarship to MSU, but only attended one semester
pursuing a degree in Electrical Engineering and a lifelong dream of being a
pilot. I left school to play with Mr. Boone full-time in Spokane. Then I got a job
so I could eat! I've been working as a low voltage electrician (licensed in
Washington) for several years. (I install sound, CCTV, TV, audio/video, and
other electronic systems in both commercial and residential buildings.) I quit my
job of five years in Seattle to go on the road again with Mr. Boone in 2005 –
seems to be a pattern here. Haven't had a "real job" since. I am currently self-
employed – doing work in real estate investing, sound systems, and of course
music. I have worked on about six recording projects with David in some
capacity or another. And yes, always drumming for food! Someday I'll get back
to that whole flying thing…"*

David Boone was a chaotic personality in high school who trivialized his
education and that of others by frequently holding late night musical jam

sessions. Seeley Lake has probably recovered since his graduation; currently he lives in Missoula and is married.

David is still recovering from a homecoming event in 1996. His band played for homecoming at Seeley Swan HS on Saturday, September 28, 1996. On Monday morning, 9/30/06, at 1:30 and 1:42 AM, shotgun blasts shattered a shrill night in Seeley Lake.

Your author was "lucky" to hear gun shots at 1:30 AM break the silence of a peaceful sleeping night. The windows to the front of the school were shattered, and my ears woke to the bang and a vehicle racing away. Twelve minutes later and ¾ mile away, an 8th grade teacher was shot to death, close range, with a shot gun. David's favorite teacher, Mr. Nelson was murdered.

"You can't get away with murder" - yet despite lovely court proceedings and local outrage, the murder remains "unsolved." David still struggles with this, but by listening to his newest CD (www.davidboone.net), one can tell some strength of life has returned.

David's favorite teacher after that became Mr. Gideon; I dislike homecoming in general due to that weekend's horrific events. I dislike homecoming dances, or being involved in murder cases in the courtroom. It was not television and being on the witness stand and staring into a defendant's eyes has given me a certain distant attitude toward guns and the power behind them.

Also in my mailbox was a wedding announcement from a student who I taught at Rocky Mountain Christian High School in Helena, MT, 2000-2001. John Larue is now married. Bob, John's father, worked with me in basketball coaching and reffing in Helena. John and Bob, it was an honor to work with you.

This summer one of my Libby, MT, baseball players from 1992-96, Bryce Baillie called me. In 1996, in the bottom of the 12th inning, Bryce hit a homerun vs. the Missoula team. The walk-off homerun gift-wrapped our Libby Loggers to State and sent Missoula home for the winter. What a feeling that was! On June 9, my youngest son Kaden's first birthday, Bryce and I talked on the phone. His wife of seven years died of a seizure. What a feeling that wasn't. Some highs and lows of life happened through Bryce. Two boys, five and three, are now without a mother. Bryce and I had a lot of conversations this summer; I called a lot of other Libby players to get them to communicate and help Bryce.

Life forms before our eyes – these harriers are in my mind and heart for life. They surely say, "I can't wait until my birthday, until Christmas, until I'm 18, until I graduate high school, until I'm 21, until Mr. Gideon stops writing this…" Yet they pace themselves well during races and adopt that attitude in life as well. Our Hawk harriers are flying high, yet enjoying NOW. Maybe there is some anticipation toward the state finish line and the destination of graduation, yet living hard and well NOW is surely printed on the insides of their eyelids.

Musical albums, weddings, and other interactions (another baseball player is my tax accountant) will make life interesting. Do I look forward to calls about spouses dying with 5 and 3 year olds? No, but life is forming, and I look forward to CD's and being a part of their life now and in the future.

(Insert Hawk cries) "Coach, no!! I thought we were done with you after October 20th!"

Depth of living: Leadership is a strong trait for this group; as leaders, "success" will trail them wherever they go. A certain quality of life exists and the wonderful personalities involved will only add to a positive depth of life.

If there were more people like the individuals on this team in the world, then we would all have a better quality of life.

With "Depth of living" as a topic, the lyrics to the greatest running song are introduced IPOD's and MP3 players! Intensity of running life hits me with this song. Only part of the lyrics are listed.

Manfred Mann's Earth Band – Runner   *from www.lyrics007.com*

Through the night...through the dawn,
Behind you another runner is born.
Don't look back, you've been there.
Feel the mist as your breath hits the air.
And it's underneath the moonlight, passing some;
Still your heart beats in the moonlight like a drum.

And you will run your time, a shooting star across the sky.
And you will surely cross the line, to pass on the flame.

Sun come up...sun go down.
Hear the beat, see the sweat on the ground.
Watch your step, keep your cool,
Though you can't see what's in front of you.

And you will run your time, a shooting star across the sky.
And you will surely cross the line.

The lyrics alone don't give me the chills. The lyrics with the music, even old 60's-70's music, give my backbone and being the shivers!

Hawks: you will run your time . . . and surely cross the line.

A headline from Sunday's *Missoulian* reads, "So long fire season – Seeley Lake celebrates end of grueling summer." Montana's fires were a smoky issue for the lungs in the last month. The past week had a lot of rain and cooler weather, firefighters worked hard for days on end, and blazes have been extinguished, finally!

Seeley's fire burned 36,060 acres over 42 days.

In TFalls, we only had one bad air day and two minor days of smoky breathing. We were lucky to never lose a practice. The team only changed one double session practice by moving it out 15 miles away to the Naegeli Ranch.

By Andrew Gideon

Tuesday, 9-25-2007, Blue Hawk Olympics

Team mileage today: 151.5   runners: 25   Avg. per runner: 6.1

Stomachs + running + Barbecue Rib sandwiches = recipe for upset bowels. Let's just say the pizza after practice was appreciated more by the stomach than the school lunch today.

Monica had this to say about our beloved coach Bob, *"There's no stopping that man."*

She said this between intervals with the girls at the State Park. Monica and CC were "on a roll" about everything and nothing, and yes, they ran well and hard, but their vocalizations resulted in a quality ab workouts. Our lady harriers may have laughed as hard as they ran today. Beca wrote, *"I feel kinda bad for Mr. Gideon who has to put up with us... By far one of the funniest practices I've ever had! 700 CALORIES!!!* ☺

It may have helped that their Terrible Tuesday intervals were moved to paths on sand, near the river, and away from the school. Today, the coaching staff interjected smaller intervals for the girls as opposed to the mile repeats.

The boys ran 3 x 1 mile hard with warm-up miles before, jogging miles between, and a cool down afterward. The top runners totaled nine miles. The top three boys totals were as follows for the three timed miles: Shane 15:50, Jacob 16:04, Mike M 16:04. RT only did two miles timed due to a bad hip, while Mike B also only had two hard miles due to knee trouble.

The girls ran 1 x 0.7 miles, 3 x 0.4 miles, and 1 x 0.2 hard; the top girls ran five miles. The top three girls totaled the following times for a combined 2.1 miles: Beca 13:51, Delcie 14:24, and JP 14:47. Mariah and Jessie cut out one .4 interval due to aching knees.

Attention people, dear readers: there is a difference between girls and boys! I know this is new knowledge, but it had to be shared, so that our society can advance in a positive direction. We coaches are trying hard to discover "perfect" workouts for each individual. Recognizing homecoming week and different body structures, like Frankenstein, we have created life, running life, in the veins. *"It's alive!!!!! Hawk Harriers are alive!!!! The Hawk dynasty is ALIVE,"* say the Victor Frankenstein coaches named Bob, Gideon, and Naegeli.

TFHS has a great tradition which started in 1987. The Blue Hawk Olympics occur early in the week of homecoming and pit classes against each other. Events include bed races (each class creates their own bed on wheels to push around the track), 8 legged races (7 student legs taped to each other), hula hoop races, tricycle races, and class cheers, as well as several others.

Seniors won all seven events to amass 70 points. Freshman took last.

Wednesday, 9-26-2007, Total Chaos

Team mileage today: 144   runners: 25   Avg. per runner: 5.8

Several weeks ago I had ranked Colstrip 1, Poplar 2, TFalls 3 for the boys in Class B Montana. After seeing times in several more meets, new rankings emerge: Poplar 1, TFalls 2, Colstrip 3, Darby 4, Loyola 5, Manhattan 6, Plains 7, Valley Christian 8, and Glasgow 9. Honestly I believe we will win it – at 2:00 on October 20th, 20 minutes after the start of the B Boys race, we will have chills down our spine; it won't be because of the weather!

Until that trophy is raised, we won't be ranked first.

My rankings for the girls programs are as follows: 1. Glasgow, 2. Red Lodge, 3. Cut Bank, 4. Whitehall, 5. Thompson Falls, 6. Manhattan, 7. Cascade, 8. Darby, and 9. Loyola.

Total chaos is a valid description of Homecoming week. Energy fills halls, bouncing off walls and acting as a shock wave of radiation through teenage minds and bodies. Heads, if not attached well by God, would fly off due to a swiveling nature of checking everyone and everything out.

Today was beach day. Seriously, how much work can kids do with sun, sand, surf, tank tops, shorts, Hawaiian shirts, and skin reflecting the sun's energy. This is not a school today; it is a festival of testosterone and estrogen.

Deer have rutting season. Homecoming week, spring, and prom are the three rutting seasons for high school. Exaggeration? This is my third year teaching at TFHS, and seven girls will have had babies late December and early January – 9 months after Prom. Five already have kids, while two are currently in God's hands forming in a much stronger way than my words on this page.

I'm not trying to make fun of this. I'm laughing in hopes better decisions for life will be made by a higher percentage of the population, not only at TFHS, but at all high schools.

Thursday, 9-27-2007, Homecoming Meet
(For the 04 October 2007 *Sanders County Ledger*)
Endurance beats new gear   *By Andrew Gideon*

Kyle Breithaupt received new spikes the night before the Thompson Falls Homecoming cross country meet. His personal record (PR) for three miles was blasted into oblivion by 2 minutes and 2 seconds. Kyle improved from 20:56 to 18:54, an amazing and awesome performance attributed purely to new shoes.

Will Kyle be wearing his new spikes next meet? "Definitely" was Kyle's response.

The Thompson Falls Blue Hawk boys sported new uniforms at the prestigious Mountain West Meet last week and were the top performing B team in Montana's largest cross country event. The asymmetrical attire also carried the team to a first place finish at their homecoming meet on Thursday, September 27; the Blue Hawk harriers bested Whitefish, Plains, Eureka, Libby, Eureka, Two Eagle River, and Arlee.

Will the team exercise the latest fashion at future meets or was first place at home the extent of believing in the power of new threads? Jacob Naegeli, senior, replied that gold in TFalls was nice, but the squad wants "first at State." The uniforms will be worn successfully again.

By Andrew Gideon

The Lady Hawk Harriers sported sizzling style and placed 2nd among B teams at Mountain West and first among B teams at the home meet. Whitefish, Class A, did beat the Class B Lady Hawks, but seasonal and personal bests showed the power of positive attire by defeating rival Plains, as well as Eureka, Libby, and Arlee.

Reportedly one Blue Hawk coach even drinks Kenyan coffee in hopes of bringing out the inner Kenyan.

Seriously, Breithaupt could run barefoot, while the Hawk Harriers baring full scale Halo gear would do just as well.

Stamina, trained brains, and precise preparation produced tremendous times, not shoes or uniforms.

Breithaupt has run over 200 miles this season in the first six plus weeks of cross country, thus his time improvement. Jacob Naegeli has trained over 300 miles, and his new PR sizzled to a 16:02, bettering his previously impressive 16:11. Nine other Hawks fashioned new PR's: Mike Morris 16:48, Ryan Sol 17:01, Bryce Miller 17:24, Patrick Jamison 17:37, Mike Kidwiler 17:37, Matt Hojem 18:10, RT Brown 18:38, Mike Barnett 21:23, and Cody White 21:39. The only two "slackers" on the team were Shane Donaldson who owns the school record (all he produced was a paltry 15:55 and second place finish) and Bryant Normandeau, who had a seasonal best of 18:41.

The Lady Hawks had two PR's and two seasonal bests (SB's): Beca Gunderson (20:41, PR), Delcie Peters (21:09, SB), Jeffreyanne Parker (21:21, PR), and Monica Conlin (22:43, SB). Four other Hawks raced their hearts out and edged the team closer to a dream top three finish at State: Ciara Normandeau, Mariah Naegeli, Lacey Wade, and Amanda Wood.

Three Thompson Falls junior high harriers also participated. Two of them wore a post-race medal after running: John Gunderson earned second, while Austin Kinser placed third. The top three received a medallion. Dakotta Kinser just missed by placing fourth.

The Hawks awed the local crowd at their homecoming meet. It wasn't because of new uniforms, new spikes, or Kenyan coffee; Heart, effort, and muscle factored into 24 Hawk Harriers having truly motivating performances.

The next session with new uniforms and endurance will occur Saturday, October 6th, in Polson, MT. The State Meet in Helena on October 20th is approaching as fast as a hawk harrier.

So I drink Kenyan coffee in hopes that this particular java will add speed to my American legs! Yes, I grind the beans 26 seconds for each mile in a marathon. Yes, I let the espresso drip through the machine for 26 seconds for my lattees. I respect Kenyan runners, their coffee, and the 26 miles in a marathon. Run faster through superstition!

Runners stretch. With political turmoil in Kenya now, my stretching hope is that some of my money for coffee helps one more runner in that country.

Lacey had tears in her eyes after the race. Her 26:27 didn't approach her '06 PR of 24:11.

Tears were in my eyes after the Missoula Marathon on July 15. My dream goal was under three hours; I wanted to see a 2:xx:xx after my name. My next basic goal was a PR – I had never worked harder for a race in my life.

Alas, my 4th best time of eight marathons was achieved.

Just as I was about to throw a pity party for myself, Derek, Shane, Jacob, Ryan, and Bryant walked up to me. Bryant was brought along as an official food tester (to make sure the star's food had not been poisoned); while the other four ran the half-marathon in fantastic times (missoulamarathon.com for results!).

When I saw them, I recalled my prayers in May, June, and July as I trained for the marathon. Lord, yes, I want three hours, but I have a tremendous deal. Take my marathon time and make it worse – as long as you strengthen the hearts, legs, and lungs of the Hawks this fall. Let each second added to my time be one second lowered on a Hawk's time at State.

My marathon time was 3:14:20. Therefore, since I was 14 minutes, 20 seconds long of my goal, and we will have 14 runners at State (seven of each sex), each runner at State will get a PR by 1 min 3 seconds, or will have improved by that amount during the season.

I ran as hard as I could, but couldn't access some strength that day. Maybe it was the 84 degree heat; maybe it was my prayers helping to improve the Hawk Harriers. My faith allows me to smile and if my time was worse, then so be it, because our season is a dream.

Still, I could see/feel Lacey's pain today. If I couldn't get a PR July 15, then I never will. I could only give a handshake to Lacey and then grip her hand a little harder as I said, *"Thanks for being Lacey Wade."* Having her as a Harrier Hawk makes us a better team.

Recall discussions about Monica. Our worry was present two-three weeks ago that she might never improve. Her seasonal best of 22:43 was achieved today - 2 minutes and 33 seconds better than Kalispell on Sept. 08.

She is off medication and removed her arch supports. Her running energy and focus is improved sans medicine, while her hips have felt better daily since removing the arch supports.

Monica, should RT, fellow hip trouble RT, remove his arch supports too?

Bryce Miller moved into the top 11 all-time today. His time places him tenth in the history of TFalls. Insert drool here - for Bryce is a freshman.

The 11th best time in our history dropped from 17:34 to 17:27. So the girls have shaved 2 seconds from the 11th best time thanks to JP entering the top 11, while the boys saved seven seconds thanks to Bryce. We are all battling time and seconds. The fight is worth it.

The weather today: at 8:30 PM, a thought blistered into my brain. There was no weather at the meet. Temperature and wind seemed perfect. Ideal conditions helped produce top results.

By Andrew Gideon

Next week we will talk with our runners about being successful no matter what the weather. 150 degrees or negative 40 with six feet of snow shouldn't affect our mind frame. Love all conditions and have a positive attitude no matter what Mother Nature throws at us.

This is another "train the brain" exercise. It must be worked on in advance. Being mentally prepared (positive visualization) for every situation, whether life or running, will lead to success. If we show up at State and the weather is not to our liking and our attitude is poor, results will show negativity.

We <u>will</u> handle anything God pitches our way in a good manner.

Today nature threw us a fastball down the middle of the plate, and we hammered it over the fence like a Red Sox homerun. (Yes, Red Sox nation.)

Today was the day that Kyle B "became a runner" according to Coach Reall. His time, effort, pace, fluidity, and stamina advanced him to a new level.

Coach Gideon talked with one boy after the meet about spring track and the future. 20 minutes later – after arriving back to the school, he finds out he has been pulled from his program, will live with a Trout Creek family for four weeks, and then leave to go back to Oregon after the quarter ends November 2nd.

Into each life a little rain must fall – some battle to find the silver lining, some the GOLD – each of us has our choices, challenges, and changes. Fancy words don't make it easier, for the battle always exists.

Tonight was Parent's Night. All the seniors are introduced at a volleyball match, along with their parents, with some of the most touching words ever written announced to the crowd.

Our seniors filled out information on length of time in TFalls, parents, school activities, most memorable school moments, future plans, and thanks.

RT – 17 years in TFalls – *"I'd like to thank my mom & my dad for always being there for me and getting me what I need to survive. My grandma for being there when my mom and dad aren't available. And all my buddies for keeping me entertained. I just want to thank everyone for being such great people and I love you all."* In the future he will *"go off to college somewhere in Montana and get a good education. After college move to Texas and settle down, find a good job, marry a good looking Texas cowgirl, have a few kids and later move back here to Montana."*

Jacob – 17 years in TFalls – *"I'd like to thank my teammates and coaches for all the fun and fast times, my family for always being there and giving me food, and of course I'd like to thank Grandma Naegeli for being one of the greatest people alive."* In the future he will graduate *"with a 4.0 GPA then attend one of three colleges (I haven't decided) to get a degree in pre-architecture. Attend Graduate school for a Masters degree in architecture."*

Amanda – 3 years in TFalls – *"Thank you Megan and Jubi for making me take so long to type this. You guys are awesome! And to all of my friends, you are the best! Thanks to my parents for supporting my decisions, and to my younger siblings, Alicia, Andrea, Warren, Walter, Sarah, and Sam, you guys*

104

always keep my life interesting. Thanks to all my teachers for teaching me all I know. And, last but not least, in fact, most, thank you to God for giving me all that I have." Her plans: *"I have lots of dreams, like singing, and going to Mars. However, no matter what happens, I will most definitely graduate from a good college, get married, and live in a nice small town."*

Ryan – 13 years in TFalls – *"I would like to thank my mom and dad for always being there for me and lending a helping hand when I needed one. Also, thanks to my friends for making high school a fun, enjoyable experience and to my brother for paving the way."* The future: *"Go to the Air Force Academy in Colorado for 4 years, serve in the Air Force, then move back to Montana and live a long, happy life."*

Bryant – 18 years in TFalls – *"I would like to thank my parents for raising me to have integrity and dreams, my friends for good times with more to come, and the quality people that I have been taught by since Kindergurten in Thompson Falls."* Goals: *"My goals in life are to design and fly my own spaceship, go to college, find the girl of my dreams and marry her, have a kid or two and never retire."*

Mike M – 2 years in TFalls – no thanks listed, what is up with that Mr. Mike? Future plans: *"My plans after graduation are to work for the forest service for a summer, move on to getting a degree in Drafting for a large company in California. Then maybe if things go really well starting my own Architecture Business like my dad. And if worst comes to worst I can fallback on what Mr. Wheeler calls a contingency plan and join a branch of the military."*

Matt – 4 years in TFalls – *"I want to thank my parents for being there through the good times and the bad, all my cross country friends and coaches for making me run, and my wrestling coaches for always pushing me to do better. I'll miss you guys and I'll hope to see you down the road."* Future plans: *"Join the US competitive eating team and eat my weight in spaghetti. My real plans are to attend the U of Montana and get a job in a small town as an elementary school teacher and a wrestling coach. If that doesn't work I'll just have to go pro at ping pong."*

Shane – 7 years in TFalls – *"Thanks to God for the gifts He has given me, my family for giving me plenty of good reasons to get out of the house and go run, anyone who feeds me, teammates and coaches for pushing me."* Future plans: *"Become a professional sumo wrestler and take over Japan. Win a few food eating competitions on the way (hot dog, pies, all the good stuff)."* Actual future plans: *"college, math teacher, own a farm, coach a XC team."*

Friday, 9-28-2007, Royalty, Brain Boggle, Parade, and Football Game
Team mileage today: 149   runners: 26   Avg. per runner: 5.7

Royalty – Our XC team has two of the four possible homecoming candidates. These words were repeated to the entire school body in an 8:30 am assembly in the gym. Yes, these students wrote their own words – yet the athletic director read them.

RT Brown – "*after high school RT attended college for two years before he was hit by a very large truck while riding his bike to class, putting him into a deep coma. While in the coma, RT's brain healed in an unusual way transforming him into some kind of super genius. When he awoke from his coma RT went on in college, as a science student, to later find the real cure for cancer, making him the wealthiest man in the world. After finding the cure for cancer, RT went on discovering new things to help save human lives and after awhile his hair began to turn white and fall out, leaving him as an image of Albert Einstein. His similar Einstein looks were later seen by the science world and he went on to be named The Modern Einstein for his great achievements.*"

Jacob Naegeli – "*After graduating from TFHS in 2008 Jacob decided to attend college in LA. While on an early morning jog through the neighborhood he was shot in the leg during a drive by shooting. It turned out the shot was just a glancing blow, but he joined a gang intent on getting revenge. During Jacob's first year of membership he put out a rap single and quickly made millions off it. He used his first million replacing his original teeth with silver ones, and the second million on a little bling. After an accumulation of about 50 pounds of random bling all other members of the gang bowed down and recognized him as their leader. The gang officially gave up on drive-by shootings (to unoriginal) and decided to stick with run-by tire slashings. Jacob is currently the gang boss of the Beefburgers.*"

Each student should give their own speech – that might alter the content.

Brain Boggle: classes compete against each other in full view of the entire student population. The game is similar to Jeopardy.

One category was "Agriculture." The 400 point question read – "What is the common measurement for lard?" It supposedly read land, but I read it as lard. Who wants an **acre** of lard, other than red neck ranchers in TFalls.

Another category: "Teachers." The 200 point question: "What teacher has TF shaved in the back of their head?" The answer of course: Mr. Gideon, your author. RT shaved the TF in this morning, painted it blue, and I paraded my head across the gym for homecoming festivities. "Their" head – that's some seriously bad grammar?

The sophomores won this event, while the freshman class was shutout. Mariah, frosh XC harrier, didn't contribute much to her team, boo! She didn't even get the shaved head question!

The parade: each team, class, sport, and royalty have a "float." Read: Flatbed with hay to sit on and toss candy at adults, various high students not involved in activities, various high school students who have been "left behind" and dropped out, grade school kids, etc.

It was a fun afternoon away from the "serious" actions of school, and, besides, my son Jaxon rode the XC float for the 2nd straight year.

Our season began with scissors; my idea to throw scissors to the crowd was vetoed. Next year we should throw packs of cigarettes to promote the healthy lifestyle we teach and coach.

We drove 10 miles to the Thompson River Road after our wild Homecoming school day.

During the workout I knocked off personal goal #2 this year - run my most miles in a year – the previous best of 1518 has been knocked off. 1524 was my total at the end of Friday.

I told all the athletes at the end of today that one goal I presented to them in December of 2006 is still left: boys first place at State, and girls - a trophy for a top three finish. October, October, dear lord, let this goal be knocked off in 22 days. Please let this happen. The prayer life gets stronger. It WILL happen ☺.

The nice thing about our run today is that Shane took last, along with Coach Gideon. Coach Gideon often takes last, running harder at the start, slowly dropping to talk/run with various harriers, and scooping up the last runner so that the vultures don't eat our athletes.

The bad thing was that Shane's knee was stiff and sore.

The nice thing about that was that it was a good day to have a sore knee; speed didn't matter, it wasn't a race, and the next two days are scheduled off or easy days for recovery.

The homecoming football game: T Falls 44, Plains 0. TFHS hasn't had a close game this year on route to a 5-0 record. The team has a great bunch of senior leaders, just like our XC team. Plains is the rival – one year the Plains Horseman shoveled too many dump loads of horse manure on our front walk.

In response, some TFHS students changed their "P" on the mountain into a gross figure.

Aw, rivalries!

After the football game was the homecoming dance. The DJ commented that TFHS has some of the strictest guidelines around for a dance. The dance was from 9-12, but at 11:25 the lights were turned on because of too much grinding (slang dance term), while the dancers close contact bothered the chaperones; students were also lifting kids up and passing them above the crowd.

Too strict, afraid of lawsuits, trying to raise the standard of living, or realizing seven students have been pregnant in three years – you be the judge. Ah, just trying to have a little fun....ah, just trying to help people move in a positive direction with life.

Lights stayed on the rest of the dance; by midnight, people had gone "home." A song comes to mind, closing time, lyrics…it's closing time, you don't have to go home, you just can't stay here. Home.

Too much testosterone?

Yes, today some students at TFHS were on the back trail with a camera as our XC team jogged by. They looked guilty as if smoking. Apparently they filmed one kid biting the head off of a snake. Confirming evidence was the snake head left in the trail.

Too much testosterone.

Maybe this is why running is being substituted into prisons and programs instead of weight training. Different chemicals are produced and continued by the body during running instead of weights.

Too much testosterone.

The snake biters were wearing TFHS football uniforms.

The people who changed the "P" in Plains – football players.

Saturday, 9-29-2007, lethargy and naps

Darby had a meet today, and my brother (coach) stated that his athletes were sick. So I bought some tea for Shane, Jacob, and Ryan, and told them Kenyans drink tea for health, even in 90-100 weather. Stay healthy! Drink tea daily; we must run like Kenyans in 3 weeks.

Poplar and Colstrip boys produced tremendous times today. Comparing our last meet with theirs today, we would place first (TFalls 34, Poplar 39, and Colstrip high 50's). Shh!!

While other teams were working hard exactly three weeks from State, we told our kids to sleep in, rest, and DO NOT RUN.

Ryan is five season miles behind Shane and Jacob. Today we devised a plot to pretend that we ran six miles together to move Ryan into first place in the mileage department. We shall unleash our attack at Monday's practice and see if it frustrates Shane's mind. Then we will tell the truth after practice and laugh. Healthy competition this is.

There was a homecoming dance last night. Our royalty candidates, RT and Jacob, found out at the football game half-time that they were not king. That honor went to a football player, imagine that! The queen was a volleyball player.

Our athletes had a homecoming week with activities, stress, running, and they even attended school on top of that! Energy becomes bi-polar from tremendous fun to a draining effect afterward. Therefore, trying to get an extra ounce of running energy just might put a bodily system over the limit. So, our Hawk harriers were nesting so the Harrier Hawks Fly High can occur at State.

Here are some times from the Colstrip and Poplar boys, as well as the Red Lodge girls for some perspective on our state (montanacrosscountry.com) Billings Invitational on 9/29:

Poplar Boys — 9th place, Azure, 16:20; 12, Brien, 16:28; 15, Knowlton, 16:33; 26, runner n/a, 17:12; 36, Reidiger, 17:31.

Colstrip Boys — 8, Blythe, 16:19; 17, T. Blythe, 16:39; 20, Oxford, 16:44; 41, Shaw, 17:38; 43, Martinez, 17:48.

Red Lodge Girls — 4, Courtney Lynde, 18:40; 6, Darcy Stevens, 18:47; 25, Kalyse Engebretson, 19:52; 33, Jordan Going, 20:26; 35, Tara Swanson, 20:27.

Fast forward to late February 2008: The all-class wrestling tournament is down to its final matches; championships are being decided in Billings, MT. Matt Hojem, a TFHS athlete, is on the matt in the 119 pound division. Matt wins the individual championship and adds his name to a second gold trophy on the year. His first will be on October 20th in Helena for cross country.

Fast forward in life: A steady job and a marriage to a "girl that loves me for who I am and not what I look like" will help Matt live out some goals.

Rewind to 4-18-90, when Matt emerged into the world. A current height of 5'7" and 125 pound weight are misleading statistics to tell what a large life Matt lives and will have in the future. Matthew Ryan Hojem was born to Randy (Forest Service employee) and Kathee (teacher in rival Plains). Both of his parents are from Wisconsin, and he spent his formative school years in Alaska.

His solid GPA is around 3.8. His solid running bests include a 5:24 mile and an 18:10 three mile. His solid wrestling resume includes a second place state individual finish. His solid ability in his favorite video game Halo 2 clinches the verdict: Matt is a solid individual.

It won't matter what choice Matt makes after TFHS graduation; all roads will lead to success because of his work ethic. Life choices consist of the U of Montana, Western (Dillon), the Navy, the Coast Guard, ROTC – become a teacher in "small town on the coast" – or even winning $100,000,000 and spending it on a wrestling room for his own personal kids to play on.

Matt was our # 4 runner last year with an 18:26 time. This year he has a goal to break 19 and go to State. However, despite a new PR on Thursday of 18:10, Matt sits in the #8 position on our team. Even though he has improved, one can tell that our entire team is much better. From a coaching standpoint, that is tremendous. From a personal standpoint, it can be frustrating; yet Matt is a team player and is happy to be pushing the team to be better.

WHEN we win state, it will be because Matt joined the team halfway through the season two years ago. In 2005, he came out too late to join, yet worked as hard as the rest of our harriers. (I actually reminded Matt of my appreciation for that effort on Tues 9-16). Matt pushed us and we were better as a result. His participation in 2006 helped us to a 4th place team finish. In 2007, his name will be on the trophy because we take seven to run with two alternates, and Matt Hojem will be a name that deserves to be engraved on a team plaque.

Matt runs despite pain in the stomach, knees, hips, and ankles. In the summer and early season we worked with him on eating habits to eliminate stomach acid. This has helped. Dear reader, please recall words from 8/30: *"Matt: He had hip surgery as a child (right hip at ages 1 and 3), one leg is shorter than another (left), and not a day goes by where there is not a little pain involved...he rarely complains."*

Both of Matthew's parents are from Wisconsin, yet don't think his advice is cheesy: *"Do your work – don't procrastinate"* Future Kenyan Hawks should realize solid wisdom in *"don't run on pavement. Listen to Bob, and Mr. Gideon, they know what they are talking about."*

Readers, apply this to life – Appreciate teammates and the gift of being a hard worker. Matt has a thankful attitude and an appreciation of commitment. As much as Matt proves he is a worker, his least favorite workouts are Terrible Tuesday's, while his most liked runs are the relaxed and easy days before meets.

Favorites include 300 (movie), a Subway sandwich (any food, seriously, after wrestling season ends), working out (hobby), Weight Training (class), XC/wrestling (sport), Mr. Wheeler (teacher), Coach Wood (coach, now teaching in Wyoming), and *"all the XC runners"* (favorite other comment).

Thanks for running Matt and good luck in wrestling.

Teammates recall the following about Matt. No name says *"something funny is he can kick anyone's a@@ & eat more than them."*

Monica writes, *"went from living on an igloo & riding polar bears to school to riding horses & being ambushed by Indians."* It's true – Matt was raised in Alaska.

Ryan says, *"part-time anorexic wrestler, forever our XC manager, my lifelong golf partner."*

CC recalls, *"Matty is amazing! Nice work on trying to stand on the inner tube!!! Someday he will be a pimp! w/ a pimp cup! U know!"* No CC, I don't "know" about that. My lack of knowledge in certain areas may be a blessing in disguise.

Patrick texts, *"Throw some D's on it. I have a secret – we always joke on the bus – he's the pimp in my hood."*

Delcie pens, *"He's making a lot of progress! Whenever his teammates are out racing, you can find him on just about every corner cheering."*

Beca writes, *"Matt is still one of the sweetest guys I know! ☺ I really like the fact that he dedicates himself to running to get in shape for his true love, wrestling. We've been good friends for quite a while now, and Matt is a great person and always supportive of me (even if we tease each other all the time!) ☺"*.

Sunday, 9-30-2007, Bye Bye September, Hello State Month

A storm is kicking up pine needles outside, but my soul is peaceful. September went well, hope exists for the future, and the team and book are moving toward a climax.

Rain beats against the window pains, while the wind begs to be heard.

A bird flies into my room turning too wide an arch and slamming into a window. This is the third bird crash during my writing; this will be the first death. Is this a sign? Two other birds flew in, navigated a nice arch, and boomeranged safely out the door.

Thank you Lord for a great month of life – what a blessing – family, health, kids, a fantastic 2nd family in this XC team, hope for a championship, and an appreciation for the journey that is already a gold medal in my heart and soul.

Training our brains and bodies to run well in snow, sleet, cold, or summer desert temperatures has to be contemplated. Success needs to be proven regardless of the weather.

Our training has frayed muscles, tendons, and joints; three weeks remain. Our scissors will cut through blizzards, slice winter winds, and be pulled from rocks like Excalibur. We will be King Arthur of the Class B court, and we will see each other with depth not apparent to the average high school student.

We will be victorious in Halo XC, Thompson Falls style.

Harrier Hawks – we are winners and to the victors go the spoils.

"Beca tackled me in the hallway one day, and it still hurts," cried Patrick. And you thought high school and cross country were non-contact sports.

He is a creative writer who has certainly never plagiarized and might be a business leader in the future; His dreams are to *"make bank, marry the girl of my dreams, spend every moment with each other doing whatever we want."*

How about a $100,000,000 winning lottery ticket Patrick? All he could say was that he would *"take the love of my life on the BEST shopping trip ever!"* A lot of people could love you for a day for that kind of shopping trip Patrick Marion Jamison, so be wary.

Patrick has an accumulative GPA of 3.2, a 5'8" 146 pound frame, and was born 4-23-91. His parents are Marion Louise Jamison in Berkeley, California, and Lee Wesley Jamison, in "like every state." His father travels with a job that combines college football / radio management. His parents were divorced this summer.

Three siblings exist: T.C. (a high school senior in Orinda, California), while Jenny is 38 years old, married, and lives in Portland, Oregon. Malcolm also lives in Portland; he is a 32 year old with a steady girlfriend.

Patrick may travel the country like his father and land at colleges such as Michigan State University, University of California, or even Missoula's University of Montana. He will have a "hell of a lot of fun" wherever he goes.

He has favorites: Garden State (movie), French toast & chicken strips (food), cuddling (hobby), My Friend Leonard (book), Lacrosse & swimming (sport), Beckman (teacher), and Gideon (Coach).

Patrick has moved himself into a #6 position on our running team. This is a very valuable spot; it breaks ties between teams at State, while it may sneak in front of other teams #4 or #5 runner and make an opponent's score worse.

He ran a 17:37 PR at home last week. This beats prior goals, but gives a new target of under 17:30 by season's end. His least favorite workout is races – don't people slightly fear challenge or areas of life when the time comes to "step it up?" His favorite workout is a mile down to the dock – in warm weather, so legs can be iced and the team can bond like ducks. Ducks like water and have legs in the water most of the time – they travel in groups – and look for handouts – just like our runners.

His running advice: *"don't spend every practice running with the girls."*

111

By Andrew Gideon

Comments from teammates let people know that he is appreciated.

No name: *"Picking on Mr. Garrison in Spanish 2 was AMAZING."*

Delcie adds: *"always has something funny to say. Hard working."*

Matt wrote, *"Patty cakes is the coolest program kid ever."* Patrick is in the 20 Peaks program because of poor decisions. We are thankful this program believes in running for rehabilitation purposes. Our team is better because of it, society is better because of it, and Patrick is better because of it. CC backs this up with *"Patty is hilarious! Yaaaa. Good thing he did "bad things" & got sent to Montana. Whatttt? Noooo!"* CC, what is up with using four consecutive letters at the end of all your words?

| Matt Hojem, Homecoming 07 | Patrick Jamison, Homecoming 07 |

Monday, 10-1-2007, Mixed-up Monday

Team mileage today: 181.5 runners: 25 Avg. per runner: 7.3

The joke – Ryan and I ran 6 miles Saturday. This was a sneak attack on mileage leaders Jacob and Shane. The team was told to take the day off, so Ryan and I devised this fake scheme. No worries Shane and Jacob, your control is still intact. The totals after seven weeks are Jacob 316, Shane 316, and Ryan 312.

The sad fact – Shane's knee was stiff Friday; he did finish his TGIF workout, but slow, with walking, and some running backwards. Today he did not run the final mile and for the first time in three years, he did not complete a workout. The mileage totals will reflect this, and after today Jacob will be the sole leader. Kak and Blivits – this may be a bad sign; message to Shane's knee: hold on tight, get oiled up, and gear up for the stretch drive.

Mixed-up Monday: because we hold an annual grade school race on Tuesday, we changed our "Terrible Tuesday" to "Mixed-up Monday." At some point during the day, before running, while racing, or after timing, our harriers will realize "it's all downhill after this."

Monday will be the hardest day of the week for our runners – get the pain over with at the start. We will experience some 400's on Wednesday and a tempo run Thursday as well, but this is the key workout.

4 x 1 mile timings today is coach Naegeli's plan. Top runners will log 11 miles (warm-ups, jogging miles between, cool downs).

As mentioned earlier, Shane didn't complete the workout. This is stated twice because of the gravity of the situation. Our # 1 runner is in pain. The top five score at state, but having a #1 get a top finish is crucial to a low team score.

Jacob had an aching knee as well, but decided to complete the workout, thereby taking the lead over Shane for total mileage during the season.

Nine others joined Jacob in completing this mixed-up Monday mania: Mike M, Ryan, Patrick, Matt (who lost his shoe after 1/8 mile in the last timing, so he ran with one shoe for 7/8 mile), Cody, Beca, Delcie, CC (even with her bad back, she is a warrior worker), and Amanda.

To make matters worse, intermittent showers cascaded our bodies as we ran. Coach Gideon runs with the team, pacing various runners, while the other two coaches record times and exhort all harriers to better times and proper form.

"Arms, Arms,Arms" – coach Bob yells this at the half-way mark of mile timings. "Arms, Arms, Arms" will forever be in the Hawk Harrier brains.

The last two miles of the day were "cool down" miles – run in drenching rain on bodies already refrigerated by the outside temperature.

Who was impressive? CC is the aforementioned warrior with mile times within a 15 second range. Austin K, 8th grade, ran three timed miles, his most ever, with each mile faster. Beca had all miles under seven minutes with a 6:36 fast (our "mile" course measures 1.1 miles by my bicycle, shhhh, don't tell the runners). Ryan's range was only nine seconds (5:29-5:38, best among males).

Tuesday, 10-2-2007, Perspective & eye color
Team mileage today: 104   runners: 26   Avg. per runner: 4.0

Perspective: life tends to give some good perspectives at times to those who pay attention. Today was one of those days.

TFHS holds a grade school one mile run each year. Today was the day. Kindergarten through 6th grade students come to the high school and run – guided by our TFHS harriers. Girls ran at 4:00, while the boys scampered at 4:30.

It interrupts our workout schedule, hence mixed-up Monday yesterday. However, each Hawk Harrier sees what grade schoolers look like while running and can remember their past.

How does a 5th grade runner appear to a senior? What does a kindergarten student seem to a freshman? Have the students made progress, yes; have the athletes grown stronger, yes.

Here are some of the scattered thoughts of our high school harriers as to perspective on the grade school kids. *Did I really look like that? Was I actually that small? These kids are much chubbier than I was. I was much more active at that age. Nine man pileup at the start of the boy's race – several were crying, don't let them drive on big city freeways. Was I really that slow. Recognition of bad form. Chaos reigns in the grade school ranks. For sure, I am happy I am not*

113

back there. Kindergarten – recess, nap time, snacks, those were the days. These grade school kids sure are dramatic. Was I that obnoxious at that age?

Here are times from our Hawks when they were in the grade school mile.

1999 – Ryan (4th grade) 7:46, RT (4th) 7:49, Jacob (4th) 8:53, Bryant (4th) 10:22, CC (3rd) 8:14, Mariah (1st) 11:34.

2001 – Ryan (6th) 6:54, Shane (6th) 7:43, Jacob (6th) 8:03, CC (5th) 7:11, Monica (4th) 7:31, Mariah (3rd) 8:08, Delcie (5th) 9:40.

2002 – Logan (1st) 10:57, John G (2nd) 9:10, CC (6th) 7:08, Monica (5th) 7:39, Beca (5th) 7:51, Mariah (4th) 8:06, Delcie (6th) 8:52.

2004 – John G (4th) 8:07, Logan (3rd) 10:27, Mariah (6th) 7:29

2007 – Logan (6th) 8:22.

Ecclesiastes 9:11 ➔ *"I returned, and saw under the sun, that the race is not to the swift, nor the battle to the strong, neither yet bread to the wise, nor yet riches to men of understanding, nor yet favor to men of skill; but time and chance happeneth to them all."*

Eyes give perspective with an overlooked blessing of sight. Eye color may give perspective about a person's personality. The eyes are the window to the soul.

Hitler, the great boon to society he was, wanted a blond haired and blue eyed master race.

All we want at TFHS is Montana Global Hawk XC domination.

What color eyes should we have? Great question.

An article from the following site indicates a certain eye color will do well in cross country. (timesofindia.indiatimes.com/articleshow/2296242.cms)

NEW YORK: *Success lies in the colour of your eyes, and those with blue ones are likely to achieve more in life than their peers as they tend to study more effectively and perform better in exams, says a study conducted by US scientists. The study did not mention anything about people with black irises.*

The tests showed that brown-eyed people had faster reaction time, but those with lighter eyes appeared to be better strategic thinkers.

Brown-eyed people succeeded in activities such as football and hockey, but lighter-eyed participants proved to be more successful in activities that required skills in time structuring and planning such as golf, cross-country running and studying for exams, the scientists said.

Louisville University professor Joanna Rowe, who conducted the tests, said the results suggested an unexplored link between eye colour and academic achievement. "It is just observed, rather than explained," she said. "There's no scientific answer yet."

Monica and Ryan took a poll and discovered eye color to see if we have the making of a dynasty. Here are the results.

Don't turn my brown eyes blue: Shane, Mike M, Mike B, Beca G, John G. The G's are sister/brother and have matching brown eyes. Beca is our fastest girl, John is the fastest junior high boy, and Shane is the #1 boy. Hmm. Don't turn my brown eyes blue by becoming injured!

Green eyes are jealous of the fastest brown eyes: Jacob, Kyle, Mariah, and Coach Naegeli. Jacob, Mariah, and Coach Naegeli are family with the same eye color.

Hazel eyes: *"Soaking in the moonlight swimming in your hazel eyes, soaking in the firelight never will say good night / Drinking in the hours and dreaming girl of making you mine"* (From "If you need me at all" by David Boone / A Tale of Gold. Since I talked of David earlier (9-24 entry), I used some lyrics from one of his songs. Hazel eyes: Ryan, Matt H, Delcie, Jessie, Logan.

Blue eyes crying in the rain (sorry, another song lyric just jumped into my head): Patrick, MK, RT, Bryant, Cody, CC, JP, Lacey, Amanda, and Coach Reall. Blue eyes are apparently the eye color of initialed runners: CC JP RT.

Combinations-green/blue: Bryce, Coach Gideon. Bryce clearly has a brilliant future.

Monica has a green/hazel combination.

What did we learn about eye color and the human running soul?

If you answered absolutely nothing, then you win a prize of absolutely nothing. It is interesting that our top runner in each area, hs boy, hs girl, and jr high boy are all brown eyed.

The eyes are the window to the soul. One item noticed by looking into our athlete's eyes is a certain degree of energy. There is a spark of life in all of our Hawk Harrier eyes; catch that reflection and fly with our hawks. The hint of a smile and an appreciation for work and life exist and will not be extinguished, even after a bad race.

The eyes are the window to the soul. Our cross country soul is multi-colored and multi-faceted. Our soul has some depth beyond the finish line, beyond the line of high school graduation, and beyond life.

If there is a heaven, and I believe there is, then we will see these eyes once more, long after the caffeine drips out the tear ducts for the final time.

Wednesday, 10-3-2007, Sprinter's workout vs. variety

Team mileage today: 143.5 runners: 25 Avg. per runner: 5.7

Ice baths: warm temperatures outside vs. cold and rainy days.

To ice on cold days or not to ice on cold days, that is the question. Whether tis nobler to slow down the blood and challenge the joints or to dispute with the coaches advice and plunge into a hot tub. Tis a question devoutly to be pondered.

Thank you, Hamlet / Shakespeare, for abuse of your monologue.

On warm days after an ice bath, bones, joints, ligaments, muscles, etc all say Thank You for contrasting temperatures – heat helps the blood flow again. On cold days, such as we had latley, the contrast is not there. The ice baths chill

By Andrew Gideon

the body, yet the body never warms back up. Muscles, joints, tendons, etc, say, BAD OWNER. Park this engine in a hot tub or a hot shower after icing.

Jacob and Shane almost gave up on ice baths this past week. However, I suggested a hot shower after icing. Jacob said it worked like a charm.

Today we ran at the Sol residence – Birdland Bay. Coach Bob was not happy with the "sprinter's workout" (approx. 6 x 250 meters) – muscles were tied in knots from the short intervals.

We did have a nice change of scenery away from the school. Our warm-up was through the State Park by the river, as well as a post sprint recovery, but we did have a longer cool down of 2-3 miles at the school upon returning. Top runners ran seven miles today.

Beca was a big winner today. We held two separate relay "races" with different sets of three per race. Beca's team won both races.

Austin, 8th grade, was on a second place team. He really wanted to know what the winners will get. Winners get the strong feeling of a job well done.

Anyone in the top 3 in either race earned a "Kudos" bar and some green tea (for health). "Extending 'kudos' to another individual is often done as a praising remark" (Wikipedia).

Thursday, 10-4-2007, Long slow Muddy Bike Day
Team mileage today: 148   runners: 24   Avg. per runner: 6.2

MK jogged with Mr. Gideon today. He needed to be corralled to a slightly slower pace, which was a good conversational pace to learn something about his mental attitude and approach with all of his life changes that are occurring – moving to TFalls, moving from TFalls, new girlfriend, running for the Blue Hawks, and the long term future.

Jacob and Shane, with sore knees rode the bike 12 miles instead of running 6 with the team. Shane found mud puddles. So did Jacob, it is just that Jacob avoided the mud and splashes and came back clean.

Thank you for the use of your bikes Mr. Gideon. Thank you for the use of your knees at State Harrier Hawks.

Bryant needs a profile, and my keyboard has all 26 letters, so I might as well go to work.

This Hawk cannot spell to save his life. Better English teachers than Mr. Gideon have tried, although I was blessed with 2 years with him. Spell checker fears Bryant's writing and usually freezes the computer attempting to offer suggestions for his writing.

Bryant was born 8-7-89. Dan Ray and Teresa Rose must have had a sparkle in the eye and transferred it hereditarily to Bryant as evidenced by Delcie's words, *"Bryant never fails to make me laugh! He's such a rebel. You know how you aren't supposed to bring any outside food into the movie theater? One time at the movie, Bryant pulls out a lump of tinfoil (that looked much like a baked potato) and asked me innocently, 'Want some licorice?' Cracked me up!"*

116

Our laugh track Bryant is known for one thing – space ships. His future plans are to *"bild a space-craft or rocket ship and exsplore this solerseston to its end. If ime still alive plote a cors for the nexst solersistem."* Bozeman (Montana State Univ.) is in the plans for Structural Engineering, Physics, and Chemistry. Spelling is a weakness, but he offers strength to our Science Olympiad team.

He doesn't list a GPA, but his main weakness would be spelling. After that, his brain works well. He will earn some scholarships by the end of the year.

Ciara, CC, is his only sibling; her profile is on 10-7. On this team, the Naegeli's, Normandeau's, and Gunderson's are all examples of fine families on our team. I love the fact that my own kids can be surrounded by these people.

Bryant's advice includes eating and laughing lots. He also states that one should *"live life like it's you only life."* Other running advice: the race of time does not compare to the races in cross country. Bryant continues the depth of thought with *"We all finis this race but no trofey go's to ferst and there is no last but how you get to the end of your time was the prize of life."*

Ending the book there enters my mind at that thought!

His 18:41 last week will be his second fastest career time; last year at State he ran 18:40.

Goals for running are to do his best; thank you for that. Life goals: *"fined a butifal woman, mary her and exsplor the univers with her."*

His $100,000,000 lottery win would turn into 10 billion after investments, and Bryant could build his space ship.

Favorites: (movie) opens up the imagination and makes him laugh, (food) everything that tastes good, (hobby) eating, (book) science books, (class) Astronomy, (sport) XC, (Teacher) Mr. Kinkade, and (Coach) Sarah.

Jacob writes, *"I think he spends his race thinking about new spaceship designs instead of about running."* After reading this, Bryant was told to think of faster spaceships so he could run faster. Sometimes songs get stuck in runner's heads, so faster tempo songs and faster spaceships may result in better times.

Beca is a good writer and will now spell out words on Bryant, *"Once Bryant and I spent like 2 hours at a restaurant waiting for our parents to show (which they never did, by the way) but we had a lot of fun driving in his car. ☺ Anyway, Bryant is definitely like an older brother to me. He is with me at 4H fairs, and ALWAYS makes me laugh no matter how upset I am. He is so smart, and I have no doubt he will build his rocket ship someday."*

Friday, 10-5-2007, The old man is snoring

Team mileage today: 95.5   runners: 25   Avg. per runner: 3.8

Tapering – the in-between world – hard work is done, weather patterns change, and State arrives as fast as Shane runs. Sept ➔ Oct; the future arrives.

One runner performed magic today? He warmed up with us, stretched with us, and then was gone. Poof. Magic. When questioned, this boy assured us he ran the three miles just like everyone else – just at the school, then down the opposite direction that the rest of the team ran. Thankfully most of our team is not a daily soap opera.

Today's run was easy as 1-2-3. Warm-up, stretch, 3 miles, go home! On an early out Friday, our kids were headed home before 4 PM. Tomorrow's bus doesn't leave until 9 AM, so it seems like a vacation!

In Missoula tonight, our # 3 State-ranked boys football team lost 43-27. Missoula Loyola, the team that ended last year's season and is our nemesis in cross country, beat them. Loyola football was ranked # 5 in Class B Montana.

The Thompson Falls Blue Hawk football team is now 5-1.

Saturday, 10-6-2007, Polson Invitational Meet
(For the 11 October 2007 *Sanders County Ledger*)
Plains and T Falls XC compete in Polson   *By Andrew Gideon*

A blustery and drizzling day greeted harriers from Plains and Thompson Falls on Saturday, October 6. The runners met the Polson wind, rain, and cool temperatures head on and produced solid results.

Coach Bob Reall of the Blue Hawks stated that Polson's course had "good, solid races – the conditions didn't let them run PR's." (PR = personal record)

The junior high two mile race led off the Polson Pirate Invitational at noon. The following times were recorded: Robert Earhart (Plains) 13:26, Felicia Earhart (P) 15:00, John Gunderson (Thompson Falls) 15:29, Austin Kinser (TF) 16:12, Dakotta Kinser (TF) 17:01, Karlena Heward (P) 17:17, and Tia Thompson (P) 23:04. Dakotta's time was a PR.

The boys Junior Varsity three mile run was next at 12:30. The Blue Hawks had six harriers compete. RT Brown (5th, 18:59) and Matt Hojem (6th, 19:00) made it into the top ten, while other finishers included Kyle Breithaupt (19:18), Bryant Normandeau (19:41), Mike Barnett (21:27), and Cody White (22:15).

The best weather may have been during the JV girls three miles. The sun peaked out to watch two Lady Hawk runners produce PR's; Amanda Wood and Jessie Drake both cut off two minutes from previous best performances. Amanda stated that she was "happy-ecstatic" with her effort. Lacey Wade was the other Hawk harrier in this event, just edging Wood at the finish with an identical 27:02 time and besting Drake by one second.

The varsity girls results showed that Thompson Falls placed 4th of 7 teams (1st in Class B), while Plains finished 7th. Hamilton, Class A, won the event.

Nine racers competed for the Trotters and Lady Hawks in the varsity race. Hawk harrier Beca Gunderson received special honor with a top ten finish with her 21:05 time. Jefferyanne Parker (TF) was next in at 21:33, followed by Delcie Peters (TF) 21:36, CC Normandeau (TF) 22:18, Mariah Naegeli (TF)

22:39, Rio Crismore (P) 22:54, Monica Conlin (TF) 23:11, Kara Bates (P) 23:54, and Zoe Banovich (P) 24:58.

On the boys side, Thompson Falls ran 2nd of 8 teams, while Plains came in 5th. Hamilton, Class A, won the meet. In the Class B ranks, Thompson Falls was first, while Plains placed 2nd.

Individual harriers Shane Donaldson (16:22, 3rd) and Jacob Naegeli (16:44, 5th) of Thompson Falls finished in the top 10, earning them special merit. Other finishers in the three mile high school race were as follows: Mike Morris (TF) 17:16, Justin Allison (P) 17:46, Bryce Miller (TF) 17:48, Ryan Sol (TF) 17:49, Patrick Jamison (TF) 18:07, Mike Kidwiler (TF) 18:19, Valin Heward (P) 18:59, Kenneth Beech (P) 19:31, and Thad LeClair (P) 22:19.

The Polson Invitational was set up slightly different than most races. The top three competitors from each school ran separate from the rest of the team. At the time of that race (2:30), a wicked wind blew in from Flathead Lake, making for hard conditions. The times were generally 30-45 seconds off each athlete's best, but Coach Sarah Naegeli of T Falls stated that the wind made the 1-2-3 race the "worst conditions" of the day.

Naegeli also said that "this course is good preparation for state with the grass and hills."

The Plains athletes were coming off some colds and flus and competed well despite not being 100% according to Coach Barb Steward.

The Hawk coaches were happy with the way the athletes battled the challenging conditions. The solid and steady results for the TF harriers in Polson were a good sign for State, because the team has been mentally working on responding well to any weather that may happen in Montana in the next two weeks – 90 degree temperatures or 10 degrees with four feet of snow on the ground.

Coach Reall is "looking forward to two good races" in the next two weeks, Runners Edge in Missoula on Thursday, October 11th, and State in Helena, on October 20th.

There are no official state rankings for cross country. This reporter currently has the boys ranked at Poplar 1, Thompson Falls 2, Colstrip 3, Darby 4, Loyola 5, Manhattan 6, Plains 7, Valley Christian 8, and Glasgow 9. Here are my current rankings for the girls in Montana Class B: 1. Glasgow, 2. Red Lodge, 3. Cut Bank, 4. Thompson Falls, 5. Cascade, 6. Whitehall, 7. Loyola, 8. Darby, and 9. Manhattan.

There was an open race at 3:00. Coach Gideon ran the three mile course in 18:56, while 6th grader Logan Naegeli finished in 27:52. Because he finished within ten minutes of Mr. Gideon, he won $30 from his parents.

Is Logan now a professional? And why is Mr. Gideon so slow?

This will be the last bus ride home that athletes were interviewed. We learned valuable information along the way.

Amanda was "happy-ecstatic" about her 27:02 today. She had "no idea" why she improved, other than the "second mile was good." How about a ton of training! We learned her favorite trees are willow and maple. She compliments Jessie for today's effort. She tells us the ice bath is colder when sitting than standing, and she really wants to run fast enough to participate at state.

Her favorite teammate is Delcie, maybe because Delcie gave Amanda no bake cookies and snicker doodles for her August birthday. Delcie was the only teammate to give her a present, so she definitely didn't share them with the team! The cookies were placed in her car and dominated her mind during that practice – *"it was all I could think about,"* Amanda said. This is a prevalent thought for a runner – the reward – lattee, omelette, cookies – at the end of a hard run.

Mike B stated that today's 2nd mile was slow and long due to several hills. He still came within four seconds of his PR despite wind and drizzle. His favorite course is Missoula and like Amanda, he has an August birthday. When I called Mike B up for his interview, he was marking up a pumpkin he had purchased with Bryce. One side had legs and was happy, while the other side had no legs and contained an unhappy face. Lesson: runners and running make one happy. The weeping willow is his favorite tree, while ice baths are "amazing." He compliments Amanda & Bryce for their efforts today. Mike's knees hurt "more in practice" than they do during meets. Hmm, maybe he will be happier on payday than the other days of the week in his adult life.

Sunday, 10-7-2007, Grape Pickers

The following seven individuals picked grapes today: Monica, Delcie, Kyle, RT, Matt, Bryant, and Ryan.

The grape picking was a fundraiser. Mr. Gideon showed up with son Jaxon because it was a decent day, and the three year old wanted to pick grapes. Unfortunately the only thing Jaxon found ripe was in his pants – wasn't that a fun treat! Vulgar / rude / bathroom humor – a sure-fire way to get laughs at a comedy club. It originates when parents are extremely excited a kid goes poopy on the pot – finally - for the first time – no more diapers, encourage this behavior with loud and positive whoops and hollers; thus bathroom humor emerges.

The previous weekend Mariah, Shane, RT, Ryan, Bryant, and Matt showed up for the student council highway cleanup.

This bunch of kids is as good as a bunch of ripe grapes – a few seeds to spit out, and kind of messy, but they sure make a fine whine.

Speaking of fine whines, here is our beloved Ciara (CC).

Ciara Rose Normandeau – a rose by any other name (CC) is still a rose. She was born 11-6-1990 and has sprouted into a 5'4½" and 130 pound flower. A few thorns (cartilage in her spine) are missing; she originally did not go out for XC because of health reasons. We are truly blessed that she changed her mind during the second week of practice.

CC is a warrior-like runner. Her attitude and work ethic is extremely upbeat, and if she weren't running off excess energy, then more words would flow from her mouth than already do. I don't mean that negatively – it's just that she can maintain a conversation with several people – all at once – on different topics – and the other person really doesn't have to be there. If you don't believe me, then listen to her favorite workout, "…long and slow days…so we can talk a lot!" Her least favorite workout is obviously Tuesday because these Terrible days are hard and fast and all energy is in the legs and not the vocal cords!

If you could see her information sheet – it is loaded with information to type – her words JUMP out at the reader.

I am thankful for her presence – she gives the team a shot at a trophy we wouldn't otherwise have. She is 7th on the girls team in mileage simply because we have held her workouts down several times to maintain long term health. Her best ever time for XC is 20:28; with a good day, she will get under 21:00 at state this year. A 21:19 showing at Mountain West is her current 2007 best time.

CC's future plans include *"become a masseuse, own a cafe or a night club, and maybe own an art studio on the side."* During one run this year, she stated she wanted to run a nail salon and massage business. Her options remain open and her energy will make anything she chooses a successful reality. The U of Montana is a likely place to find her in four years; Europe is not! She will work toward a small business management degree, a master's degree in culinary arts, graduate in massage therapy, spa and treatment.

She works now at ACE hardware – 40 hour weeks during the summer and weekends around XC now. In college, she is eyeballing the Outback Steakhouse as an opportunity to pay some bills. Call ahead for reservations and call ahead to warn them – CC is coming your way.

Parents - Teresa Marie married Daniel Ray Normandeau. Teresa is from Minnesota, while Dan is from Montana. Her brother is senior Bryant (10-4 profile). Either Beca is a sister, a wanna-be sister, or else CC has adopted her – that second family shows up again.

Advice to younger students is *"always be nice…it never gets old, work hard…it pays off, love life and live in peace."* A heart and a peace symbol follow that quote. Her running advice sounds similar to Delcie's (9-02 entry) – *"Push yourself…it might be tough but it is so satisfying, the best feeling in the world when you know you did your best!"*

CC has a good team attitude – her goals include, *"beat my best time ever! Get top 15@ State, or maybe just a trophy with my girls!"*

Her goals for life are as follows: *"Be happy…own a log cabin…go snowboarding & swimming daily. Run a fantastic night club or some other small business. Adopt! Marry the nicest guy alive, probably Channing Tatum!"*

With $100,000,000 she would buy 20 acres on the coast, a log cabin with *"3 bathrooms, 12 bedrooms, a swimming pool (hot tub) all that stuff. Then adopt like 7 kids and raise them all as good as I could. I might buy a club. Oh, and I'd send them all to college!"*

Her favorites: Movie (<u>Gladiator</u>, <u>Peaceful Worrier</u>, <u>White Chicks</u>, <u>Practical Magic</u>), Food (Kettle Corn, veggie chips, cupcakes, cookies), hobby (running, swimming), book (<u>Message in a Bottle</u>), Class (Art, study hall), sport (XC, track), Teacher (Nelson, Stuckey, Gideon, Dyer), Coach (Gideon), Other (phrase with Beca..."I'd marry him!), Other other ("Delcie...don't start talking. I'll fall asleep!"), and then there were a lot of other things written down that the average teacher would demand be typewritten for lack of understandable use of language (a lot of phrases such as "Oh, baby ... I,I ,... Whaaaaa? ... Neooooo!").

Delcie writes, *"She and I have been through a lot together. We became friends in third grade. Both of us were completely crazy...One time we rubbed dandelions all over each other's faces & CC got an allergic reaction to it."*

Beca pens, *"CC also is an amazing at running. She is a big motivator to me. I consider her an awesome friend (we'll always be loyal to the original four!) And I always laugh with her. I don't know where she gets some of her random facts! 700 calories!!"*

Jacob is *"still trying to figure out what kind of creature her IPOD speakers are."* CC was definitely mad at RT during our homecoming meet when he tossed CC's creature to the ground and broke it. Bad RT. Her IPOD speakers are a combination of a rabbit, space creature, and marshmallow man.

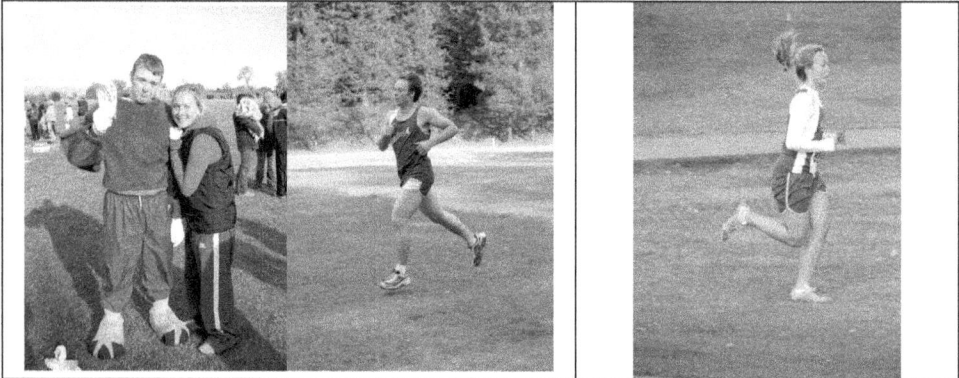

| Bryant & CC State 07 | Bryant, Homecoming 07 | CC, State 07 |

Monday, 10-8-2007, Thoreau

Team mileage today: 135 runners: 25 Avg. per runner: 5.4

One last memory trip through the Forest Service trails in the fall leaves. That path always takes me away from running – one must watch the feet and trail; the focus becomes narrowed so that roots, pine cones, and bear scat are not stepped on. Trees block out buildings and nature replaces man-made pavement.

Thoreau would appreciate a walk through our Mule Pasture. He said, *"I wanted to live deep and suck out all the marrow of life."* - *"In the long run, men hit only what they aim at. Therefore, they had better aim at something high."* - *"I have learned that if one advances confidently in the direction of his dreams, and endeavors to live the life he has imagined, he will meet with a success unexpected in common hours." - "The cost of a thing is the amount of what I call life which is required to be exchanged for it, immediately or in the long run."*

Thoreau's eloquence helped me love reading him (college) and teaching him (American Literature). Two of the four quotes use "in the long run."

After eight weeks of the season our team, not including coaches, has run 5835 miles – 3916 by 18 boys, and 1919 miles by 9 girls.

5835 miles is an astounding amount of "advancing in the direction of dreams." 3916 miles by the boys aims directly at that gold trophy in twelve days.

Tuesday, 10-9-2007, The old man is snoring

Team mileage today: 135   runners: 25   Avg. per runner: 5.4

If it is the journey and not the destination, then when the journey nears an end, where will the destination be?

It is our second to last Terrible Tuesday. Last year we did 3 x 1 mile hard, but after random harrier sampling, soreness, tiredness, and lack of energy popped up. We adjusted our workout to a 2 x 1 today. Less is more in this case.

This season has been a phenomenal journey, and it is with sadness that the end of the tunnel roars its future light toward us. The oncoming future light from the sun is delayed approximately eight minutes. Calculate the distance from the sun to the earth and divide by the speed of light = between 8 and 9 minutes. So, the light we are living in is always in the past.

Our journey must end with a championship dream. Accepting a broken heart and a less than gold finish just will not do. I have had to do this several times in my life, and the feeling is too much right now.

Bryce Miller hurt a knee in PE (our # 5 runner). Kak and blivits.

Positive weather, 73 degrees after a rainy week, greeted muscles today.

Wednesday, 10-10-2007, Easy Day, easy entry!

Team mileage today: 95.5   runners: 24   Avg. per runner: 4.0

Another easy day – bounce energy back into our legs for State – 10 days. I can't eat, can't sleep, just dreaming of you....our little trophy!

An easy entry, my easiest this season – let the keyboard and brain rest for State! I can't eat; I can't sleep, just dreaming of you...a best selling book!

Thursday, 10-11-2007, Divisionals

Two weeks ago on Homecoming Friday, I allowed RT to shave "TF" into the back of my hair/head. He then painted it blue – so I had a blue TF in my hair for the parade; the TF is still distinguishable today. Today RT came to school with "TF" in his head/hair shaved out. If we used cut and paste techniques, we could fill the TF in my head with RT's hair.

(For the 18 October 2007 *Sanders County Ledger*)
Thompson Falls Junior High XC runners   *by Andrew Gideon*

123

By Andrew Gideon

On Thursday, October 11, a junior high cross country race was held in Missoula at the University of Montana golf course.

Four Thompson Falls Hawks ran in the 1.33 mile event.

John Gunderson edged teammate Austin Kinser by one second; John's time was 9:16. Dakotta Kinser continued to show improvement running as he clocked a 10:33 time; just 19 days ago on the same course Dakotta timed in at 11:14, an improvement of 41 seconds.

6th grader Logan "Work Horse" Naegeli came in at 11:09. This was Logan's third race in nine days – he ran the local mile run at the high school on October 2nd, and competed in a three mile run in Polson on October 6th that he finished in 27:52. This was the last meet of the year for the junior high. Austin Kinser led the junior high members with over 150 miles of training during the season.

(For the 18 October 2007 *Sanders County Ledger*)

Blue Hawks fly well in Missoula   *By Andrew Gideon*

Almost ideal conditions existed for a cross country meet in Missoula on Thursday, October 11. Temperatures at sixty degrees with little wind made for a pleasant day to run.

The Thompson Falls Blue Hawks responded with eight personal bests from 22 possible athletes, while another runner posted a season best.

Missoula Loyola and the Runner's Edge hosted the event at the University of Montana Golf Course. The high school girls and boys participated in a three mile race.

The Thompson Falls Lady Hawks can be considered Divisional Champions. The race in Missoula did include the three Missoula AA schools and some Class C schools, while serving as an unofficial "divisional" race for the B teams. Thompson Falls was the leader of all Class B teams, but did fall to AA Hellgate and Sentinel.

Beca Gunderson led the way for the Hawks with her 20:58 showing. The next three runners fed off of each other's energy to score some good points for the Lady Hawks: Jefferyanne Parker ran a new Personal Record (PR) of 21:15, edging CC Normandeau's season best time of 21:15, while Delcie Peters ran a strong 21:24. The other racers were Mariah Naegeli 22:42, Monica Conlin 23:09, Amanda Wood 26:48, Jessie Drake 26:50, and Lacey Wade 27:48. Wood and Drake set their PR's.

The boys can also be considered Divisional Champions. Hellgate and Sentinel again took first and second overall, yet the Hawks third place overall showing bested other B teams Loyola, Darby, Deer Lodge, and Valley Christian. Plains did not compete due to homecoming activities.

Shane Donaldson led the way for the Hawks as he has done all year by placing 4th overall in 16:00. Twelve other Hawks flew in pattern following Donaldson's lead: Jacob Naegeli 16:14, Mike Morris 16:38, Ryan Sol 16:58, Patrick Jamison 17:22, Bryce Miller 17:31, Mike Kidwiler 17:39, Matt Hojem

124

18:17, RT Brown 18:44, Kyle Breithaupt 19:04, Bryant Normandeau 19:15, Mike Barnett 21:20, and Cody White 21:35. Morris, Sol, Jamison, Barnett, and White all set their PR in this race, while Jamison's time moved him into 10th place all-time on the Blue Hawk running list.

The next and last event for the Hawk Harriers is the State B Meet in Helena on October 20th.

The Blue Hawk boys have been the first place Class B team in every meet this season that they have competed in. This coach believes this will continue on October 20th in Helena at the State Meet. Last year the boys placed 4th.

The nine Lady Hawks have run hard in practice this season by logging over 2100 miles so far. The girls placed 8th in 2005 and 6th last year. That showing will be better this year, and with a solid all-around team performance on State race day, a top three trophy is conceivable.

Cody White wrote the following for an English assignment on 11/26/07; I include it here because this was his best race; he finished his season with a PR. *"The man trudged through the snapping track. Every step drew him nearer the cheering crowd, the mocking finish line, and the trophy calling out to him. The man responded by running harder, laughing at the biting pain in his chest. His foot hits the white line, and the applauding crowd explodes into cheers."*

Friday, 10-12-2007, First forecasts

Team mileage today: 118   runners: 20   Avg. per runner: 5.9

I've already predicted gold for our Hawk boys at State next weekend.

I am not a weatherman, so that prediction will probably be right.

First forecasts for Helena, MT, weather on the October 20th showed a high of 59, 34 low, with a 10% chance of precipitation. Today's weather.com site predicted 60 high, 39 low, and 10% precip. Almost ideal conditions seem to be possible for an ideal book and an ideal ending.

The team ran a little longer today – junior high athletes are done, while the high school team has been cut to the seven state runners and the alternates. Several runners showed up to run as an option - a great sign for the future.

Saturday, 10-13-2007, 50 miles

Crazy Horse is credited with the saying, "It is a Good day to die." This is a warrior's theme and good for Montana history; the quote states that today I will sacrifice myself if necessary for a cause. The warriors don't want to die necessarily, but the time to fight has arrived and the duty can not be shirked.

Today was my day to battle the Le Grizz 50 mile ultra marathon. I have been coaching, teaching, writing, and parenting; I have also been training for this tiny Ultra-Marathon.

Miles (splits) 8:16, 8:02, 8:33, 9:33, 7:47 (5 mile 42:10), 7:42, 7:26, 9:40, 7:34, 8:17 (10 mile 1:22:48), 9:42, 8:40, 8:32, 9:33, 9:22 (15 mile 2:08:38),

8:26, 8:06, 9:51, 9:04, 9:40 (20 mile 2:53:45), 10:06, 8:31, 9:26, 10:26, 9:03 (25 mile 3:41:16), 9:31, 10:34, 9:52, 23:46 (2 miles) (30 miles 4:34:59), 10:28, 11:07, 10:50, 10:19, 10:31 (35 miles 5:28:15), 13:30, 10:43, 11:28, 12:42, 12:30 (40 miles 6:29:09), 11:50, 12:53, 12:24, 11:45, 13:06 (45 miles 7:31:07), 11:58, 12:21, 14:06, 12:02, 12:20 (50 mile time 8:33:55).

Here are the estimates of my finishing time that I gathered from the athletes on Friday.

22 time estimates: **(BOYS)** Mike M 7 hr 15 min, Matt H 7:00, RT 7:26:13, Jacob 6:47, Bryce 7:05, Ryan 7:11:39, Patrick 7:02, Shane 8:03, Bryant 7:30, Cody 6:52:13, Mike K 7:23:07. The closest boy was Shane, who had the slowest guess. Hey, I tried!

(GIRLS) Amanda 9:35, JP 6:35:17, Monica 6:52:04, Lacey 1 min and 1 sec (she did say she had no idea), Beca 7:42:31.73, CC 7:23:19, Delcie 6:30, Mariah 7:15:02, Jessie 7:22:22. Beca was the closest girl – at least Amanda's guess didn't happen! It could have been worse!

Coaches – Coach Bob 6:58:22 and Coach Naegeli 8:10. Coach Naegeli was the closest coach guess and the closest overall guess.

The closest in each category, Shane, Beca, and Coach Naegeli, all won a Le Grizz shirt, courtesy of Coach Gideon's sweat and pain.

The battle raged on longer than this warrior wanted to fight; nevertheless, fight I did until the end. My fight gradually became slower and less confident, but my goal to finish remained.

I ran 50 miles today! How many people can say or write that! Trust me, it looks great in the log book!

This was more than a physical battle – it was a mental and spiritual war. The weather and scenery was amazing – I couldn't imagine this race with snow or rain; I have seen pictures of this run during horrible weather.

At times I am weak; this is the time to call on the strength of God and life. I appreciate the blessings of health and strive for the collective energy of my soul to move in a proper direction. Today it was 50 miles along a beautiful Montana scenic reservoir; this Harrier Hawk season has been with 22 wonderful high school students and two other coaches.

I wish I could pen thoughts of the agony/ecstasy of the LeGrizz 50, but our Hawk season dominates my mind. I care more about their performances than my own personal race. If this 50 mile ultra-marathon were to motivate them (an original goal), then run this race to show that one person can run farther and faster than ever imagined. I spent most of the race praying for the team's performance at State and for the lives of the Hawk Harriers post cross country.

At mile 15, my right foot began hurting – way too early. At mile 35, I changed shoes. This helped, but mostly, for the last 30 miles, I had a slight cramp in my right foot. This was worrisome because my stride changed slightly – with changing strides an injury could follow.

My wife Deborah and kids were along the course to cheer me on. Deborah probably ran 13 miles with me during the race. If this run helps my boys see life as a challenge, then great. I just wonder what a 1 and 3 year old could see from a Dad who runs for 50 miles.

I had gel and a camelback for Gatorade. However, at mile 36-37, there was an aide station. I grabbed an orange slice candy – exquisite, beautiful. Wow, that hit the spot. I savored that bite for several miles.

At mile 42, halleluiah - another aide station and the aforesaid chew candy. The taste was so dissimilar than the gel and goo I had been eating for energy, that I had a little slice of orange heaven again.

At mile 47, I finally understood that medical marijuana is a necessity for some people. At mile 48, I was one of those people.

My left neck and arm went numb for the last three miles, but I decided not to worry my wife with that silly information until several hours after the race.

Sunday, 10-14-2007, Funny bone

My only item not sore is my right funny bone. Seriously.

I demand a re-race of the Le Grizz 50 mile – I am positive it was 100 meters short – I could have beaten that 85 year old lady ahead with another 100 meters – or at least gotten close enough to dive (okay, trip) and knock her down – I am sure I could have gotten up faster.

State Champion – I was the first Montanan to finish in my age group of 39 year olds. Okay, I was in the 18-39 age group – and I was the only Montana entrant. Actually there were five Montanans aged 18-39. I may have beat all Montanan's, but people from Arizona, the other 49 states, Canada, Puerto Rico, Kenya, and Cuba beat me.

cheetahherders.com ➔ Le Grizz Ultra-Marathon. The Le Grizz Gazette, Volume 26, 07, has my fancy honor box (Montana Champion) on the last page.

There were 85 finishers – 28 first time finishers, including me.

One couple earned the "10 Bears award" for competing for the 10th time.

Enough of others, I may have to amputate my right foot/ankle. I only changed stride for the last 35 miles because of the pain on the bottom of my foot.

It's not so much ankle swelling or knee pain, or the stomach pain, but the internal bleeding, the coughing of blood, and the rash up my side that is painful.

Whose idea was it anyway to run 50 miles? It took two hours to drive to the start line – doesn't that give a guy a clue!!!! Hello, sanity.

The first mile was okay because it was dark, I hadn't "waked up" yet, and I forgot I was entered in this long of a race. (Jaxon says, "I waked up Dad." – that is why my grammar is poor.)

I should have carried scissors.

The first 15 miles were great – it was the last 35 that really hurt.

By Andrew Gideon

I edited out my writing on medical marijuana once again. See, you didn't just read that. Feel no pain, therefore there is no pain. An ice bath actually numbs the pain in more ways than one.

In fact, I think they measured the miles wrong – each one became increasingly longer. I'm sure I probably ran 70 miles.

A finish line never tasted as sweet as this 50 mile one.

Yet, Saturday's State will be sweeter than orange slice candy.

Monday, 10-15-2007, Picture Day

Team mileage today: 110   runners: 24   Avg. per runner: 4.6

Never interrupt school and the classroom so that learning can occur at the best possible pace. The administration interprets this as interrupt the classroom, on average, of at least 10 times a day, and then have picture day steal the entire extra-curricular day as an inconvenience. It is good our coaching staff pays attention to detail and factors in the daily challenges that hinder (mostly) and help (rarely) from the "non-interrupted" school day.

Anyway, today is/was/and forever shall be PICTURE DAY.

Beca and picture day . . ."*I tend to like picture day, because of the camaraderie and chaos.. The coaches would whole-heartedly DISagree…we were all laughing so hard (giving our abs a workout). The day is always a week before state, so excitement is building, the team is wired, and the photographer is pulling out his hair. Goofy pictures occur and everybody is shoving each other good-naturedly and making fun of each other. Good times, good times.*"

Hottie Harriers 07	Seniors and their guns/pipes 07

(For the 18 October 2007 *Sanders County Ledger*)

State XC Preview   *by Andrew Gideon*

A hawk swoops down to Helena, talons gripping a trophy to bring back to the Hawk nest. The prize meal, a first place gold, slides straight to the taste buds. A fish in the belly wouldn't taste as good as this trophy on the school shelf. By savoring the gold, a future dynasty is built with solid food.

The Blue Hawk boys have been the first place Class B team in every meet this season that they have competed in. This coach believes this will continue on October 20th in Helena at the State Meet.

Head Coach Sarah Naegeli's best place boys finish was second in 2001; she said that "we hope to make the dream a reality."

Coach Bob Reall said that the team is going to Helena with the four C's in mind: "be cool, calm, collected, and very calculating."

Shane Donaldson, senior, has led Thompson Falls all season long. Even though it is State, the fearless Hawk Harrier is approaching Saturday's finale as "just another meet."

Following in formation for the Hawks will be seniors Jacob Naegeli, Mike Morris and Ryan Sol. Joining the squadron will be juniors Mike Kidwiler and Patrick Jamison. Bryce Miller, freshman, will make his State B debut. Alternates are seniors Matt Hojem and RT Brown. Along for the ride, and very important in his own right, will be senior Bryant Normandeau, who will sport the Hawk mascot uniform.

Last year at the State B Boy's Meet in Helena, Donaldson (2), Naegeli (3), and Sol (17) ran the competition into the ground. The 22 points combined for those three harriers was better than any other school. However, cross country at the class B level scores a team's top five runners, with the sixth place member used as a tie breaker. The terrific trio was followed by Blue Hawk harriers running the fastest races of their life: Hojem (50th in 18:26), Kidwiler (56th in 18:32), and Normandeau (63rd in 18:41). Champion Missoula Loyola, Colstrip, and Poplar all had four, five, and six runners place better. The final team scores were Loyola 93, Colstrip 97, Poplar 99, and Thompson Falls 128.

This year looks different – it is conceivable that six Hawk Harriers could be in the top 15 and earn All-State status. If that happens, then a first place trophy is assured. A current and unofficial ranking by this reporter has the top seven B schools as follows: Poplar 1, Thompson Falls 2, Colstrip 3, Darby 4, Loyola 5, Manhattan 6, and Plains 7. The reason the Hawk Harriers are not ranked first is this: Winning the championship as an underdog satisfies a romantic vision for all the "little guys." Poplar won State in 1996-1999, so they have a strong history. However, the Hawks and their young are hungry; solid food is a first place trophy. Loyola has won six of the last seven State titles.

On the girls side of the State B Meet on October 20th, the Lady Hawks look to progress again. In 2005, the Hawks placed 8th, improving to 6th in 2006. The top two teams, Glasgow and Red Lodge look mighty impressive and should lock up the top two spots. Five other teams will be competing for the third spot and the final trophy. The best runners on the day will snag the prize.

Here are my current rankings in Montana Class B: 1. Glasgow, 2. Red Lodge, 3. Cut Bank, 4. Thompson Falls, 5. Cascade, 6. Whitehall, and 7. Loyola.

The advantage for the Lady Hawks is momentum and adrenaline. The momentum is continued improvement throughout the season and a first or second

By Andrew Gideon

place Class B finish at every meet in 2007. The adrenaline will come from the boys – the boys run at 1:45 PM, and the girls will witness the boys win the Gold. The rush of adrenaline may be the difference in the muscles and spines at 2:40 when gun fires for the Lady Hawks to have a tremendous day.

Nine Lady Hawks have run hard in practice this season by logging over 2150 miles. Sophomore Beca Gunderson has led the way during all the meets, except for the first Libby meet when junior Delcie Peters was the top Hawk Harrier. Beca stated that the "girls are looking more toward a team trophy than individual status; however, individual honors are attainable."

Sophomore Jefferyanne Parker vaulted into the top 11 All-time runners in Ronan and improved that performance three other times during the year. Junior CC Normandeau continues to show her warrior-like attitude with her season best last week. The other three athletes on state day will be senior Amanda Wood, sophomores Monica Conlin, and freshman Mariah Naegeli. Alternates will be sophomore Lacey Wade and freshman Jessie Drake.

The current forecast for Saturday in Helena is a 47 degree high, a 33 degree low, 60% chance of precipitation with 13 mile per hour winds.

Hawks don't care about temperature when attainable food exists for the talons to grab. These Hawks will feed the Thompson Falls family well on Saturday night.

Trophy – get in my belly!

Tuesday, 10-16-2007

Team mileage today: 101   runners: 21   Avg. per runner: 4.8

Today's workout was one race pace mile, 12 accelerations men, 10 women, and six total miles. There hasn't been this easy of a Tuesday since August 7 – six days before XC started. Accelerations, aka pickups, for us are done at 200 meters. We start at a jog and "pick up" the pace until the last 50 meters are run at 90-95%; then the athlete jogs back and does it again.

Jacob, Shane, Delcie, and JP lifted weights for eight minutes after running. Jacob and Shane (boys) used three pound dumbbells, and that is exactly how Shane acted – like a three pound dumbbell. Delcie and JP (girls) used five pounds in a routine that moves some strength to the arms and shoulders. This gives the legs a chance to say it's about time something else around here did some work!

Our Hawk Harriers only lifted the last two weeks – 5 boys, 5 girls (1 Monday, 2 Tuesday, 2 Wednesday) – and for only 8 minutes with dumbbells – a very light upper body workout.

Wednesday, 10-17-2007,

Team mileage today: 80   runners: 21   Avg. per runner: 3.8

Helena Saturday forecast: 47 high, 34 low, 60% chance of precipitation, 12 mph winds.

Exactly which team will benefit from which type of weather cannot be predicted. Several parts of the course may become muddy and slippery after rain, snow, and five races of individuals, but how each individual and each team reacts is a mystery.

My brother in Darby did not like my forecast for his team at State – a possible 3rd place. Steve sounded stressed and said predictions are worthless – it all comes down to who races well on Saturday. I agree – forecasts can give one an idea of what is in store – how the mind reacts is TBA (to be announced).

Yesterday is a fact – in Helena the high was 60, the low 36, and 0.12 measurable inches of precipitation landed in the history books.

On Sunday, the history books will have been written. A wave of excitement just shook me – that history to be written is making me smile. ☺

TFHS Pep Assembly 2:45. Five coaches – one bowl of ice cream, marshmallow crème, and three candy corns. The contest was a bob and weave type of eating challenge with hands tied behind the back. The competitor needed to dive in with the mouth and find the three candy corns and spit them out. Yes, this cross country coach was the first finisher – prelude to state. I was a winner because I am a competitor, and I have watched my one and three year old eat.

Coaches Gideon and Naegeli gave speeches, as did Jacob Naegeli.

Coach Gideon's joke – used in the pep assembly – *Two hikers on a trail came around the bend to find an enormous brown bear about 75 yards up the trail. The bear spies them and begins running toward them at a full gallop. One hiker drops his backpack, sits down, throws off his boots, and starts lacing up a pair of running shoes. The other hiker says: "What are you doing? You will never outrun that bear!". The first hiker replies: "I don't have to outrun the bear..."* www.runtheplanet.com/community/humor/jokes.asp

Coach Naegeli had the entire student body (214) move up to the top three rows of the gym bleachers to feel what a cross country starting line is like. She had a contest – whoever could name the source of the following quote would earn a bag of gummy bears – *"The will to win means nothing without the will to prepare."* (Mr. Gideon won – gummy bears are vital nutritious elements and a key to Hawk Harrier running success. Sssssshhhh, oops, the secret is out.) Then Coach Naegeli listed mileage run during XC seasons only for the past six years for our harriers. The amazing amount of mileage piled up:

Jacob – in 6 seasons of XC running (52 weeks), 7th-12th grade = 1952 miles
Shane – in 5 seasons of XC running (46 weeks), 8th-12th grade = 1802 miles
Ryan – in 4 seasons of XC running (40 weeks), 9th-12th grade = 1594 miles
Delcie – in 5 seasons of XC running (42 weeks), 7th-11th grade = 1303 miles
CC – in 5 season of XC running (42 weeks), 7th-11 grade = 1131 miles

Please remember – these totals only indicate mileage during XC season – not during track – or summer – or winter. These Hawks have dedicated legs, hearts, and Hawk minds to success.

The top seven boys were blessed to receive a massage today – two harriers optioned out, so two alternates swooped in to take advantage. It is a nice prize for hard work and sets the runners up for a good relaxed run at state.

Thursday, 10-18-2007, No school, lots of energy

Team mileage today: 71   runners: 19   Avg. per runner: 3.7

No school today – MEA (Montana Educator's Association) meetings in Belgrade. I don't have to go because I have taken enough recertification credits in these areas already. Our school has some optional days in August that can be used in place of these meetings.

9 AM practice – mile warm-up, stretch, and run three miles.

Today the top seven girls get sports massages from a therapist. Our massager, Carmel, received an $85 stop sign violation this morning. Welcome to TFalls, here's your ticket (this is a theme of our police department and sheriff's – it boosts the local economy in a backwards type of way). Don't go over 25 mph in TFalls or Plains; our appreciation for your visiting is an $80 speeding ticket.

Massages slow down the circulation and lower body temperature. I know this first hand after my 50 mile Ultra Marathon; a free massage awaited me after the "race." For 8 hr 33 min I ran and the body worked decently well. After a 10 minute massage I was freezing – four or five layers, a blanket, and heat turned up in the car semi-helped the situation.

CC had the biggest smile after a massage both times. Recall one of her options is becoming a massage therapist. Maybe she can recall her own feeling and smile and reward others with a gift of massage.

"The time with CC went the fastest – 20 minutes with her was over too quickly," stated our massage therapist – a compliment to CC's personality.

The teenage # 7 runner adventure continues....not at practice – slept in – a missed practice means no meet – so we did call him and he arrived late.

The life of a teenager is not one I want to live anymore. As a teacher, vicariously it happens. Today was the definition of bi-polar – mood swings – high and lows of life.

Today is one day of the next 22,000 (60$^+$ years) of our Hawk harriers lives. Today's choices do affect the future, but blowing one day and choice out of proportion in our infinitely complex, yet simple, life is wrong. Trust me, this has been done too many times in my life; it is a weakness.

I pray for our # 7, as I pray for myself, and I pray for our Harrier Hawks: wisdom, good health (and an appreciation of that health), success, and happiness. I pray we take one day at a time (1 mile at a time, 1 step at a time) and use this daily gift successfully. Some days seem poor, but we can have the best "poor" day possible. We can replace negative habits, thoughts, words, and deeds with positive ones. I have used this Bob Feller quote before, but we can *"build on yesterday's successes, or put its failures behind and start over again."*

One Hawk really needs prayers today and will for a while. Where he will live next week is to be determined. Where his life will be in the next year is TBA. A heavy burden this is for a 15-18 year old high school student – yet too many kids in the US have this on their shoulders. How many adults have this on their shoulders and can't handle it, yet somehow it is thrust upon our youth?

In this regard, I pray for wisdom to guide my own children, Jaxon (3 years old) and Kaden (1), to bring out all of their physical, mental, and spiritual gifts that they have been born and blessed with.

Yes, I pray for wisdom and guidance.

I have also prayed for success for these two teams and all of our individual harriers. Dear Lord, our TFHS XC student-athletes deserve the best. Please let the first place boys team be Thompson Falls. Please let the girls sneak into a trophy. Amen.

Team pasta feed/carbo load at the Gundersons. Beca's mom is a master chef – yummmmmm - others brought wonderful food, and good group bonding.

From the *Sanders County Ledger* today, *"Not guilty pleas were again entered by John Bennett to a new round of charges....new information alleges Bennett was driving the pickup that wrecked, killing Christina Gomez-Debruyker, while possibly under the influence of drugs from cold medicines and/or the ingredients in canned air, like that used to clean computer keyboards. Bennett was charged following an accident in Thompson Falls August 13 in which he allegedly sped down Haley Avenue in Thompson Falls, lost control of his vehicle, it overturned, resulting in the death of Debruyker...."*

We started our year with this on the first day of practice. Running with our team will stay with us. Our health will lead us. Our choices to continue to work as a team and make solid choices will lead us in a positive direction…just as the choice to get in the car that day will stay with each of the occupants.

Friday, 10-19-2007, No school, lots of energy

Team mileage today: 56   runners: 19   Avg. per runner: 2.9

A final forecast before the bus leaves with a four hour ride in the rain. High 50, low 35, winds 14 mph, 40% chance of precipitation.

Isaiah 40:31➔ (my.homewithgod.com/mkcathy/inspirational/eagle.html)

Isaiah 40:31
*"But they that wait upon the LORD
shall renew their strength;
they shall mount up with wings as EAGLES
they shall run, and not be weary;
and they shall walk, and not faint"*

*Did you know that an eagle knows when a storm is
approaching long before it breaks? The eagle will fly to some
high spot and wait for the winds to come.*

133

> *When the storm hits, it sets its wings so that the wind will pick it up and lift it above the storm. While the storm rages, below the eagle is soaring above it. The eagle does not escape the storm; it simply uses the storm to lift it higher. It rises on the winds that bring the storm.*
>
> *When the storms of life come upon us ... and all of us will experience them ... we can rise above them by setting our minds and our belief toward God.*
>
> *The storms do not have to overcome us; we can allow God's power to lift us above them. God enables us to ride the winds of the storm that bring sickness, tragedy, failure, and disappointment into our lives. We can soar above the storm.*
>
> *Remember, it is not the burdens of life that weigh us down; it is how we handle them. –*   *Author unknown*

A final forecast for the boys – this is our weather, our year, our first place. It is "just another meet" to Shane, yet this meet is going to bring smiles to a lot of faces in our community. This "just another meet" is not one to get nervous at – it is the first meet of the rest of these student-athlete-people's lives. Their lives will be successful, because they are leaders. This meet will be a springboard to a wonderful future.

Thompson Falls best boys finish was 2nd place in 2001.

If, by chance, heartbreak befalls us, then we will pick ourselves up, brush off the dirt and grime, and move on, knowing that our great journey in life has just begun. We are winners.

A final forecast for the girls – improvement on last year's 6th place finish. Twice the Thompson Falls girls have placed 6th at State; the best finish ever for a Lady Hawk Harrier team. This year will be an improvement on that finish. Our girls will run well, run strong, and they too will use this as a spring board to.....

State Champions 2008, oh YEAH!!!!!!!

For this year, improvement, team respect, and a trophy will do.

Today's entry was written and printed out so the Hawk Harriers would have my words in their hands and trained brains on the bus.

Friday night at the Helena Super 8, I gave the following Bible verse to Shane and Beca, 1 Corinthians 9:24 ➜ *"Do you not know that in a race all the runners run, but only one gets the prize? Run in such a way as to get the prize."*

Shane asked for a Bible verse – apparently I had given him one last year because of what Bob calls "toilet mouth." So Shane and Beca, run that race tomorrow to get the prize. This text continues, 1 Corinthians 9:25 reads, *"Everyone who competes in the games goes into strict training. They do it to get a crown that will not last; but we do it to get a crown that will last forever."*

These two harriers are our #1 runners and inspire me to be a better person and coach. They run (and live) well, and they run (and live) in such a way that individually they are winners, and the team is winners because of them.

Saturday morning, 10-20-2007, Zero days until State

My motivational speech for State today involved mathematics. Seven boys will be racing three miles each; seven girls will be running three miles as well. That's 42 total miles – *what's the problem? ~!*

I have had that speech in mind since deciding (in July) to run the 50 mile Le Grizz Ultra Marathon. He he he.

I went on to say that each person in the room could run 42 miles INDIVIDUALLY if he / she wanted to. Three miles is no problem compared to the 7000 miles our team ran this season. Three uncomfortable miles to glory and then a winter of contented and comfortable rest!

CC said that my speech gave her the idea that really three miles one time is not much compared to what work has been done.

Coach Bob Reall is amazing with all of his statistical effort. He goes through each race during the season and tracks individuals from all Class B teams. At state, he lists each individual in Class B in order of fastest to slowest, for both boys and girls, and then estimates team scores.

Boys: If each individual were to run their best time of the year, the team scores would be TFalls Harrier Hawks 53, Colstrip 107, Darby 107, Poplar 116, and Loyola 173.

Girls: If each individual were to run their best time of the year, the team scores would be Red Lodge 52, Glasgow 97, Whitehall 179, Cut Bank 196, TFalls Lady Harrier Hawks 220.

JP said the numbers made her edgy; her 21:15 would place 45th.

At our morning meeting to motivate and talk of times, some harriers painted smiley faces on their toes. At the beginning of the year, our "Train the Brain" article and handout included an advertisement with a picture of a person with smiley faces painted on the toes.

Happy toes = happy feet/legs = happy heart/mind = happy coaches…
And championships.

Saturday afternoon, 10-20-2007, State. . .

(For the 25 October 2007 *Sanders County Ledger*)
State Champions – TFHS Boys XC   *by Andrew Gideon*
State Champions – these words sure have a nice ring…and the Thompson Falls Blue Hawk Harriers answered the call. On Saturday, October 20, in Helena, the Blue Hawk cross country team won the Montana Class B Boys State Championship.

By Andrew Gideon

Seven Hawks confidently lined up at 1:40 PM in box # 20 at Bill Roberts Golf Course. Seven harriers were set to run three miles each – 21 total team miles stood between the starting line and a gold trophy.

Twenty one miles is nothing compared to what put these harriers on the firing line. Please rewind to senior Jacob Naegeli's 7th grade year when he ran 140 miles in the six week junior high season. In 2007 he ran 416 miles in the 10 week high school XC season. In between he ran track, he ran in the winters, he ran in the summers; Naegeli competed in half-marathons, team relays, and ice bathing contests. In six seasons and 52 total weeks of cross country, Naegeli ran 1952 miles.

Senior Shane Donaldson started cross country as an 8th grader and ran 206 miles in that six week junior high season. In the ten weeks of the 2007 season, he ran 410 miles. Donaldson also did a bit of summer running, including an outstanding 1 hour 22 minute half-marathon in July. In five seasons and 46 weeks of XC running, Donaldson compiled 1802 miles, not to mention winter running, track, and ice, ice, baby.

Senior Ryan Sol began training for this state championship as a freshman; he logged 1594 miles in 40 weeks during four seasons of TFHS XC practices. Summer sun, winter snow, and spring track ovals all witnessed Sol logging serious and comical miles.

In other words, this overnight success took years to come to fruition. As freshman, this group placed fourth. They went to 5th and 4th the following two years, before instant success luckily fell into their legs.

Donaldson (2nd place individually), Naegeli (3rd), and Sol (25th) are the heart and soul of the Class B Boys Champions.

Senior Mike Morris joined the team this year (thank you), earned All-State status with a 9th place finish, and scored some terrific points for the Hawks, while freshman Bryce Miller ran the fastest freshman Class B time in the State; Miller's 26th place finish rounded out the scoring for the State Champion Blue Hawks.

The top five teams and scores at the State Meet were Thompson Falls 65, Poplar 78, Darby 91, Colstrip 105, and Loyola 156.

Donaldson led the race for the first 2.5 miles before Paul Abrahamsen of Darby took over and closed out the individual title. Donaldson's silvery finish earned him All-State Status for the fourth straight year.

Naegeli earned the bronze, as he did in 2006, and garnered All-State Honors for the third straight year.

Times for the Hawks were as follows: Donaldson 16:44, Naegeli 16:50, Morris 17:08, Sol. 17:47, Miller 17:49, junior Patrick Jamison 17:59, and junior Mike Kidwiler 18:27. All seven TFHS athletes placed in the top 36 runners; there were 140 total participants in the race.

Three other seniors rode along for the state trip and earned their name on the first place plaque: Matt Hojem and RT Brown were the alternates, while Bryant Normandeau wore the Hawk mascot uniform.

Normandeau is a huge reason that the Hawks won the state title – he didn't score, he didn't even run – he simply wore the Hawk mascot uniform. Evidence of how he helped the team win exists: In six seasons of XC from 7th grade until Saturday, 52 weeks of practice occurred – Normandeau ran 1568 miles in that time.

This state championship did not come easily; it came with commitment, dedication, time, and effort. Running year round, ice baths, good teamwork, and effort in the classroom are all ingredients to what makes these individuals successful and what helped the team earn a state championship trophy.

"The journey of 1000 miles begins with one step" is a quote attributed to Lao Tzu. The journey to a state championship began years ago with junior high steps for Naegeli, Donaldson, Sol, and the 2007 Montana Class B Champion Thompson Falls Blue Hawks.

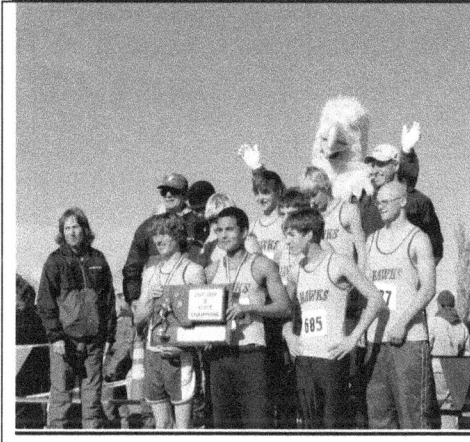

| On the Victory Stand | Holding the Trophy |

(Also for the 25 October 2007 *Sanders County Ledger*)

Best Ever Finish – TFHS Girls XC   *by Andrew Gideon*

The Thompson Falls Lady Hawk Harriers battled a howling wind during their race at state on October 20th. Wind is probably the hardest racing factor – even worse than hills – to most runners. By the time the gun fired at 2:56 PM for the last race of the day and season, the temperature may have been the day's highest (48), but the conditions were the worst for runners.

The Lady Hawks battled the rolling hills course and 20-30 mph wind gusts well. After finishing, individual Hawk smiles agonizingly fell onto the Helena course. When team results were announced 20 minutes later, attitudes perked up. The harriers' efforts were rewarded with a Thompson Falls best ever

137

By Andrew Gideon

4th place finish, changing some frowns upside down, and picking smiles up off the leaf-stricken ground.

Fourth place is the best finish ever for a Thompson Falls girl's XC team, topping last year's 6th place. Before the race began, the team heard the following inspirational quote: "The strength of the team is the individual, while the strength of the individual is the team."

The Lady Hawks exemplified these words and worked well from a team standpoint with only 46 seconds separating the first place runner (sophomore Beca Gunderson) from the 5th place runner (junior Delcie Peters). This solidarity helped the team top Loyola, Manhattan, Cascade, Whitehall, and Darby – all traditionally tough teams.

Final team results showed the scores as Glasgow 56, Red Lodge 62, Cut Bank 185, Thompson Falls 195, and Loyola 212.

Looking at development from year to year, the Hawks Harriers showed more improvement than other individuals. The top ten returning Class B girl runners from last year dropped 97 spots in the points department, while the five returning Lady Hawks improved 16 points. For clarification, last year's state champion dropped to 18th place, while the 2nd place 2006 individual dropped to 44th this season. Meanwhile, for the Hawks, Gunderson improved from 23rd to 22nd, while sophomore Monica Conlin gained eight spots from 50th to 42nd. These significant numbers indicate Thompson Falls netted positive change, while other teams and individuals performances were comparatively worse between years.

Add in freshman (rookie) Mariah Naegeli's sizzling 38 second Personal Record and the Hawks showed progress that other teams didn't. Conlin also set her PR.

The times in the three mile race weren't blistering because of the conditions – the wind warped the clock's functioning. The best times for all classifications came earlier in the day when the weather woke up mellow.

Lady Hawks timed in as follows: Gunderson 21:01, junior Ciara Normandeau 21:35, Conlin 21:44, Naegeli 21:45, Peters 21:47, sophomore Jeffreyanne Parker 21:52, and senior Amanda Wood 26:55.

The lady Hawk harriers worked together on this day and finished with a strong group finish – the # 2 through 6 runners finished in places 38-42-45-48, and 50. That is a solid team performance.

The Lady Hawk TEAM finished 4th – the best finish ever...until next year!

Last year the boys placed 4th, only to win Class B this season. 42 weeks exist between now and the start of next season. In 42 weeks of cross country season between 7th grade and junior year, Peters ran 1303 miles, while Normandeau logged 1131.

How much will these girls run, and what does the future hold? Only the incessant Edgar Allen Poe ticking of a stopwatch will tell the tale of the Lady Hawks heart.

This year's team was amazing – solid GPA's, 4-H involvement, student council participation, super personalities, and a fantastic effort for a challenging sport indicates the depth of the Lady Hawks character.

Thank you to nine Lady Hawks for an outstanding year; the 2007 season and the cumulative running miles in your shoes gives proper perspective on your spirit. These miles are the first steps to the rest of your life, and that future is bright and positive.

Sunday, 10-21-2007, The day after

There was no champagne last night or hangovers for the team today. Waking up to thoughts of the best finishes ever surely brought smiles to faces.

The boys won State!!!!!

The girls finished 4th – beating a previous best 6th place finish!!!

Smile~! ☺

The parade – A victory parade . . .last night. . . when we arrived back to Thompson Falls after a fabulous meal at Hu-Hot restaurant (Mongolian grill) in Missoula (our victory feast, Genghis Khan had conquered another battle) – a nice commemoration awaited the Harrier Hawks who Flew High. The coaches knew about it, and we tried to keep it a secret, but surely cell phones and text messaging may have ruined the surprise.

At 10:15 PM, a police officer led the Hawk bus on an escorted aerial flight display through town. Ten to fifteen cars followed us, and horns honked, causing blurry-eyed bar patrons to wander out to see crystal-clear Harrier Hawks flying through the night. Deer surely wondered why the last day of peace before hunting season was being ruined by noise and lights. Traffic was disrupted all the way to California, or maybe even four or five blocks, provoking smiles and cheers on our Blue Hawk faces. Another memory was added to our portfolio.

The police escort led us to a bon fire on the school property. It was initiated by our superintendent Dr. Pauli. The team, parents, and others not camping in the woods for the first day of hunting season, stood around, listened to several impromptu speeches, and just enjoyed a hillbilly time in TFalls, MT.

My own kids and wife came out to see the fire, even though it was past bedtime. Some memories at an early age need to be forged onto brains, synapses, and neurons.

Beca wrote the following:

Instead of being the usual type of bus trip, that four-hour ride home was something I will always look back on as one of my most memorable moments in high school. Our boys, the crazy, laughing, jovial bunch that they are, had only hours before become the State Class B Cross-Country Champions. To understand what this meant to them, picture a shiny, gold trophy being handed to you and your teammates, realizing how much hard work and dedication that it represents.

139

By Andrew Gideon

I don't know what the boys were feeling, but I had a flurry of emotions. I was happy to be with these girls and guys, and content with the fact that the girls had placed fourth, missing out on third by a mere ten points. The whole experience became very bittersweet when I realized how much my world was going to change now that these friends were not going to be here for another season. However, my most prevalent feeling was that I was so proud of my boys, who had won something that had been coming their way for a while. I watched them through the season, all of them devoting themselves to that dream finish. To see them receive that trophy made me more proud than any mother hen.

As the team neared Thompson Falls, we became aware of many cars idling on the side of the highway. At first we were confused. We soon realized that this was actually our welcoming committee: a victory parade! As the bus went by, a least fifteen cars followed, blasting their horns behind us. By this time, we had every window open on the bus, screaming out to the sleepy town that the Bluehawks were champions. Everyone on the team realized the fact again and we celebrated all over. It was amazing chaos.

After we had taken our trip through town, we pulled into the football field where a giant bonfire, complete with parents and friends awaited us. The fact that all those people cared about our success was awesome. We ran over to the edge of the football field, and under the stars, in the lights of the field, we rang the Bluehawk victory bell. It had never sounded so sweet.

Oh yes, the MoHawk haircut.

Monica made a polite request to Mr. Gideon for a MoHawk haircut if she were to get her best time ever at State.   Mr. Gideon responded with another option – if the girls were to get their highest place ever, then he would also shave the head for MoHawk support. That incorporates the team concept, in addition to individual performance.

Both happened: Monica ran a PR, while the team had the best place ever.

On the bus home, Coach Gideon received his Mo-Hawk haircut, courtesy of RT Brown.

RT's hair transition during the year – fuzzy, bulky hair at the beginning of the season added 3-4 inches to his height. In early season, he shaved his head. Late season, he had an opposite TF shaved OUT to contrast Coach Gideon's shaved in TF. At State, his TF was painted blue and gold school colors.

And then the thoughts come..what about next year..what could we have done to add a little more oomph to the girl's legs at the end of the race to help them get 3rd. Quickly, thoughts are forced into positive memories of the team, the quality of people, and a job well done.

For 10 weeks (not to mention summer running), we ran together, laughed, probably cried, but surely our MoHawk haircut in the mirror says, "I'm good enough, I'm strong enough, and gosh darn it people like me." Thank you Stuart Smalley and Saturday Night Live.

The Lady Hawk Harriers all received the following canned version of hope yesterday before the race, "the strength of the team is the individual, while the strength of the individual is the team." This quote fits our team spirit. Our ladies worked well together and finished with a strong group finish - # 2's through 6 runners finished 38-42-45-48, and 50. That is a solid team.

Let's get this solid team to the 8-10-12-14-16 range next season!!!!

There is a zen saying that I read in Dharma Bums – "When you get to the top of the mountain, keep climbing."

State Champs – resting on laurels – or continuing to climb?

I ordered two books on cross country today: Training for Young Distance Runners and Coaching Cross Country Successfully.

There is work to do to get back on top next year! There is no rest... Please insert the Yiddish saying, "Man plans, God laughs." We can study, plan, and work, but our lives are in God's hands.

Since I wrote on several other coaches earlier in the book, here is how their teams and individuals finished up.

Mark Albert's Hamilton team placed 2nd in Class A Girls – top two finishers 8th and 9th. His Class A boys placed 2nd (by 8 points), with his top two runners 3rd and 6th. Another runner's 14th place finish earned All-State status.

The Darby Tiger Girls placed 10th with the #2 overall girl.

Steve Gideon's Darby (Class B) boys earned a 3rd place trophy. Individuals placed 1st (Paul Abrahamsen), 10th, and 11th. That made three of his athletes All-State, as many as the Hawk Harriers had (2nd, 3rd, 9th).

Monday, 10-22-2007, Bittersweet

When the 3:15 PM final school bell rang today, my heart wandered in two directions – one, yes, cross country time, and quickly followed by two, NOOOOOOOOO, and emptiness. The glow of success exists, but our XC 2007 destination has been reached.

"Weird, sad, weird, it sucks, ok" – were several of the athletes responses to what they felt like when leaving at 3:30 without practicing. "It's weird, but I'll enjoy it," said another.

Our journey of the next 1000 miles begins today.

Some harriers will run tomorrow after school; enjoy that one day break!

In the school bulletin for today were the following three announcements.

(1)   "State Champions – Congratulations to the boys cross country team – State Champs! Shane Donaldson, Jacob Naegeli, and Mike Morris earned All-State Awards. Ryan Sol and Bryce Miller rounded out the scoring for the 1st place Class B Boys!"

(2)   "Girls Cross Country – Excellent work! Best ever finish for a girl's team at Thompson Falls High School with a 4th place finish. Beca Gunderson, Ciara Normandeau, Monica Conlin, Mariah Naegeli, and Delcie Peters earned the points for the girl's team."

141

(3)   *"Boys and Girls Cross Country Members – Thank you for your hard work running this year and thank you for the solid efforts in the classroom. – Coach Gideon"*

It's interesting to note that four positive things were written about our school on the board in the teacher's lounge. # 1 was the football CONFERENCE championship won last Friday night (T Falls 45, Eureka 6). Our State Championship was relegated to # 3. At least we were basically mentioned in the same paragraph as the football team. I do hope the football team does well. Success is as contagious as apathy and a flu virus.

1992 Libby Loggers Legion Baseball: Tears were shed by Coach Gideon at season's end. Bittersweet was an apt word for that summer. I had three amazing 18 year olds that I would never coach again – good grades, positive, tremendous baseball players, and a willingness to improve the program.

Those three heroes of mine (Ryan Schrenk, Scott Foss, and Chris Kuennen) raised money for new lights because they had a dream to play at night. Half-way through the season the lights were up and night games were played. We didn't have enough games to satisfy them on the schedule, so we practiced extra with the coaches pitching and played ball all summer long. They, along with the team, were always up for more practice, hitting, games – what a life~!

I wrote letters supporting Scott Foss to the Montana Legion Baseball Chairmen. If I have ever written anything necessary, then this was it. Scott was named the Montana player of the year.

Tears were shed because we had won the Western Division of Montana Legion Baseball (one of four divisions), yet placed a slightly disappointing fourth at State.

If I could live a summer of my life forever, that would be my pick. Baseball, winning, and young health, immortality!!! – What a place to live in eternally.

If I could coach a team forever, the TFHS Hawk Harriers are my pick. If only time could stand still and we could be young enough to run forever…

Time keeps on ticking, ticking, ticking into the future...

Bittersweet.

Tuesday, 10-23-2007, What's Next…?

My son Jaxon learns the words "What's next?" Jaxon is three, and he has not perfected the art of patience like us mature adults and teenagers. Incorporating the idea of letting go and moving onto something else is not programmed into his system completely yet. So I say to Jaxon, "What's next? What's next?"

No, Jaxon, it is daytime, you can't play with the flashlight, what's next?

Jaxon, we are turning the television off now, 16 straight hours is enough – what's next! (Reality – a half hour per day.)

No Jaxon, you may not have your 73rd piece of candy in the last half hour, what's next on your list of things to rot your teeth?

Yes, Jaxon, that's it; your toy was carried off by a hawk, so you have moved onto the next toy. Great job. NO, don't jump off the rail to try and fly like a Hawk, not THAT NEXT!

What's next...in life, for today, for the future?

What's next for the Lady Hawk Harriers is a 2008 State Meet – less than 365 days away!

Seriously, choices made now – food, habits, exercise, mileage, safety, ice baths – will show up when we run the State Meet in 2008.

Analyzing our season as coaches will help us for next year. Maybe team and individual running success is really as simple as more mileage = better results. That surely is a huge ingredient to victory, but what are the smaller intangible items, like mental and spiritual health?

Here are some mileage totals for our brains to analyze.

2006 team - 7008.9999 miles (28 total runners = 250.3 miles per athlete)

2007 team - 7035.0001 miles (27 total runners = 260.6 per set of two feet)

2006 high school girls – 2624 miles / 11 runners = 238.5 per athlete

2007 high school girls – 2391 / 9 = 265.7 per athlete

The top three girls for 2007 mileage: Delcie 356, Beca 319, and JP 305.

The top three girls for 2006 mileage: Delcie 339, Beca 337, and CC 306.

JP moved from 218 (06) to 305 (07), Monica improved from 133 to 289, while Mariah went from 143 in 06 to 251 for this season. CC dropped from 306 to 238 (remember the back).

A slightly higher percentage of running in 2007 was hard/timed/interval mileage.

The top three boys for mileage in 2007 were Ryan 417, Jacob 416.0001, Shane 410. In 2006, the leaders were Shane 425, Jacob 424.9999, and Ryan 408. Yes, Jacob runs .16 meters different each year, strange kid!

These totals all represent the 10 week cross country season.

Even though our XC journey ended Saturday (What's Next?), we still have one race left. On Saturday, 10-27, the Montana Cup will have 15 of our runners competing (8 boys, 7 girls).

The Montana Cup is an open-aged race. The race distance changes each year, as does the location; this year it is in Missoula. Montana is broken into seven areas – our 'team' is Kalispell. The race is scored like a regular XC race with the top five runners earning team points. Adults are on the same team as kids, so I will be a teammate this weekend instead of a coach.

The Big Sky Conference finals college races will also be held this weekend in Missoula. The 8K men's (11:45 AM) Big Sky Conference Championship will be run, as will the 5K women's race (11 AM). Our runners will watch and then have their own event two hours later. It will be a good

143

experience, individually and as a team. Hopefully some athletes will be motivated to continue on to college.

Even though the season ended Saturday (What's Next?), we still had runners working out. Jacob, Shane, Ryan, Kyle, Mike M were the five boys (I ran 6 miles at 7 minute pace with Shane) (Kyle ran 5.5 miles), while Monica & Mariah were the two girls. Beca would have run, but she had to baby-sit. CC might have run, but she had to baby-sit my kids while I played at running. Matt (wrestling is what's next for him) and RT (golf is next) lifted and then ran.

This season is over. What's next is the future. There will be more races and more life. It was good to see seven runners today.

Three major goals I set at the beginning of 2007 have been met.
(1) Run the Missoula Marathon on July 15 (sub goal – have Hawk Harriers fly along on the half-marathon route) – check.
(2) Run the most miles ever in a year (or every day of the year) (sub goal – motivate TFHS XC runners with this goal) – check. (I will end with 2007.4 miles in 2007.)
(3) State Championship Trophy for the boys (sub goals – boys at least third, girls trophy) – check and the girls came close.

That is a successful year – I should be able to relax and relish the triumph of hard fought and victorious battles and wars.

Yet, my obsessive personality drives me on (What's next) – the Seattle Marathon is Thanksgiving Sunday. Former Hawk Harrier Derek Naegeli is running his first marathon, so I will support him by running.

Maybe I should add multiple personality disorder to my resume and argue with myself about stopping.

Alas we don't live in a vacuum. No Hoovers here, bowling balls and feathers drop at different speeds, just like younger harriers may move faster than lattee gulping coaches.

This vacuum doesn't allow belief that running is the only activity that our wonderful Hawk Harriers engage in. What, they may not be 100% excited about State Next year, only 363 days away?

Sadly, runners "need a break" and "don't want to get burnt out." They will move on to basketball, cheerleading, wrestling, indolence, lethargy, recovery, skiing, snowboarding, and causing distress for teachers in the classroom. Maybe, just maybe, there will be time for "school" and "academic" matters. However, first quarter ends on 11-2, and I guarantee some seriously good grades for our harriers. Stay tuned for that.

Maybe it is good to not run in winter, slipping while carrying sharp scissors has killed 42.7% of people who make up statistics.

"Time for something else" pops onto our computer screen and into our vocabulary. Whatever. Life is running; the rest is just details.

Hawks don't carry scissors during basketball – the ball will pop!

Ears will be struck off in wrestling. John 18:10 ➔ *"Then Simon Peter, who had a sword, drew it and struck the high priest's servant."*

Combining cheerleaders and scissors is like mixing paint and three year old children - MISTAKE.

Successful runners maintain a razor-sharp mental edge. A trained brain and mind need to recover (stress and recover). Thanksgiving turkeys need to be digested (after a run or it will be a sleepy tempo pace), while Christmas presents, quilting hobbies, (reader: insert a personal winter activity here), and singing in the shower need to be revisited for sanity. Maybe even a New Year's Polar Bear Plunge (jumping in an icy Montana river on January 1) will need to happen.

Yes, even I took yesterday off.

These harriers ran long in track, summer, and cross country. Hawks are not equivalent to Kenyans, although surely we put some serious fear into our XC opponents. Hawk laughter is contagious and without a break from our silly jokes, the abs would not recover fully.

Neil Young sang that it is better to burn out than to fade away, and that's admirable, but next week, after the Montana Cup, we will probably request kids take a week off. My obsessive, I mean, quality focused personality, leads to success, but maybe a break is needed. ☹ but true.

My personal break will be in January as several more "new" goals exist between now and December 31; I hope my body, legs, and joints hold up until then.

There will be a handout on winter running, blood volume, and maintaining fitness given to our XC heroes. Some will get some weight lifting information for total body work for other sports, while some will just get a dumbbell workout routine discussed with them.

Good luck to all Hawks for the next endeavor.

To let go of something and move on is often difficult. Losing a loved one to death or separation and letting go is easier said than done (for example), but what's next must be considered. Part of the reason Jaxon is being taught these words is because his dad (minus DNA test, that's me) has a hard time with this aspect of life.

For example, adjusting from high school to college was difficult and not handled well. Making the step from college to "real" life threw me for a loop. Helping people make this step in a good and easy way is part of my impetus to teach; with successful habits, the transition should not be hard; what's next and moving on should be relatively easy.

Another example is that I interviewed for the Head Girls basketball coach at TFHS on October 2. Despite quality work in many areas of life and 21 seasons of basketball coaching, I did not get the job - despite being the only coach interviewed with a win at State as (1) a head coach, (2) as an assistant girls coach, (3) as an assistant boys coach, not to mention (4) being at a state tournament as a basketball coach in the 2000 decade, and (5) I felt I had been promised the job for two years by one (of three) person on the interview committee.

Letting go of my REJECTION has been a struggle. Despite a successful 50 mile run, a State XC Championship, the Red Sox in the World Series, and health, my emotions have not been happy.

I quit teaching in 2001 for several years partly because I went 0 for 7 interviewing for Head coaching jobs. What's next was a four year banking career.

I stated once that I wouldn't teach Journalism in high school again. Here I am at TFHS teaching Journalism. However, when I said that, I didn't have kids to put in diapers or feed (not necessarily in that order).

So do I whine, complain, quit or is it my job to be successful at responding to unpleasant situations? This should serve as a positive example; Oh kids at the zoo exhibit - look at the adult handle challenges in life in a positive manner. STOP WATCHING ME, because I don't want to be a good example. Ladies and Gentlemen, please move on to the next exhibit, this display animal is experiencing irritability.

I wanted the Head Girls basketball job. I did not want to teach Journalism. 0 for 2. What sounds good to me is reverting back to being a kid and throwing shoes through windows, getting technical fouls, and running away for several hours until I get hungry (then going home). So I will pout a little while, get over it, and then move on. What's next?

Several ideas come to mind here: (1) God has a plan, (2) be thankful and appreciative for the blessings in life, (3) in running one must learn to take the good workouts with the bad, and (4) having a team attitude is good.

In the Bible, Jesus, in Gethsemane, prayed the following, "My Father, if it is possible, may this cup be taken from me. Yet not as I will, but as you will." (Matthew 26:39). This quote bonds reasons # 1 and # 2 above. God has a plan and be thankful and appreciative for blessings.

Things that are unwanted in life happen – some bad and tragic events, yet some are not tragic. It is not life or death that I did not get a basketball coach position. At the same time, when I came to Thompson Falls, I was not a part of the cross country program. I have always loved to run and have been competitive for a long time (17,000 miles over the past 17 years). I asked coach Naegeli if I could run with the team.

The first year, fall of 2005, I just ran daily with the team and offered little coaching. It was good to be an "athlete" again and learn from coach Naegeli and coach Reall.

The second year, coach Naegeli went to bat for me and hired me as an assistant coach. This was a huge blessing – I would now get "paid to run." I mean, of course, "paid to coach."

Now I have "State Championship 2007 XC" on my coaching resume.

I deduce I should complain of my blessings as a XC coach as opposed to complaining that I am not the Head Girls Basketball coach.

This thought melds into reason # 3. Some runners do not like Terrible Tuesdays or other workouts. However, good runs, liked runs, and the bad runs must all be mixed into an overall running recipe. One must take the positive with the negative. The hard runs are not fun, but they produce better times - be uncomfortable to be comfortable.

Running causes discomfort and pain a lot of the time. Occasionally it seems relatively easy and the body moves like melting butter on a frying pan. However, longevity is related to good health, but running is a necessary for a better QUALITY of life.

Understanding "team" is good. TFHS needed a Journalism teacher, so the job to be a good team player was mine. My brother-in-law received the Head Girls Basketball position, so being part of a team and family means saying congratulations and good luck to him as well.

Eat your vegetables; they are healthy. Learn to take the good with the bad, appreciate blessings and positive times in life, and realize God has a plan.

Job 2:10 ➜ *"...Shall we accept good from God, and not trouble?"*

A thought – I wonder if my two boys will ever stop whining or throwing tantrums. I wonder if God looks down on all of us and wonders the same thing.

My mother told me – just wait until you have a kid just like yourself. Based on temper tantrums my kids can throw, her wish has come true. Jaxon and Kaden, my prayers are with you because of DNA. Staying focused on one thing is good and propels a person to higher levels, but let go when the time comes. Let "what's next" become part of your vocabulary.

What's next, what's next… is school, family, next year's trophy for the girls cross country team, and the Seattle Marathon on November 25 and shooting for 2000 miles on the year (currently I have 1657).

Time to get to work and quit being lazy!!! Time to quit pouting, look on the bright side of life, and move on.

In other words, going into this season, I knew it would be one to remember; thus the book, the trophy, and the current poignant theme of writing. Letting go of this team will not be without a fight. Keep on typing those memories fingers, keep on running across the keyboard. Remembering in the *Harrier Hawks Fly High* way is a victory in itself.

Let this season continue – I want to keep running, talking, working with these athletes. The season is over – bittersweet, because this group did so well, but the journey is one of those situations I will love to live with forever.

It was fun to ask Ryan, Jacob, and Shane what it felt like to be *"has beens."* Seriously, that's kind of funny. *"It's all uphill from here in life,"* I told them on our jog today.

They are Has-beens who can honestly recall a State Championship.

147

By Andrew Gideon

Wednesday, 10-24-2007, Mariah's Storm

We don't want to call our remaining harriers leftovers; that may be a harsh and politically incorrect term, depending on the meal. However, several individuals did not get a profile yet. Our team is made up of # 1 through # 22; all are important to our success as a team, as a family, and as a society. We are only as funny as the least humorous on the team.

Mariah's Storm may be a horse that inspired the movie <u>Dreamer</u>. That filly certainly put on the speed. Our Mariah's Storm is a filly named Mariah Naegeli who shed 38 seconds from her PR at the State XC meet. She has three years of XC races left, for she is just a freshman.

Mariah Elizabeth Naegeli (initials M.E.N.) is outnumbered by men in her family and lives on a ranch, yet she still manages to not be a complete tom boy. Born 2-8-93, she has three brothers: Derek is a college sophomore, Jacob is a senior Hawk Harrier, while Logan is a 6th grader. Mariah's mom (Sarah) coaches the XC team, while Dad, William (Bill) ranches and works as the county's OEM (Office Emergency Management) supervisor.

Sarah is from Ohio and thus understands Coach Reall (30+ years in Ohio); she is also able to read <u>Harriers</u> (book) with some understanding of geography. Dad Bill is from the TFalls / Trout Creek area; so is Grandma Naegeli, a very proud lady who has a State Champion Grandson. It is good somebody from Ohio was brought into the valley, so new blood exists and two less cousins had to marry. Bad red neck Montana joke = family tree / no forks.

Mariah is a quaint quilting queen. She quilts, ranches, runs, involves herself with 4-H and student council, and otherwise never stops; yet she is always seen with a beautifully bright smile. Recall that a bull stepped on her toe during the second week, but complaints about a broken bone were never voiced by Miss Naegeli. At State she sizzled with a 38 second PR that moved her into the # 12 All-Time slot on the Girls running list at TFHS. And that's no bull.

She is the tiniest Hawk Harrier at 5'3" and 98 pounds, but don't mess with her – she is a Naegeli = tough! Mariah's advice to future runners sounds tough too, *"run fast! Who cares what other people think about running, it's amazing, and more work than you think."*

How about some advice to younger students: *"have fun in school. Participate in extra curricular activities. Stay out of trouble."*

Goals were broken early in the year. Her new goals were broken. Last week she wrote, *"break 22 in the three miles."* Done – check – at State = Nice!. Her other goal may be a life-long project – *"get my knee healed up fully."*

Future plans for our rookie include going to college, possibly getting photography and education degrees, and to *"live life as it comes."* She isn't a picky freshman about future colleges as long as they fit with her majors. Mariah does *"want to teach something."*

Maybe she will be a mom some day – is that a lifetime job without schooling or is it a job that comes with the school of hard knocks? The Naegelis

148

have probably had a few hard knocks in their time, but positive attitudes always abound and surround those who know the family. A Naegeli without a smile is like a Coach Gideon without a morning lattee. It just doesn't happen!

Mariah life goals are to *"run the rest of my life, live in the country, maybe even on a ranch. Run a marathon. Live life to the fullest."*

Living cheaply is a good concept to teach and live by. Mariah will do that – just as brother Jacob did on his 9-02 entry. If she were to win $100,000,000 she would *"first, buy the $600 digital camera that I want. Then probably buy a few more things, and put the rest of the money in the bank."*

Mariah enjoys long slow walks on the beach, oops, long slow runs. She dislikes the mule pasture – what is wrong with her…a beautiful trail, trees, path, no houses or pavement – nature – shade - she wants to live in the country, what could be better than this trail? Oh well.

(I interject here with a paragraph written in English 2 class by Kyle B – Mariah, pay attention…*"The mule pasture is a beautiful place to walk or run. You see so when you are there. You see nature – birds, deer, elk, and some may see a creature named The Gideon running in the pasture every once in a while."*)

Other favorites: Facing the Giants (movie), all but kiwi because I'm allergic to it (food), sewing / quilting, photography, running (hobbies), Time Capsule (book), PE (class), track or XC (sport), Mrs. Petteys (teacher), Mr. Gideon or my mom (coach), boys (other, but this was erased, but not enough for me to see it with my x-ray teacher eyes).

Mariah worked hard this spring to rehabilitate her knee. She participated in junior high track, but also did many exercises for long term knee health.

Her first meet was 23:43 in Kalispell. Her State time was 21:45. Thank you, Mariah, for the 8.3% improvement during this season.

Mariah's running style is typical Naegeli – a cross of gazelle/cheetah/squirrel. In others words, some bounce, fast, and kind of nutty. Watching Derek, Jacob, and Mariah run is always worth the price of admission. There seems to be a hint of enjoyment, even through the pain and struggle of a race or practice. Surely there is pain involved, but rarely is it voiced.

Derek literally ran until he dropped and then ran more. Jacob probably had more knee pain than he indicated, while Mariah lets bulls trample her toes, yet the Naegeli family members are all winners, and keep on running.

Delcie writes that Mariah is *"usually pretty calm & collected, willing to help you out in times of need! Very talented in sewing & running."*

Nine harriers logged mileage today – 4 boys, 5 girls – some good "off-season" running!

Thursday, 10-25-2007, Seattle Marathon letter

What's next for me…besides continuing to type this future best-seller?

A Seattle Marathon fundraiser is next. Here is a letter and email I will send out to people.

By Andrew Gideon

Andy Gideon ran the Missoula Marathon (26.214 miles) on July 15. He also ran the Le Grizz Ultra Marathon (50 miles) on October 13th. Andy enjoys talking and writing about himself in the third person and realizes he has been blessed with good health.

The Thompson Falls Blue Hawk cross country team had a phenomenal season. The boys won the Montana Class B Boys State Championship. Our girls had the highest finish in the school's history (4th) – narrowly (10 points) missing the third place trophy. Thank you Team Hawk Harriers! These student-athletes are blessed with good intelligence, health, and promising futures.

Some people have more struggles than others. Having a child in the hospital can be a terrifying experience (trust me). Kaden, born 6-9-06, spent his first two months of life in the hospital, but he is now an eating, growing, and smiling/laughing machine. Kaden is blessed with good health despite a slow and scary start.

Candlelighters exist because "kids can't fight cancer alone."

Candlelighters of Western Washington has the following Mission Statement,

> "We are an organization dedicated to serving children with cancer who are being or have been treated at Western Washington hospitals and their immediate and extended family members, survivors, health care professionals, and bereaved families. This includes families who come to Western Washington from other states seeking the latest treatment for their children in facilities such as Children's Hospital and Regional Medical Center, the Fred Hutchinson Cancer Research Center, and Multi-Care's Mary Bridge Children's Hospital. CCCF-WWA is run by volunteers, mostly the moms, dads, siblings and survivors who know what its like to face childhood cancer and want to help each other through one of the most difficult journeys imaginable.
>
> There are no membership fees and all of our funding comes from individual donations or fundraisers." (http://www.candlelighterswa.org/newsletter/June2007.pdf)

In 2001, I ran the Seattle Marathon, while my wife Deborah ran the half-marathon. Our goal, besides appreciating our own health, was to raise money for Candlelighters. We were blessed with $622.11 in donations from friends, foes, and family.

My goal for this race (Sunday 11-25-07) is to raise at least $622.12. I will meet this goal because I will write the check for the full amount if I have to! However, I am enlisting your help ☺!

Please send a check to "Candlelighters of Western Washington" to me so that I can turn it in at the Seattle Marathon (they were a sponsor of the event in 2001). My address: Gideon, PO Box 2214, Thompson Falls, MT 59873. This is a tax deductible gift.

If you want to make an anonymous donation and thus avoid the newsletter that they send out, then make the check payable to me. I will send you a receipt (plus you should have your check) verifying that your gift will be given to Candlelighters.

If you can't donate, then I understand – I will still love you for being on my email or mailing list; sometimes my monthly paycheck doesn't cover the silly bills that insist on being paid (who needs food!).

If you can donate, then I will send you a thank you note after the marathon.

Here are some bible verses to consider.

Hebrews 10:24 ➜ *And let us consider how we may spur one another on toward love and good deeds.*

Galatians 6:9 ➜ *Let us not become weary in doing good, for at the proper time, we will reap a harvest if we do not give up.*

Here is some information on the son who was in the hospital for the first two months of life, as slightly mentioned in the letter above. **Kaden James Gideon** was born 6-9-06 at approximately 8:03 am. His due date was August 29. Kaden was born going 90 mph in the back of a GMC Sierra extended cab pickup about 1-2 miles from Johnsrud Park. Andy was "lucky" to help deliver his second child. It is an amazing story. A lot of little miracles happened to keep him alive and a lot of little miracles have happened since. Kaden James Gideon was born into this world a little 2 lb 6.5 oz, 14 3/4 inch miracle!!!!!!

Two girls (Beca, Mariah) and four boys (Shane, Jacob, Mike M, and Cody) ran four miles after school today.

What the XC program is doing is more than running; we "pretend" to care about helping people become high quality individuals. One quality people need is thankfulness or appreciation for others.

Today, five days after State, we wrote thank you letters. They were to someone who donated $1000 to our XC team, someone who made cookies, a couple who support us at every race during the season, our massage therapist, and Runners Edge (Missoula running store that works well for our athletes).

Thank you Thank you Thank you Thank you Thank you. Surprise – even if we hadn't won State, we would have still faked thankfulness.

Friday, 10-26-2007, John Hamilton article

John Hamilton is the REAL sports reporter for the *Sanders County Ledger*. He fought fires in August, so I substituted for football, volleyball, and cross country articles for the paper. When he returned, I was asked to keep penning the cross country words.

John traveled to Helena last weekend, took a lot of pictures, and wrote fantastic words about the team. I am pleased to reprint his October 25 article of the *Sanders County Ledger* here.

By Andrew Gideon

State championships don't grow on trees, but they do grow like trees – slowly, but becoming sure and strong, and well established in the end.

Take cross country programs as an example. They start as a seed of a thought and then develop into a plan of action, a time to run with and grow.

With the proper care, intense nurturing and lots of work during the entire year, not just during any particular season, these teams, these growing living championship trees are allowed to prosper and eventually produce the fruits of victory.

The seeds to this year's Thompson Falls cross country teams – the new State B championship boys team and a very competitive girls team, which finished fourth in Saturday's team race (see other stories) – were planted years ago, and nurtured along by many different people along the way.

Shane Donaldson, Jacob Naegeli, Mike Morris, Ryan Sol, Bryce Miller, Patrick Jamison and Michael Kidwiler, the 2007 State B Thompson Falls boys cross country team and the Lady Hawk team of Beca Gunderson, Ciara Normandeau, Monica Conlin, Mariah Naegeli, Delcie Peters, Jeffreyanne Parker and Amanda Wood owe a debt of gratitude to a lot of people.

Not only to predecessors from years past like Adam Oswald, Kellyn Gross and Derek Naegeli, but also to other members of this year's teams, to mention only a few, guys like Matt Hojem and RT Brown with the boys, and girls like Jessie Drake and Lacey Wade with the Lady Hawks – the teams' alternate runners in Helena last week.

Thompson Falls' cross country head coach since the second season of the program's existence in 1999, Sarah Naegeli now knows fully well what it takes to grow championship timber in high school cross country.

"You have got to have buy in from at least five or six kids, not just one or two," she said. "These kids have to commit themselves to it, and work hard all year around. Only then can you begin to start thinking of success at the team level."

Coach Naegeli can now think freely of such team success, and relish the championship tree that has since grown deep roots in Thompson Falls' sports history.

Here are a few observations made from watching that tree develop and mature over these past several years.

****

One of the best runners in Montana at any level this year and the past several falls, Shane Donaldson capped a splendid cross country career by winning second place individually for the second straight year to lead the Hawks to the elusive State B team title.

On top of that, Donaldson became the first Hawk harrier in history to earn All-State B honors all four years of his high school career, a feat even the great Adam Oswald did not achieve during his star-studded career. Besides his second place wins in '06 and '07, Donaldson also copped top 15 finishes in '05 (ninth) and '04 (fourteenth).

If not slightly height challenged, Donaldson could well be enjoying a second straight individual championship, but his comparatively short stride does him no good during the last quarter-mile stretch of the course in Helena, which is severely downhill oriented, giving taller, longer strided runners a decided advantage on that portion of the course.

Using gravity and their naturally longer strides, Cut Bank's Ben Jacobsen last fall and Darby's Paul Abrahamsen this past week managed to move past Donaldson and into first place in the State B race.

"It would have been interesting if the race ended with an uphill stretch instead of downhill," coach Naegeli said. "Shane's turnover (the amount of strides he takes) is very rapid; he just might have won the race with an uphill finish."

Naegeli knew she had a winner with Donaldson during his freshman year at the State B race. "I caught up with him about two-thirds of the way through the race, and he was in sixteenth or seventeenth place at the time," she said. "I told him he really needed to move up, and he did it, getting into fourteenth by the finish."

Interestingly, when asked by his coaches who inspired him most this fall, Donaldson identified Oswald as the person he most admired. Still, while showing the utmost respect for the all-time great Hawk, who went on to a successful career running cross country in college, Donaldson went ahead and broke Oswald's school record of 15:51 (set in 2001) by running a 15:45 at the Mountain West Invitational in Missoula last month.

As good as Donaldson naturally was, he probably would not be near the runner he is if it wasn't for classmate, teammate and running soul mate Jacob Naegeli, the coach's second oldest son.

Seemingly inseparable during the past several years of running, either in training, in cross country or in track and field, Shane and Jacob, the cross country comrades are fairly inseparable when it comes to the State B race as well, as they have gone two-three in the season finale the past two seasons running.

Not coincidentally, Jacob holds the third fastest cross country time ever ran in TFHS history with a 16:11, also clocked at the Mountain West last month.

****

Only the toughest survive in cross country running, and no one is tougher than Lady Hawk junior Ciara Normandeau.

The Hawk junior, in spite of a back problem that was only recently diagnosed correctly, ran to a strong 38th place finish in the girl's race Saturday, and continued to impress coach Naegeli with her incredible effort.

"Ciara has a bad back, the doctors say she is missing some cartilage in her spine and that she will require corrective surgery within the next six years,"

By Andrew Gideon

Naegeli said. "To keep on running, and run well like she has, tells you a little about how tough of a person she really is."

****

Giving credit where credit is due is always the right thing to do.

Naegeli had no problem in sharing her team's State B championship glory with valued assistant coaches Bob Reall and Andrew Gideon.

"Those two just complement each other so well," she said. "Bob is really good at the statistical side of things. He is our bookkeeper and scout, he keeps an eye on all of Montana cross country, and keeps us up to date with who has done what in the past."

Gideon, besides doing most of the cross country reporting for this newspaper during the season, is a coach of a similar but different color.

"Andrew is very good at talking with the kids about race strategies, split times and what they need to be doing," Naegeli said, "and he is very good at motivating our runners, he gives some very inspirational speeches."

Saturday, 10-27-2007, Montana Cup

Most of the fun of the Montana Cup may have come from friendship, time together, and an appreciation for a solid season. Last night coach Naegeli and her husband kept an eye on the Hawks as they nested at a hotel in Missoula. Needless to say, the harriers spent several hours in the pool and didn't have the same curfew they did for State last week. The race was secondary.

On Saturday Coach Gideon drove CC and Amanda to Missoula. They watched a movie on a portable DVD, thus avoiding any in-depth conversation with the coach. Therefore I didn't subject them to my poor attempts at humor – that will teach them for ignoring me.

Fuddruckers stole our money after the race, but dumped pounds of burger and root beer floats into our systems in return.

(For the 01 November 2007 *Sanders County Ledger*)

***Montana Cup runneth over**_____By Andrew Gideon*

Just when a reader thought it might be safe to wade the waters of the sports pages again without seeing a running article, the Hawk harriers again showed their fins.

Last week, The Thompson Falls Blue Hawk harriers finished their season on October 20th with a boys B State Championship, while the girls finished with a school best 4th place finish.

These runners did not go on an immediate vacation to a shark free beach. Instead, eight boys and seven girls ran yet another race on October 27th. They must be crazy to continue to "run for fun," instead of resting on laurels! The senior running-with-scissors boys might be "has beens" already for cross country, but they will have a track season in the spring, while the girls will test the waters as a team next XC season to swim to a top three trophy.

154

The Montana Cup started on Halloween 1992 as a competition between different areas of the state. Montana is divided into seven areas for competition: Billings, Butte, Bozeman, Great Falls, Helena, Kalispell, and Missoula. Thompson Falls competes with the Kalispell team.

In terms of team competition the Kalispell team lost by one point to the Missoula team. The girl's team for Kalispell placed 5th.

Any runner is able to participate, all are welcome. The high school at Thompson Falls sent 15 of the 225 total runners, as well as 2007 graduate Joe Sol and teacher / coach Andrew Gideon.

Head coach Sarah Naegeli said that she "wanted the kids to do this for fun, and they did. Some had fun competing, and some had fun just running and being with their teammates for one more race."

For the boys, Shane Donaldson earned himself yet another hat for finishing in the top echelon. This is his third hat received in calendar year 07; Donaldson finished 3rd among juniors (18 and under), while Jacob Naegeli finished 5th and earned himself a hat also. Donaldson's time was 27:32, while Naegeli clocked a 29:29. Those are fine results for an 8K (4.97 mile) race.

Other boys competitors were Mike Morris (30:07), Ryan Sol, Matt Hojem, RT Brown, Cody White, and Mike Barnett.

On the girl's side, Beca Gunderson (37:59) led the way, followed by Delcie Peters (40:48) and Mariah Naegeli (42:20). CC Normandeau, Monica Conlin, and Jeffreyanne Parker helped themselves to an abdominal workout during the race with laughter for the entire 8K (4.97 miles) distance, as well as a somersault 150 meters from the finish, and an arm-locked skipping finish. They were a team! Amanda Wood, who distanced herself from the terrifically thrilling trio for sanity reasons, was the seventh Lady Hawk harrier to run.

The Montana Cup has the following quote on the home page of its website (www.montanacup.com), "To go through life without ever running over rolling hills, flat fields, rocky gullies, shifting sand, sloppy mud, clinging clay, and fresh firm grass where your feet spring like lambs, is like going through life without ever touching your lover's face." (Roger Robinson of New Zealand).

Thompson Falls runners again made the community proud for its positive participation that exemplifies hard work. And if a reader ever believes this sports page will be without running as long as Naegeli's exist, then they might not want to swim in a shark infested area.

Side note – Shane gave back many gifts this year. He won races and watches, gift certificates, and hats. He didn't accept them to maintain his amateur status – we wanted no part of lawyers or those complaining of the $20 rule. Way to be honest Shane – another top trait of our Hawk Harriers.

Sunday, 10-28-2007, More Characters

We have characters on our team - time to discover one more.

By Andrew Gideon

Michael Thomas Barnett is a quiet personality on our team. His best three mile time coming into our 2007 cross country season was a 23:41. Mike, stealthily, under the radar, like the furtive character he is, improved his PR to 21:20. We will take another 9.9% improvement next year, which will move his time to 19:13. Who really knows about Mike B? Let's find out more.

He was born August 19, 1992; he already knows that will be a Tuesday next season. Happy Birthday 2008 - here is a Terrible Tuesday workout for you.

Mike is calm; His information sheet is as quiet as he is. I am not sure he has completely bought into the running idea and the next level still waits. For example, whereas Mariah spent all spring and summer doing knee rehabilitation exercises and building mileage slowly, I didn't see Mike's extra care and concern for his knee. Mike worked hard, 230 miles this year compared to 193 in 2006, but several workouts were abandoned to a bicycle and cut short to a knee. His improvement was 9.9%, but for him to reach that level of gain next season, a higher level of commitment will have to occur.

It was tremendous that he was able to watch the team at State. It was fantastic this season for Mike to be surrounded by harriers Jacob, Shane, Ryan, and the rest of the State Champion crew. Time will tell how this will add to his running mileage and determination. Hopefully it will add up in a positive way, because Mike B will be one of the four returning male athletes in 2008.

Mike B's advice to future runners is, *"Run hard and don't stop. Your body will make it to the finish."* He doesn't like long runs or speed sessions; his favorite workouts are the "short & sweet...☺ Random days." May I have your attention please; in one respect leaders need to like speed and distance to be successful at cross country – just a strange thought that went through my head.

Let's not solely ponder on Mike's running for analyzing his character. He maintains a 3.8 GPA. He is well-liked by the team and lists teaching and engineering as possible directions for his life.

Eric and Deniese are his parents; both came from Michigan. Brother Dave was our # 7 / 8 runner last year, a good student, and a good track hurdler. Dave graduated in May 07 and is currently working instead of attending college. If Mike imitates his brother, that would be great – he worked hard. Both have the idea of working for a year after high school before college.

Despite being in education for 30 of my 39 years of life, I do advocate that more people take a year off after high school, work, and **then** attack college with enthusiasm. If the zeal isn't there, then maybe college isn't for you. This road is better paved in my opinion / book than attending college and dropping out, never to return. Statistics I have read indicate that 65-75 % of people who go straight to college or university drop out after less than a year, never to return.

Mike does have advice to the future high school students of the world, *"work hard on your school work + it'll pay off in the future."*

Speaking of a pay off, if he were to win $100,000,000, he would *"buy a few nice cars, take an amazing vacation to Europe, and donate some."*

A man of few words and short stature he is (5'6" and 125-130 lbs). He is getting a good, solid education and has a pleasant classroom work ethic. His life goals include "*Be successful. Travel to Europe.*"

Favorites: The Haymeadow (book), The Benchwarmers (movie), cereal (food), running (hobby), Gym/English (class), Track/XC (sport), Gideon/Naegeli (coach), Gideon (teacher), Mountain West (running course), AMAZING (word).

Delcie wrote, "*Pretty random, always coming up with funny ideas.*"

Mariah and Monica, Homecoming 07   Mike B, Homecoming 07

Monday, 10-29-2007, Red Sox Win

The Red Sox swept the World Series over Colorado. 37 arrests were reported for disorderly conduct. I am a Boston fan, and my son Jaxon, 3 years old, has already witnessed 2 Red Sox World Series crowns. We celebrated Sunday night's clincher by going to bed with a smile within five minutes of the last out, a strikeout by Jonathon Papelbon.

Needless to say, there were not 37 arrests in Thompson Falls for disorderly conduct for celebrating our State Championship.

Now, if the football team had won......

The 2007 Lady Hawks (all nine) were asked to analyze days, meets, weeks, etc. that may have been the best for them. A writing assignment (yes, for our STUDENT-athletes) was given them yesterday – analyze the top two peak times during the season.

Mariah (frosh, rookie) turned in her assignment first; she wrote, "*The two meets that I felt the best at were state, even though it was cold, and Ronan. Also, I felt really good the week that you trained us through the meet (Mountain West). I have learned the cold weather makes my knee hurt more, but if I stretch it out a lot and do a bit of warm up, it doesn't hurt as much.*"

Beca Gunderson, Pulitzer Prize winner, responded to Monday's homework with a great season analysis. She wrote, "*I think the practices that were hardest for me were Tuesdays until the last two weeks. However, I also think those ones were the most beneficial, because when you have to do repetitive miles you get to where you just let yourself run and not think about it, and it*

157

builds confidence because if you can handle that hard work, then you can handle any XC course. Also, the first practice the girls did at the State Park was hard, but the last one there felt <u>awesome</u>! The extra track workouts & weightlifting was all very appreciated and I would love to do more of those next season, like two or three times a week at the beginning. I would also like to do more long runs. I thought you guys (coaches) did really well at planning our workouts and worked us very hard. BUT, next year I want to be worked VERY hard, because this year I was very disappointed that the boys did awesome but the girls didn't even trophy, and by SUCH A SMALL AMOUNT. So work us all harder than ever, because next year is <u>our</u> turn and I want to win."

WOW – good focus Beca. She mentions being more competitive / working harder, so we have set her up with several extra workouts.

Let's get this (win NEXT YEAR) done for Beca.

Monica writes in all colors and sizes of letters and pens, yet the computer just doesn't bring out her character: *"peak: Mountain West, the first time, and State race for sure. Worst: Libby and Kalispell. My legs felt exhausted for almost every race except for Mt. West + State. And also Thompson wasn't bad. It was mediocre. I was pumped for State! My legs felt pretty good, and they were fresh. I think it was just the adrenaline though. I'm not sure what it was at Mt. West the first time."*

CC wrote, *"I liked my race in Missoula. Both Mountain West and Divisionals. I felt the best in those two races! Woo Hoo..That was easy!"*

Yes, CC that was easy, but DEPTH – add more depth!

Delcie's evaluation: *"# 1Our home meet. Why? It's a fast course and I was feeling really strong so I took advantage of it! I think that week we went to the State Park for speed workout. # 2 Ronan Meet. One of my favorite courses!"*

Tuesday, 10-30-2007, Awards banquet

A successful leader delegates authority to ensure more work gets done. I have been taught *"if you want something done right, do it yourself."*

However, Since I am lazy and don't enjoy writing, I enlisted Jacob and Shane to write articles on our end of the year potluck awards night.

This 11-15-07 *Sanders County Ledger* article is *by Jacob Naegeli*

Tuesday October 30 was the 2007 cross-country end of season potluck. The food selection was excellent ranging from good old Mac-n-cheese to scrumptious moon pie. Varsity letters were given out to everyone who went to state, and other awards were handed out next.

According to the athlete's votes, Most Dedicated male went to Ryan Sol, Jacob Naegeli, and Shane Donaldson, all seniors, while the Most Dedicated girl was Beca Gunderson a sophomore.

Also from the Athlete's votes, the Most Inspirational guys were Bryce Miller, a freshman, and Mike Morris, another senior. The Most Dedicated females were Mariah Naegeli, a freshman, and CC Normandeau, a junior.

For the Junior High boys the Most Inspirational was John Gunderson while the Most Dedicated was Austin Kinser. The Coaches also had some say on who gets awards. For MVP, dubbed the "best legs" award by Derek Naegeli (06 TFHS Hawk Harrier graduate), Shane and Beca were selected.

To finish off the night, Coach Naegeli gave individual awards to every athlete ranging from the push up queenNOT award...to the chicken wing award.

That's quite a list, but there is no doubt in my mind that every award is well deserved after seeing what these runners go through. In fact, during the 2007 Cross Country season the entire team, junior high included, ran 7035 miles. Of these, the girl's team racked up 2391 miles, 4221 by the guys, and 423 by the junior high team.

Only two more awards were given out during the meeting. Ryan Sol won the male award for most miles with 417, while Delcie Peters, a junior, won the female one with 356.

By Shane Donaldson (another 11-15-07 *Sanders County Ledger* article)

The successful cross country season officially ended on Tuesday, October 30. Like the rest of the season, the end came with great fashion. The coaches once again allowed us to have a potluck. (However, the coaches were smart enough to make the runners' bring their own dishes.) These dishes included, but were not limited to, fried chicken, spaghetti, moon pie, ice cream, and even a few pops were seen floating around. While the runners' were wolfing down their dinners, the coaches and parents were actually doing something important. They were handing out awards.

The awards on our cross country team come in a range of topics, from speed to miles, to such random stuff as noisiest runners and everything else you could think of under the sun. The first awards were divided by varsity and junior varsity. The varsity letter was awarded to the runners who ran at the state meet. Thus, 18 people, ten boys and eight girls, were awarded varsity letters while the rest of the team was given junior varsity. From there on, the awards were as diverse as the people who received them.

However, the one thing that I felt wrapped up the season was the booklet each harrier was given. Throughout the whole ten weeks of our sport season, the coaches took pictures, cut out newspaper clippings, and even took random notes about the team. Towards the end of the year, coach Naegeli compiled all these artifacts into a book. One of this reporter's inside contacts told me that making all the books, just putting the pages in order, took almost three hours. (From the quality of the book and the number of pages, I believe that statistic.) With this keepsake, the runners' of the 2007-2008 team will be able to look back and remember the year they placed fourth (girls' team), and won the Class B State Meet, guys' team.

Our athletes vote on several awards – *most inspirational* and *most dedicated*.

Jacob, Shane, and Ryan were most dedicated – this definitely works with this book's dedication page. They were/are the program's heart and soul.

Next year, which girl(s) and boy(s) will step up to become the most dedicated and future heart and soul of a program is an entirely different question.

Beca was named most dedicated for the girls this year.

Today was our post-season awards banquet; congratulations on the past, but what's next?

Does this qualify as dedicated...or crazy runner with scissors? Derek Naegeli (see dedication page) literally ran until he dropped and then ran more. During several races in 2006, he fell to the ground, got up within 15 seconds, fell, got up, fell, got up, and then finished his races. The coaches original thought was hyperventilation. Later we found he actually flat-lined (no pulse). Now he has an implanted heart monitor and will run his first marathon next month in Seattle.

Wednesday, 10-31-2007, Halloween

Maybe my house can get egged again. My humble abode is 2 for 2 in getting egged on Halloween in my Thompson Falls teaching career. Thanks for the State Championship – egg, SPLAT. Thanks for working hard in English. SPLAT, drip, stain. Thanks for having a family in Thompson Falls, here's some omelet ingredients - SPLAT, drip, drip, fried (if sunny), and frozen (if cold).

Breaking Stride arrived in my mail box today. Amazon.com stole my kid's food/candy money on Halloween; the pages were devoured like a long slow run with some tempo intervals thrown in - between 5 pm and 11 pm with interruptions for candy, trick or treaters, and diapers. I recommend this book, but not more than Harrier Hawks Fly High. I don't recommend diapers, but just as diapers come with great kids, many miles are logged for running success.

Thursday, 11-1-2007, Ultimate Frisbee

Okay, no eggs for Halloween; Yeah for small victories. Maybe winning State helped and the girls should win state next year.

Instead of what's next – and the only answer is more running, there are options available. Basketball is an choice for at least four girls, while one may be on the new cheerleading squad. One girl will work, while another will lift and prepare for pole vault in the spring, along with running. The boys will mostly take the winter off, concentrate on school, scholarships, and rebuilding their faulty characters by living in the past of their glory days. One boy will play basketball.

What's next today was Ultimate Frisbee. While Mr. Gideon ran 4.25 miles in the morning and 6.75 after school to go above and beyond 1700 miles on the year, at least 10 individuals got together to play Ultimate Frisbee.

We probably need to define Ultimate; when I jogged by at 4:20, they needed a serious coach to put an end to the comical game they attempted to play.

The baton was passed to Kyle to read <u>Breaking Stride</u>. Last year I started passing around running books to hopefully generate enthusiasm and love for the sport. We read books, and then pass them like a baton to the next runner.

<u>Finding their Stride</u> and <u>Harriers</u> are two other books on high school running currently being passed around TFHS. These books are recommended, but please, buy a second copy of this book before purchasing others. Think of my kids, my family, let them eat, please…

Friday, 11-2-2007, End of the First Quarter, Congratulations

This is probably a great day for our athletes. The season ended two weeks ago, with an encore race performance last weekend. However, today was the end of the first quarter, and that is a source of relief.

Our harriers earn good grades – Beca and JP both produce A+ grades in English 2 class – thanks for the great work - while others will put some impressive marks on their permanent file.

The United States Air Force Academy emailed me an electronic form for Ryan. It has been filled out and sent off (successfully!). One of my comments was that Ryan is one of my All-Time favorite people (and I have said that to less than twenty people in my life).

What I wrote on Ryan is top secret – bring out the old standard joke – I could tell you, but I would have to kill you. I'm sure this book violates privacy laws and US National Security is breeched because of <u>Harrier Hawks Fly High</u>.

"Coach Naegeli, Reall, & Coach Gideon, Congratulations on your recent State Championship. A finish like that takes hours of dedication, sweat, & tears, and I'm not just talking about the runners. I am very proud of your accomplishment," Chadd Laws, TFHS basketball & football. Mr. Laws is also a World History, General Math, Algebra 1, and Consumer Math teacher.

Thank you for those kind and true words.

Saturday, 11-3-2007, Positive Statements

We run a positive program. Having our Hawk Harriers write about teammates to respect their personalities has helped our team be just that, a TEAM.

Coach Naegeli collected newspaper articles, pictures, and comments such as these. Each athlete received a packet of good memories and experiences.

Here are positive statements written by Hawk Harriers about teammates.

RT - Mr. Clean hairdo; Always keeps us entertained, keeps CC's music in check for the rest of us who are too polite; really driven at whatever he does.

Shane- Funny! Never late; Always encouraging and eats a lot; leader; Above and beyond mental capabilities. pushes himself well; school record;

Matt - very dependable; Great wrestler! Always willing to try something new, helps that he's good at almost everything. A great competitor.

Mike M - He makes me laugh so hard! He's just an innocent bystander, and he's always working hard. He is always teasing me, but I love him anyway.

161

By Andrew Gideon

Jacob- He's my brother and he's amazing. Great captain. Always cheers his teammates. a marvelous baker! smart, down-to-earth. longest hair.

Bryant - always ready to help anyone; always positive, never seems to have a bad day and gives everyone something to smile about; his laughter is contagious; Never a dull moment around him. Makes practice fun.

Ryan- stays under control. so random…and it makes me laugh really hard. always encouraging everyone; Ryan works hard, off season and in season.

Patrick- good running form. ridiculously hilarious when the music is turned on. His dancing moves are hilarious. never a dull moment with him!

MK - crazy for eating 2 hot dogs before a meet; Real team player. Had chance to leave but decided to stay. Really committed to running. Determined.

Mike B - The only kid as random as I am. Very positive attitude. Brave. Takes after his brother. he's finally realizing that he really can run.

Kyle- Great enthusiasm; Easy to spot - Head and shoulders over everyone; 2 minute improvement …I'm jealous; Finally realizing he can run!

Cody- Funny, hard worker (runner); The only one that will sing really loud with me at random times "Peanut butter Jelly Time!" He's good to pace off of; Can't tell where his compression shorts end and where legs begin.

Bryce - Hyper, works hard, always polite and respectful - has almost smoked the freshman record; Funny, positive; improving a lot, Has nice legs.

The entire girl's team: *We are doing so well! Do you realize how good we could be? Our potential? Believe, because we are fast as a team.*

Amanda- worker! improving magnificently! 2 minute improvements. …I'm jealous; Diligent, nice; Stubborn, in a good way, about not giving up.

CC - even with her hurt back, she never complains; respectful; positive, good friend; Funny; She ALWAYS keeps things interesting. Great team leader.

Monica- Kept working hard and trying to improve, even when she hurt so much and didn't know why. She runs hard, even when she's really injured.

Delcie- cool curly hair; calm. Her spikes make her ankles look fat. enjoyable personality. encouraging. an awesome friend, and she is chopping time off like nuts and is GOING TO CATCH ME! a lot faster than she thinks.

Beca - always helping everyone. leads the girl's team for the second year in a row. Happy; Very determined runner; Good spirited. good friend and good leader. Nice target painted on her back. That's the problem with being in front!

Jeffreyanne- cute, Makes me go faster! JP is going to catch me! I hope she realizes what a great runner she is. A hard worker we can always depend on.

Lacey - makes me laugh. enjoys Wallace and Gromit! willing to push herself. kept working hard even when others would have given up.

Jessie- will bust out laughing in a race while Cody and I are singing and dancing to "peanut butter jelly time"- Great determination; positive attitude

Mariah - puts up with 3 obnoxious brothers and hasn't gone insane yet! best freshman runner ever; 20 second improvements per race? Dang.

Our volleyball team won two matches and lost two at Divisionals and placed 4th. Only the top two teams move on to the State tourney, so another season at TFHS has finished.

Our football team was in the elite 8 after last week's win. However, Fairfield beat them 38-6 today. This season ends with an 8-2 record.

So, XC, volleyball, and football were all successful. Boys XC first in State, Girls XC 4th in State, Volleyball approximately 13-16 overall, and the football team made the final 8.

A statement on the faulty logic of our football program is ready to be inserted after much thought. At a teacher development day in September, two football coaches stated during a "Love and Logic" presentation that TFHS should have no standards for grades. Everyone should be allowed to compete, regardless of classroom effort. All "F" report card = ok to the football coaches.

Wow. I couldn't believe my ears that two respected coaches and teachers would stand up and say, let alone believe, that schools should lower our standards to absolutely nothing. It fits right in with the "no homework" idea of "Love and Logic." My only comment on our district's "Love and Logic" philosophy is a quote by King Edward VIII, *"The things that impresses me the most about America is the way parents (adults) obey their children."*

Successful people keep raising the bar and challenging the self to higher standards. Galatians 6:9 ➔ *Let us not become weary in doing good, for at the proper time we will reap a harvest if we do not give up.*

Successful people do homework. Whether it is writing a book, studying the stock market, raising cattle, getting wood for winter heat, playing with kids, raising kids, getting up with kids at 3 AM, reading the Bible, or exercising (physically, mentally, spiritually) above and beyond the call of duty…that is homework . . . that is what successful people do.

Therefore schools should set higher standards, not lower, and we should teach students that life is a 24 hour per day job, and yes, homework is required for success in life. Our schools produce doctors (on call at all hours), soldiers (fighting for our US freedom), waitresses (want good service?), car mechanics (paying attention to detail is important) – if our schools don't set higher standards, then we don't produce quality workers or people.

If a student-athlete cannot make the effort to learn in the classroom, then that shows a choice / lack of commitment to learning / effort. It logically follows that our football team will never get past the final 8 in State in any season – the extra effort is not there – on or off the field. Other teams also work harder in the summer lifting weights, etc. Do your homework!

Sunday, 11-4-2007, New York City Marathon

Paula Radcliffe won the women's marathon in New York. An adept reader recalls (8-17 entry) the fact that she is an ice bath proponent. We salute a fellow champion ice bather!

By Andrew Gideon

A Kenyan, Martin Lel, won the men's marathon. Kenyan coffee works.

37,866 people finished this race in 2006; multiplied by 26.214 = a total of 992,619.324 miles covered – almost a million miles.

In Saturday's US Marathon trials in New York, 131 men tried to make one of the three spots for the Olympic team. Ryan Hall (2:09:02), Dathan Ritzenhein (2:11:06), and Ryan Sell (2:11:40) made the team, while a runner (Ryan Shay, 28 years young) died trying. Meb Keflezighi, silver medallist in the 2004 Olympic marathoner, finished 8[th,] while Khalid Khannouchi, the American record holder finished 4th in 2:12:34.

131 tried, 3 were "successful," yet 128 definitely did not fail. Four-five months (in reality, a lifetime) of training, lives devoted to work, and only a small margin get the spoils of victory. We live in a competitive society.

If I were to die racing a marathon, or just running, I would die happy.

Tuesday, 11-6-2007, Humor in everyday life

It was an honor and a privilege to run with the heart (Shane, Jacob) and soul (Ryan) today. Shane ran at warp speed and didn't converse with us, but Ryan and Jacob jogged at conversational pace for six miles of Gideon humor. After my humor, they might think about running with Shane next time.

Neither Jacob nor Ryan watched the NY City Marathon Sunday.

It was my second jog of the day. At 6:20 am, I ran 4.5 miles, and with an extra ½ mile cool down after school, I ended with 11 for today.

Wednesday, 11-7-2007, Air Force

Ryan took a field test for the Air Force today – he will be measured in distance running, curl ups, and pull ups. If he doesn't pass the running test, he is fired from our cross country team – even if he is a senior and he is done anyway.

Jacob, Beca, and Delcie ran after school. I was not invited. ☹

Thursday, 11-8-2007, Mobile society

We have lost two of our twenty-two high school harriers.

Patrick went to California or Utah, depending on which rumor is true. His parents are in California, while Utah is the rumored new program for him.

Bryce moved to Cut Bank, MT, to live with his father. Cut Bank XC should be thankful for receiving the top freshman Class B runner in the state.

We are in a mobile society.

Our eight seniors (9-27 entry) have been in TFalls for 81 years of life. Divide that out and the average stay is 10 years for our seniors.

Another senior this cartoonist has not sketched is RT.

With RT Brown, life is always an adventure, whether chugging a gallon of chocolate milk which didn't stay long in the system or getting a TF shaved out in his head and painted school colors, he is as fun as a long run-on sentence.

164

Robert Tyrel Brown was born 1-14-90 to Bob & Carla Brown in Thompson Falls. His brother Aaron is currently 19 and graduated from TFHS. RT stands at 5'7" and weighs 145.

His 3.333 GPA will lead him to a future to "live life as it comes." College will land him somewhere for law enforcement. He may just work after high school instead of college *"only if I'm good at something and don't need an education to do it. And it must pay pretty fair."*

RT's list of favorites: "Anything with Jackie Chan or a lot of action" (movie), don't have one, just a lot of them (foods), hanging out with my friends (hobby), don't know (book), Media Arts, Weight Training (Class), running & golf (sports), Mrs. Stuckey, Mr. Wheeler, Mr. Dieterich (Teachers), Mr. Thompson (coach), purple (color), of course, Dr. Pepper (drink).

RT gave up his beloved Dr. Pepper for XC; it is rumored he is back on his 12 pack a day diet so he can cough up fur balls like a mange stricken cat.

His advice to younger students: *"don't hold back. Do mostly everything you can do, now. Always stay positive and happy."* RT has advice for future runners; his name is on a State Championship XC trophy, so listen, *"Don't step in holes or fall down hills. Always push for more. And laugh a ton."* That doesn't sound like pure running advice, but a main fear is that he is an accident waiting to happen. In Libby two years ago, he fell on a hill on the year's first meet and injured his hip. With several weeks left this season, a hole gobbled him up, and he missed part of practice. RT improved – his 18:38 PR occurred at our home meet, and he basically matched it with an 18:44 at Divisionals.

RT's breaking of 19:00 on 9-27 was huge. Accomplishing goals always feels good. His 9-10 goals were *"self – recover from injuries enough to run at State; academic – a 3.3 GPA."* He did run well enough to run at State – this was the only year out of the ten years of TFHS XC that his time and effort would not have been good enough to qualify as one of the seven runners on the team. With about 3-4 weeks left, he could see that he probably was not going to make the top seven, yet he worked hard for several reasons. One was to push himself and give his best effort. Two was to be ready in case an alternate was needed. Three was to be a positive example for the younger runners. All three of these reasons were discussed with him during the past few weeks to help keep him motivated.

RT earned respect for his three years of effort in XC. His least favorite workout is the mule pasture. I love that path, but maybe he feared injury. I recall the clicky-top entry (9/4), running behind him on this route, listening to the clicks of his body each step. His favorite runs were the relaxing days before meets.

Life Goals: *"live happily, have a great family, a great job, live a long time. do amazing things."*

If he were to win $100,000,000, he would buy a "dream corvette. Buy my mom and dad their dream cars. Pay off my parent's debts & bills. Put half in the bank and not touch it. Go to college. Help Bryant build his space ship."

By Andrew Gideon

Most memorable moments exist, *"All the bus trips with the cross country team and the band. Stealing and signing the cone from the Ronan cross country meet."* Let it be known the 2006 team apologized once the coaches found out, and the team sent money to pay for a new cone. More RT memories: *"trying to drink a gallon of chocolate milk on the way back from the Ronan (2007) and throwing it up in the garbage on the bus. Freezing my rear end off in Bob's ever so wonderful ice baths. All the movie nights and halo parties with the guys."*

RT is not allowed to go Ronan again (stolen cone, milk chugging, anything else?). Let's not forget he filmed biking off cliffs in August, giving Ryan a scar on the shin just before our season started. This surely did not stress out the coaches; thus, it is mentioned. (note: RT will be injured in a video-taped snowboarding accident at school in December.)

RT raised funds for a golf trip to Australia last summer. His donation from me hinged on running effort last February, and he made a great effort, so my donation was higher as a result. Golfing down under was a great experience, and when he came back from it in the summer, he ran hard with the team to get into State Championship shape.

Delcie writes: *"always doing something crazy. Seems to find great delight in eating as much as possible, and then puking it back up. I don't get it! Isn't there a happy medium somewhere? ☺"*

Spaceship builder Bryant (in his own words): *"ak 'brown eye' good times worker in Science olipead eathing top romen RT owes Juner year pooshed him a down a hill on a bedracer down a hill."*

Some anonymous person wrote that RT is "bald." Yes, it is a bald head that sharply contrasts his formerly wild & wavy & unpredictable hair. Does this mean there is a new RT straining to get out and away from the old RT?

CC pens that *"RT is the BOMB! I ❤ movies @ his house! Remember the time he <u>almost</u> did a back flip off his rope swing!"*

Patrick and RT share some connection; Pat only writes, *"Yea...."*

Matt, fellow senior, emotes, *"Rope swings, tubing, golfing, gallon of milk, bald head, movie nights, hip problems."*

Ryan's pen inks out, *"Mr. Clean, Mr. Clean, Mr. Clean!! Hobbies include mooning, flatulence, bike jumps, & making kick-a@@ videos."*

Remember RT, we are laughing near you and not at you.

Jacob writes, *"Wow, the exact opposite of Lacey. The gallon of milk challenge was unsuccessful."*

Two years ago, I wasn't sure about RT and his future. His English 2 effort left something to be desired. His efforts in XC were good, but often hindered by injury. RT tipped over in a kayak on a calm Thompson River last June – rescued by the rest of the XC team. He seemed like a future injury to society waiting to happen. His fun-loving nature has proved to be good, mainly with the addition of respect. RT will be successful; his efforts have convinced many the future will not only be fun, but bright as well, for Robert Tyrel Brown.

Today Jacob and Shane jogged 14 miles after school to the Naegeli ranch. When asked why, Jacob replied, *"for a change of pace."* - A healthy change of pace!

Ultra running is ultra living.

"Live deep and suck the marrow out of life" is a quote by Henry David Thoreau. Ultra-marathoning is living deep. Reading, ranching, and running too much is sucking the marrow out of life.

At mile 37 of my ultra marathon, I had an orange slice candy from the aide station. My heavens, that tasted unworldly, and those orange slices have been my favorite candy since. Wow, did that hit the spot. If running 50 miles is what it takes to appreciate orange slice candy, then I highly recommend it.

Friday, 11-9-2007, Ultra Living

Ultra Living is a newly created phrase, by yours truly, not patented, nor copyrighted, but produced solely by this brain.

Ultra Running → an ultimate challenge.

Ultra Living is what the kids on this cross country team do.

The healthy way to overdo life, brought to you by the cross country team at Thompson Falls High School, TFalls, MT, USA, - Work hard in school, sports, 4H, Science Olympiad, Envirothon, ranching, running, photography, Upward Bound, and student council. Get good grades, be family oriented, strive continually for success, and by all means, occasionally push beyond the limits of what a person thinks can be done.

This Ultra-Living is experienced daily by these Hawk Harriers. I once said Jacob makes me sick sometimes with all his multiple activities. Maybe running an ultra marathon 50 miler makes people sick. However, it is better to be a shooting star and burn out, than die slowly each day of life.

Personalities have been covered, running has been covered, positive life has been covered, and Ultra Living is now being covered.

These kids and this way of life are to be admired. Our XC team didn't have drug or alcohol problems, we had fantastic grades, and it was a joy to be alive each day of the season and year surrounded by these athletes.

Monty Python said, *"Run away, run away,"* but TFHS XC runs to a good life.

May the reader join in the tidal wave of Ultra Running and Ultra Living.

RUNWYLD (my license plate). RUNBYND (what I would like my next license plate to read). Run wild and run beyond (live wild and beyond) what you think you are capable of doing.

Monday, 11-12-2007, Positive attributes

At the banquet on October 30th, everyone received a packet as discussed by Shane's article (10/30 entry). One liner "positive" attributes for each Hawk

By Andrew Gideon

Harrier were listed in the back. Coach Naegeli goes above and beyond to give good memories to these student-athletes.

Always leave on a good note is a good piece of advice, so our runners are left with positive memories; positive characters are our <u>Harrier Hawks Fly High</u>.

The individual comments are left out here because of similarities to the 11-03 entry, but comments on the coaches and overall team are now listed.

<u>Coach Naegeli</u>: *amazing mom, caring, is a second mom, food, runs at her house, serious/fun, laughs easily, fun, shades, running, careful, the best, nice, "Montana coach of the year 07", mom*

<u>Coach Reall</u>: *"boob", statistical, surprising, ice bath, back in Ohio, hilarious, enduring, legendary, Ohio, Ohio stories, scotch-Irishman, too funny, amazing, supportive, protective*

<u>Coach Gideon</u>: *obsessive, competition!, inspirational speeches, tea and chicken noodle soup, dedicated, obsessed, awesome—50 miles, comics, encouraging, Mohawk, my hero, Runforestrun*

<u>Our season</u>: *the best ever, good/sad, my 1ˢᵗ and not my last, excellent, spectacular, stupendous, 1ˢᵗ rate, fantastical, crazy, out-of-control in a good way, amazing, too short, bittersweet, too fast, inspirational, the best yet, fantabulousgreatfantasticgodlikealmightygrandwonderful, state champs!*

<u>Girls team</u>: *Hair, "hottie Harriers", state champs 08, chatty (especially at state park), Friends, tenacious, nylons, fun to run with, crazy, hairy, amazing, they're nuts, impressive, my best friends, ecstatic, wonderful*

<u>Boys team</u>: *hilariously immature, eat a lot, my best friends,, fast, "smirking sasquatch scaries", state champions, incredible, loud, crazy, wow, definitely not the most mature, #1, State champs 07, steak champs!, incredible*

Tuesday, 11-13-2007, pacing & writing

22 High School Harriers – 69 days of the season from first practice (8-13) to State (10-20). Dividing 69/22 yields a result of just over three. Therefore, from the start of the season, it would have been wise to do a student profile every three days or at least two per week.

Ooops.

So, at the end now exists an abundance of profiles left to write. Started too slowly, now I need a final sprint to win this race of book life. One would think a wise running coach would allocate energy and pace himself properly.

Oooops with an extra o!

However, not all TFHS XC harriers chose to be profiled, so my pacing has been saved!

Miles not run. . . .Profiles not written. . . yet success will still be achieved. My scissors will provide a short cut through the pages.

That is a silly way to introduce our final Hawk Harrier profile.

Amanda Eileen Wood is a senior, although she is only in her third year of high school. She is skipping a year in high school, just as she did in grade

168

school. Her birth date of 8-14-91 and simple mathematics lets us know that she will be 16 when she graduates from TFHS.

Amanda wasn't entirely convinced that she would join XC this season. However, Mr. Gideon, the author, was lucky to be able to teach some summer school. Amanda did not make a mistake by coming to summer school, but she did hear about the benefits of cross country for two weeks straight at the end of July. Amanda finished several classes in the four week summer school, which freed up her time to be part of the "best finish ever" Lady Hawk team.

If high school graduation were the finish line, Amanda just might be first place in the state of Montana this year.

Amanda's first race of the year on 8-31 ended in 30:35. Her best time by the end was 26:48. Most improved during the season was a certificate she received at our banquet. 231 miles of hard work earned an improvement of 3:47, 12.4%. Wow. If we could all improve that much each year in pay, performance, or pacing, then we just might write the best seller.

A 3.9 GPA and early graduation will help her to embark on future plans of college, marriage, and kids. The last two mentioned items lead us to family.

Family is in her structure as parents Randy August and Symona Rena decided to have a large group of kids – seven to be exact. On parent's night (9-27 entry), Amanda appreciated her siblings for making life "interesting." Sam is four, the youngest, while Amanda is the oldest. The next oldest sister, Alicia, skipped 8th grade and will follow in her sister's footsteps to the first place line of being the youngest class graduate.

Amanda is 5'6" and 135 pounds; she uses her frame to run, sing, and be positive. Her time may not have earned us points at state, but her improvement, attitude, and effort made her a welcome addition to positive team chemistry.

She enjoys singing and has reached the highest level of singing competition in Montana, each year at Montana's State competition. In addition to musical skills, it is obvious that she enjoys work and appreciates the use of her brain; otherwise she might not have listed her favorite classes as "Band, Choir, Geometry, Physics, and Chemistry." Or maybe she isn't picky as her favorite teacher is "undecided" and her top coach is "all."

Other favorites include <u>Lord of the Rings</u> and <u>Star Wars</u> (movie), food (food), singing, reading, playing piano, making up songs (hobby), fantasy and sci-fi, too many to name, and most fiction novels – not love stories (book), honey bunches of Oats with Almonds (cereal), and 2% (milk). She enjoyed our two scavenger hunts on the first two Wednesdays of the season, although timings of more than one mile won't be getting any Christmas presents from her.

Amanda will graduate at 16, so future students listen up, "work hard, pay attention, don't be like me, actually study, and do your homework when it's assigned (I don't do this)."

She may be gifted musically and school-wise, yet running was not easy for her. She worked hard and thus this is a solid reason for listening to her advice to runners, "run fast, you're capable of running a lot faster than you think, and the ice bath is only bad the first time."

Another victim of the ice bath survives to tell her story! Her life goals include traveling to Mars and becoming a professional singer. She could be the best singer ever on Mars.

If she were to win $100,000,000, she would *"pay for college, take flying lessons, and singing lessons. Buy a house, and a car. Save the rest."*

Amanda has some words from Delcie, *"very intelligent! Also stubborn."* With friends like that, who needs enemies?

Persevering is a synonym for stubborn, and the connotation is much more positive. That's surely what Delcie meant!

To be successful at Ultra-Running and Ultra-Living requires perseverance and stubbornness.

Maybe we should all surround ourselves with stubborn and persevering people to enjoy life better. These can both be good traits.

Stubborn and persevering lead to the next focused step: obsessive!!! ☺

| Amanda, Home meet 07 | Six senior boys – RT is the bald one |

Wednesday, 11-14-2007, GPA's

My strict orders are not to divulge GPA's. A warning from the TFHS counselor: It is an invasion of student privacy. Tongue out, make noise, for I have parental permission slips.

National Honor Society members can have their names printed. These people are Delcie, Beca, CC, Amanda, Ryan, Jacob, Shane, Matt, Mike B. Nine of 22 is 41%; this is much higher than the overall student population. Runners are smarter than the average two-legged human.

When I asked the office for Hawk Harrier grades, one would have thought the world exploded and I was the terrorist. Sorry I showed concern about my athletes! The counselor was very concerned I would print these and invade privacy. Parents and students have okayed the release of the information in this book. God won't sue me for caring about my athletes.

First quarter GPA's do not factor into the overall GPA. Only semester grades factor into that. "Honor roll GPA's" can be disclosed to the public.

Here is the 1st quarter honor roll: Beca 4.0, Ryan 3.86, Matt 3.83, Jacob 3.83, Mariah 3.71, Mike B 3.71, Shane 3.67, Amanda 3.57, Lacey 3.5, Delcie 3.5, Kyle B 3.33, and Jeffreyanne 3.33. 12/22=55%. 55% of our team is on the honor roll. Runners rule the Hawk knowledge roost.

My entry about GPA's is simple and two-fold.

One – we have some winners on the running field and in the classroom. Leaders abound, even those in 2nd and 3rd place at state, and will help our society. Some will earn Academic All-State status (3.5 GPA and above, and a varsity letter winner). Congratulations and nice work!

Two – if a person had low grades, it gives a coach/teacher another option to go to our student-athletes and arrange for help. So I talked to a student-athlete today about grades. We can move this person on a solid track and give options to keep running in a straight line. Or curvy line. Or circular. As long as this person keeps running, writing, reading, and moving in a POSITIVE direction.

Science Olympiad, a MHSA sponsored contest, begins Monday. Here are the Hawk Harriers doing more Ultra-Living by competing in Bozeman – RT, Jacob, Bryant, Ryan, Beca, Mariah, and Shane. Seven members with science knowledge – including one horrible speller who wants to build a spaceship.

Our team was entered into the Army National Guard Academic All Team Award. Our ten varsity boys combined for a 3.333 GPA, while the eight varsity girls earned a 3.494. Based on last year's entrants, both would place us third.

The deadline for entering TFHS is December 14.

Thursday, 11-15-2007, Shoe Size

Walking a mile in someone else's shoe gives good perspective. The wise-old saying is that one should not judge another until walking a mile in his shoes. Nothing in these two statements has anything to do with shoe size! Running more than a mile might give blisters.

We can go back to the perspective of eyes being the window to the soul and comparing ourselves to what we were as younger runners (see 10-02 entry).

Kyle at 12 ½ has our largest shoe size on the team – those were his spikes. However, his regular shoes are 13. Therefore, since he improved so dramatically with smaller, tighter shoes, then we can falsely conclude that putting people's feet into smaller shoes is wise. CC and Bryant, brother and sister, both wear 7 ½ (our smallest shoe size). The family that has small feet loves each other, so I'm going to chop off some toes.

Size 8 boys: Shane, RT. Size 8 Girls: JP, Monica.
Size 8 ½ boys: Mike B. Size 8 ½ girls: Delcie, Lacey.
Size 9 boys: Matt. Size 9 girls: Beca (her spikes are 8 ½), Jessie
Size 9 ½ boys: MK, Cody W. Size 9 ½ girls: none.

By Andrew Gideon

Size 10 boys: Bryce. Size 10 girls: Mariah (now wait a minute, 98 pounds, smallest girl, yet second largest shoe size, 10, is this like a dog's paw and she will grow taller?). NO, I am not calling Mariah a dog – but I am digging a hole with my paws.

Size 10 ½ boys: Jacob (only ½ size bigger than his sister).

Size 11 boys: Mike M, Ryan, Patrick (3 of our top 6). Size 11 girl: Amanda

Coaches: Naegeli size 10, like her daughter, they can trade shoes; Gideon 9, and Reall 9.

A good reader paid money for this book. You have seen how the other better, smarter, running half lives. Hopefully walking, no RUNNING, a mile in our shoes has added perspective to work ethic, dedication, high school Montana harriers, and a job well done.

All week long I told TFHS harriers I would be running after school, so get your excuses ready. I was looking forward to running with some kids again.

Today arrived, and...no runners. Sadly, Coach Gideon ran alone. 4.5 miles before school, and 8 miles after was logged. Three of the eight were miles in 6:47, 6:59, and 6:48 with a half-mile easy between the harder push miles.

"The Runner" (written by me in 1991) comes to mind and is included at the end of the book.

Another *Sanders County Ledger* issue was printed today in its normal Thursday release. John Hamilton wrote the following.

"All in all, a pretty special fall for some of Sanders County's finest athletes and most devoted fans.

So far this school year, Thompson Falls teams have enjoyed the most success, but Hawk and Lady Hawk teams were not the only ones to find their times in the sun before their seasons truly ended in this little slice of heaven we call western Montana.

Let us take a look back before the still-fresh memories begin to fade into sports history.
***

"The Thompson Falls boys' State B cross country championship, won last month in Helena, was probably the biggest memory maker produced by any Sanders County sports entity this fall.

Coaches Sarah Naegeli, Bob Reall and Andrew Gideon watched their team at Bill Roberts Golf Course in Helena as Shane Donaldson (second overall in 16:44), Jacob Naegeli (third in 16:50), Mike Morris (ninth in 17:08), Ryan Sol (25th in 17:47) and Bryce Miller (26th in 17:49) totaled up the low total score of 65 points to hold off Poplar (78) and Colstrip (91) for the State B title, the first ever in cross country for Thompson Falls.

Patrick Jamison (17:59) and Mike Kidwiler (18:27) were also part of the Hawks' State B championship effort.

172

Nobody will relish the championship or cherish the moment more than the seniors who were so responsible for making it finally happen. Donaldson, Naegeli, Morris and Sol all ran their final prep races, in State B championship stride, at Helena.

The State B title is officially Thompson Falls' sixth ever in a boy's team sport.

The legendary Hawk football teams of the 1970s produced the school's first State B championships ever in '73 and '74. An equally legendary Thompson Falls wrestling team copped consecutive State B-C titles in '79 and '80.

Most recently, Coach Randy Symon's boy's track and field squad corralled the 2002 State B championship after a stirring team performance at the Missoula County High School Stadium.

***

Not quite of state championship caliber just yet, the Lady Hawk cross country team looks to be poised for great things in the next few seasons.

Coming off a sixth place team finish in 2006, the Hawks ran to an impressive fourth place this fall without the benefit of a senior among their scoring five in Helena.

Juniors Ciara Normandeau and Delcie Peters, sophomores Beca Gunderson, Monica Conlin and Jeffreyanne Parker, and freshman Mariah Naegeli could very well be right in the thick of the hunt for more State B metal next year.

Could this be another Thompson Falls State B team championship cross country team in the making?

Stay tuned, only time, and the times the Lady Hawks eventually post, will tell.

Thompson Falls has one only one other girls State B team championship – the 1984 Class B track and field title."

Friday, 11-16-2007, Dinner Time

For birthdays when I was young, my family always went to Shakey's Pizza in Missoula. Shakey's is now gone, sadly replaced by the Dominoes and Pizza Huts of the World. (Grumble, grumble at corporate America here.)

However, loving pizza will go on forever.

Our team of runners is no different and loves pizza.

Favorite types of pizza will be remembered for long forgotten birthdays.

Pepperoni (Jacob, MK, Matt, Jessie), Supreme (Delcie, JP, CC, Coach Gideon), Combo (a.k.a.supreme?) (Ryan, Monica), Hawaiian (Mike M, Coach Naegeli), Meat Lovers (Kyle B, Mike B, Beca), Cheese (Bryce, Lacey), Pepperoni & Sausage (Patrick, Mariah), Meat or cheese (Shane), Sausage (RT), Pepperoni & Meat Lovers (Bryant, Cody), not plain cheese (Amanda). Coach Bob was not present on the day/time I took this order.

By Andrew Gideon

I say dinner time, because the climax of the day/entry, book, story, and 2008 Hawk Harrier XC season is over. It is time to sit down to a family pizza, review the day, book, story, season, words (editing time), and eat dinner. It is time to do something constructive with what happens after the main events have ended. What's next can wait until tomorrow morning; I smell pizza, and too many pages of editing.

Girls - Mtn West Start 07

Girls Huddle before State

Boys and Hawk in Ronan

August Practice 07

PS (Postscript)

This is not really a post-script, as the plan is to go through the school year and end with graduation. However, the entries might be slightly different from this point on.

The season and championship is huge, but it is one small part of the successful lives of our Hawk Harriers.

11-19 and 11-20: *Bird's Eye View* (the TFHS school paper). article *for 11-30-07, issue 8 – advisor Mr. Gideon.* Please notice names that are consistent with the cross country program.

Science Olympiad Individual Results
There were fifteen categories of competition at the State Science Olympiad. These different types of events are rotated each year.

Students from each school work in pairs for every event. The variety of events is then scored to get the team total.

Three sets of students earned 2nd place honors. In the "Boomilever" event, RT Brown and Bryant Normandeau garnered the silver. The "Electric Vehicle" competition saw Jacob Naegeli and SK drive away with second, while HP and VB did CSI proud with a detailed job in the "Forensics" department.

Four sets of THFS teams placed 4th. These great students and the categories are as follows:

"Cell Biology" – JG and Mariah Naegeli

"Chemistry Lab" – KP and Ryan Sol

"Ecology" – RP and HP

"Herpetology" – Mariah Naegeli and MF.

HP deserves recognition as her 2nd and 4th results in each competition led the way for the Blue Hawks. Miss Mariah Naegeli also had two categories of top four performances.

Three other sets of students placed in the respectable top eight finishes. MF and RT Brown knew how to operate in the "Physics Lab" department with a 7th place. On an octagonal tray, KP and Bryant Normandeau served up an 8th place result in "Food Science." VB and Beca Gunderson brought the hills to life in the "Sounds of Music" competition and an 8th place result.

Finishing in the top 8 meant a top 25% finish. Quite a few students combined to do well individually and thus help the team to its 4th place (top in Class B) finish at the State Science Olympiad.

Thanks for being scientists and helping Gallileo happily roll over in his grave.

This year's competition was held Monday and Tuesday, November 19 and 20, in Bozeman

Overall the team placed 4th of all schools in the competition, regardless of school size. TFHS was the top Class B school.

11-29-07: (29 November 2007 *Sanders County Ledger* article)
Seattle Marathon   by Andrew Gideon
Two Thompson Falls residents competed in the 11-25-07 Seattle Marathon.

Derek Naegeli, a 2006 TFHS graduate, and Andrew Gideon, a teacher and coach at Thompson Falls High School, ran in the 26.214 mile race.

This was Derek's first marathon and his time was 3 hours, 22 minutes, and 45 seconds. He placed 167th overall out of 1236 males that finished. Derek was 10th in his age bracket. Derek is currently doing a research project on squirrel hair and is in his second year of college as a Pacific Boxer in Forest Grove, Oregon.

By Andrew Gideon

Gideon finished his 9th career marathon just 6 weeks after running a 50 mile Ultra Marathon. His final time in Seattle was 3:38:52. An average time for Gideon's 9 marathons is 3 hours, 26 minutes.

Gideon asked for donations and raised $795.12 for Candlelighters of Western Washington. This is an organization that deals with children's cancer.

Author's excuse: I was beating Derek after the first 385 yards. It was only the final 26 short miles he crushed me.

12-09-07: **Life is good** has a great motto on the inside of my running hat (a little running man logo) – *do what you like, like what you do.* After my runs I glance at the expression – it is a good reminder. Go read about the history of this company – small start (selling shirts from the back of a van), rough start, and odds seemed impossible, but now the founders are doing what they like and liking what they do.

Thank you TFalls XC 2007 team – I liked the season and the running. The Hawk Harriers Flew High; this helped us to do what we liked (even though the pain of running was present at times), so that we could like what we did.

12-10-07: Monday – lunch. Matt went for a run at lunch. The crazy man does this quite often. I talked with him about his wrestling season so far – this is the update: He runs at lunch for cardiovascular endurance and hopefully a stronger third round. This year, at 119 pounds, he is 10-1 with 9 pins. Last year he "almost killed himself" by wrestling at 105, and his record was 24-15. He chose 105 last year as the route that would have the easiest competition for him at State. This year he feels much stronger, especially in the third round. Matt is focused.

12-11-07: Mr. Gideon ran 6 miles in 11 degree temperature before school. This helped him top 1900 miles for 2007. After school, he ran another 5.5 miles with Ryan and Jacob. It was cold – what kind of crazy people run with scissors in the middle of winter. Scissors not like cold; scissors freeze. Cody, with an IPOD, and Shane, after lifting weights, were also seen being crazy, I mean running.

Beca had some eye trouble in the middle of December. Her eyes experienced the same crisis as Delcie's in spring 07 (entry 9-02). Fortunately, her problem was diagnosed slightly sooner than Delcie's and she was back to school and basketball much quicker. Both girls' eyes are healthy, but there was a loss of sight scare.

I thought about deleting this – but it shows we are human – and even though we had a successful season and are doing well with life, there are always bumps in the road. Obstacles pop up to be overcome.

Two girls on our team had a bout with not being able to see. This is probably scary for anyone – I would be sick to my heart if it were to happen to my own children. Therefore I spent a lot of time praying for eye health for these two girls – just as I have spent a lot of time praying for the entire team's health.

An appreciation for that health is also part of the prayer.

12-13-07:   (For the 13 December 2007 *Sanders County Ledger*)
Freezer Burn Run   *by Andrew Gideon*

Eleven local students in the Thompson Falls area competed in a race in Frenchtown on Saturday, December 8, 2007. This race was the 2nd Annual University of Montana, HHP Freezer Burn.

Three high school students ran the 13.1 mile half-marathon event. All three are seniors at Thompson Falls High School. Mike Morris placed 1st in his age group (fifth overall) with a stellar time of 1 hour, 23 minutes, and 52 seconds. Jacob Naegeli finished 2nd in the age group (7th overall) with a 1:25:16. Taylor Bradley timed in at 1:40:54.

Eight other youth ran the 5K (3.1 mile) race. Times for these eight are as follows: John Comunetti (23:54), Jack Pruett (24:15), Charles Clark (25:20), Luc Comunetti (26:30), Mariah Naegeli (27:28), Joe Frields (30:44), Payton Frields (30:54), and Logan Naegeli (31:01). Joe, Payton, and Logan are grade school students, Jack is in junior high, and the other four listed are TFHS students.

Coach Naegeli ran her first 5K in 3 years today. Her back has been bad, and she has been working herself back into shape. Also, Future harriers are getting into Hawk Harrier form!

Shane and Ryan took the ACT test for the second time to try to better their previous results.

12-27-07:   From the Sanders County Ledger 12-27-07. "*A plea agreement may be in the works for the Plains man accused in the death of a girl in Thompson Falls last August... Bennett stands accused of vehicular homicide while under the influence after an accident that occurred in Thompson Falls August 13. In that accident, Bennett was allegedly driving a pickup truck at a high rate of speed east on Haley Avenue when the vehicle left the roadway, flipped and crashed into a tree. One female passenger survived the crash with injuries while another passenger was declared dead at the scene... the matter will likely end up in plea agreement...Bennett's charge of vehicular homicide while under the influence, is based on an allegation that he had been huffing canned air before the accident.*"

The reason I include this is that there is nothing to do in TFalls – the only choice is obviously huffing canned air, getting drunk, or driving fast and crazy.

Maybe we can get kids hooked on Ultra-Living: running fast, huffing and puffing oxygen and going into oxygen debt from mile timings, winning state championships, and 4-H, studying, Envirothon, ranching, education, running, running, and more running.

By Andrew Gideon

<u>**2008**</u>

<u>Happy New Year</u>

<u>**2008**</u>

1-1-08: Happy New Year

Monica Conlin wrote an English 2 assignment on 5-06-08. These words are a great way to start a season and a year. Thanks for running your fingers across the keys Monica!

Cross-country is the sport to be in! Some of my favorite memories happen in the fall when we lace up those brand new Brooks. Running takes a lot of mental training, physical training, dedication, and you also make a few friends along the way. I can't think of starting the school year any other way! You may find that this intense sport deserves more props than it usually gets.

On a hot, humid September day, running a grueling three mile race is probably the last obsession on a person's list of to do's. This harsh sport of cross-country is not only physically hard, but it is also a mental strain on one's brain. Pushing yourself through a five-kilometer race is painful, but once you have acquired a tolerance for it, you can begin to build up psychological strength and eventually reach further and further distances. While some may argue (football players) that we cross-country runners couldn't run a hill as fast as them, I think the question here is "Who can run it longest?"

Maintaining a good physique is one of the more important qualities of cross-country. If you are not "in shape" before the season begins, you will be by the state meet! Building your muscles up in your arms, legs, and core, you will find your times improving immensely. Even if you are not in this sport because you like it, it will keep you in top physical condition for your next activity in the winter (especially doing all those push-ups and curl-ups after there has been a profanity uttered!).

If it is one thing you can take away from the x-c season, it is dedication. To be dedicated means to work hard and be devoted to what you do. Running anywhere from 3-8 miles everyday, except for Sundays, can tell you one of two things: either we are crazy people who run with scissors or that we are extremely committed to what we love. You can decide between the two!

Some of my closest friends have been made in the fall when practices start. There are always new and fresh faces I look forward to meeting from the junior high, as well as returning veterans. At meets I see all the friendly competition and the many girls and boys I have met over the course of four years in the sport (seventh-sophomore years). I can always find myself laughing at jokes my teammates make or chatting it up with an acquaintance from another

178

school. I enjoy seeing everyone sharing the same interest as I do and getting to be with them!

Mental toughness, a conditioned body, dedication, and a great way to make new friends; what more can be asked of a sport? People may say that kids in x-c are crazy, whack, or my favorite, "psychotic," but we have something that they don't have: something to work for. I can't wait until the next season when the girl's team pushes to achieve state, like the boys' team this year!

1-3-08: Here is an originally hand-written letter (per directions) for Jacob to Gustavus Adolphus College in St. Peter, Minnesota.

Jacob Naegeli is truly unique and I look forward to hearing of his accomplishments for the next 5, 10, 15, and 20 years. His future is unlimited.

Jacob's talents are exceptionally varied, and he tackles each challenge of life with 100% effort.

Welding, farming, school-work, social skills, Science Olympiad, National Honor Society, 4H, Envirothon, baking, laughing at my jokes, all around good guy, I'm sure I missed a few positive attributes, and he also smiles constantly despite all the effort he puts into every aspect of life...the list of his abilities is far-reaching. Looking at all he does, one would initially think it impossible to be successful in all his endeavors; however, he thrives in activities and shows tremendous integrity and enthusiasm.

Jacob is definitely an original person with great leadership potential, as demonstrated by success in the aforementioned capabilities listed above. He is also well-schooled in the 3R's of a true Montana education: reading, ranching, and running.

Gustavus Adolphus College would be a better place with Jacob Naegeli as a student.   *Andrew Gideon*

I also sent in another letter (different structure) to Earlham College, Richmond, Indiana – in a more "formal" constitution.

Just look at the school names: Earlham College and Gustavus Adolphus.....is this your typical teenager?   Jacob Naegeli is one of a kind (unique) – we need more Jacob's in the world.

1-4-08:   I finished with 2007.4 running miles in 2007. The .4 stands for my two completed 26.2 mile marathons. It is a quick reminder when I look back on my running charts that two marathons were completed during the year.

There is a song, a current favorite, "2000 Miles" (*The Pretenders*) that my wife burned onto a CD and onto my IPOD shuffle.

I remember completing my 2000th mile December 27th, 2007. It was 15 degrees out with too much snow on the ground. The roads near Placid Lake, Montana, were partially plowed, but it was slick and tough running. Mile 2 of my 3 mile jog finished the 2000th mile. It was snowing; a good feeling of accomplishment, as well as respect for being physically healthy (health = blessing), flooded my brain. I stopped and said *Thank You* to God for all my 2007 blessings. The cross country team and state championship came to mind.

By Andrew Gideon

Every step of the way my wife was with me on this run; every step of the way she has been a hero in my life with running, work, and kids.

Derek Naegeli buried this old man by running 2367 miles. His goal for 2008 is to run every day (minimum of 10 minutes) of the year.

We are all given 24 hours per day. Time demands for me included (1) two energetic boys aged 3 and 1, (2) the overtime I put into my teaching, (3) the amount of energy and research that I have done with XC (hint – you are reading this book, and hint – State Champions), (4) paying attention to financial investments, and (5) reading the Bible.

One might wonder how I had time to dedicate 40 miles per week to running. I don't waste time on MySpace or playing computer games. I don't spend time in bars. I find ways to be productive. Students like Jacob (read previous entry) energize me and help me learn to put energy into proper areas in life. A high percentage of my running is in the two hours before the family wakes up in the morning.

1-7-08: written by Shane about the New Year's Day Run (1-1-08).

If you haven't looked at a calendar lately, it's a new year. Also, if you didn't pay attention, there was a local race on that day. The New Years Race is a growing tradition, especially among high school students.

When the 9th annual race was about to go off, nineteen students and three teachers could be seen among the throng. 12 minutes and 2 seconds later, Mr. Wheeler finished the 2K race. 6 minutes and 26 seconds later, Shane Donaldson was the first to complete the 5K race (first place among all entrants in 18:28). Classmates Jacob Naegeli and Mike Morris, who earned second and fourth, respectively, finished the race soon after. Mr. Gideon was the only high school teacher to complete the 5K. He did so in 20:41.

The first high school female student to finish the 3.125-mile race was Beca Gunderson. She crossed the line 25 minutes, 3 seconds after the gun went off. Jeffreyanne Parker was the second girl and Mariah Naegeli the third to finish.

If one were to break down the high school runners by winter sports, the results would stand as following; Two Cheerleaders, Three Girls Basketball Players, Three Wrestlers, One Boys Basketball Player, and numerous people who don't participate in any school related winter sports. Fourteen of twenty possible cross country runners competed.

1-8-08: The Yearbook staff pondered the following: "Our theme this year is *Everything You Never Expected*. What unexpected things happened during your lifetime? Answers could come from life events, your career, the school, politics, technology or anything you want."

My response is/was as follows –
I never expected to see *"Life is a Miracle"* the way I have through my children. Jaxon was born 9-16-04, while Kaden was born 6-9-06.

Jaxon's birth and the development in the womb are miracles. We take for granted our hearing, eyesight, muscles, tendons, heart, spleen, blood flow, brain, as well as physical, mental, and spiritual dimensions of life. God blesses us all in mysterious ways.

With Kaden, life itself became a miracle – delivered in the back of a GMC Sierra extended cab pickup at 90 mph, 20 miles from Missoula, near Johnsrud Park – 3 months early – he weighed only 2 lbs 6.5 oz – and came out with the cord wrapped around his neck – left foot first - too blue for black words on white paper. Each day doctors told of horrible possibilities while Kaden struggled to breathe. Many people prayed for Kaden, and today he is alive and well and shows the human spirit, i.e. life is a miracle.

I didn't expect to deliver both of my children, but their daily development brings unexpected joy to my heart.

<u>1-11-08 (Friday)</u>: The Montana Coaches Association and the Montana High School Association announced the coaches of the year for fall sports. Sarah Naegeli of Thompson Falls won the Class B Boys Cross Country Coach of the Year Award. Congratulations. Yeah!!!!!!!!!!!!!!

<u>1-14-08</u>: A TFHS student was carted off by ambulance Friday at 12:45 PM. At lunch some pills were ingested and the student went into convulsions. Another girl was hauled off in handcuffs as part of the ordeal. The boy and girl were not in cross country - they should have learned to run!!! Running can cure a lot of ills - by adding a lot of wills; running does not make a person perfect, but it does force better habits.

<u>1-17-08</u>: Happy 40th Birthday to Mr. Coach Gideon. This moves me to the Master's category for racing and youngest in age brackets (40-44, 40-49). Nice!

My best present of all was the honor of running with Ryan. Last year on my birthday I ran with Jacob and Shane. Today, while running with Ryan, he told me the Air Force Academy accepted him.

Yes!!!!!!! On 11/2/07 I filled out an online evaluation for him – hearing him appointed to the Air Force were great words to hear.

And for an encore birthday present, I refereed some basketball. The crowd did not always have pleasant words for me to hear.

So I shall remember "accepted to the Air Force." Nice!

<u>1-26-08</u>: Jacob played the Star-Spangled Banner on the accordion before the girl's basketball home game today. He has three accordions.

Accordions remind me technology has passed me by. For example, the newest type of sticky notes folds like an accordion. What is up with that? New sticky note technology confuses me; I spend time figuring out which side is sticky and which way to write. I'm old fashioned, so the old style was just fine.

Maybe Jacob can teach my sons to play the accordion.

<u>1-28-08</u>: **Cross Country team wins Army National Guard Academic All Team Award** *By Ryan Sol* (appeared in the 2-07-08 *Sanders County Ledger*)

181

By Andrew Gideon

Congratulations to the Cross Country team, who, even three months after the season, are still receiving awards. In a competition honoring the top five average GPA's of Montana B cross country teams, the Thompson Falls' boys and girls' teams took an impressive 3rd and 4th places, respectively. The girls' varsity runners averaged a 3.494 GPA, and the guys averaged a 3.333. Although not quite as exciting as the state championship, this award is still extremely gratifying, as it shows how well-rounded our student-athletes are.

Valley Christian, with a combined 3.800 GPA, led the Class B boys programs. Whitehall led the girls with an impressive 3.900 team GPA.

Information from the Montana High School Association at mhsa.org.

2-05-08 (Super Tuesday):   Ron Paul for President.

"Ron Paul stands for limited constitutional government, low taxes, free markets, and a return to sound monetary policies." (ronpaul2008.com/issues)

Ron Paul won the Sanders County Montana Republican caucus vote today; Paul also won the Missoula County vote; Missoula is home of the University of Montana.

"Ron Paul for President" signs are plastered on house windows and other areas in our lovely metropolis. Ron Paul wants the United States to get back to the constitution. Despite winning Sanders County, little hope exists for Dr. Paul as the next US President.

Yes, let's get back to the constitution. Thomas Jefferson signed it – he owned slaves (despite "all men are created equal."). Only white property owners could vote at that time. Women could not vote.

This entry gives a little insight to rural Montana. Please, come and drink our arsenic-laced water and think like us; together we could change the world.

Kurt Vonnegut once said, *"There is a tragic flaw in our precious constitution, and I don't know what can be done to fix it. This is it: only nut cases want to be President."*

2-07-08 (Thursday): Eight of our XC crew played Ultimate Frisbee in heavy Montana snow after school. They played on the football field – stepping on the precious football team's grass.

I laughed when I also saw the footprints on the football concession stand roof – the remains of a hard fought snowball fight.

What – that's dangerous – somebody could fall off the roof and get hurt. Stop the madness. Some teacher report these kids. I'm writing my report now.

It's not Ultimate Frisbee until you play with scissors too.

Where was this snow in August when Montana was burning down?

2-09-08: **Scrumpy Jack Scramble** *by Jacob Naegeli (Sanders County Ledger)*

Last Saturday, February 9, the third annual Scrumpy Jack Scramble was held in Missoula. The scramble is a two by two mile relay. Teams compete in three separate categories, male/male, male/female, or female/female.

Last years defending champion M/F team, Shane Donaldson and Beca Gunderson, strived to defend their title, but fell to third this year after intense competition. Following them closely were four other teams from Thompson Falls. In fourth were Jacob Naegeli and Jeffreyanne Parker, fifth Ryan Sol and Mariah Naegeli, and sixth Andrew and Deborah Gideon. Cody White also competed in the M/M division with Thadd LeClair from Plains. Times for all were not record breakers, but it was a great break from monotonous winter mileage. It was also a good sign that our runners are still healthy enough to run even as various strains of the flu and colds sweep the school.

After this race, Beca and JP were driven to Plains to compete in their last regular season basketball game. Beca would play JV and Varsity, while JP would step onto the JV court.

What is wrong with these kids – it is INCONCEIVABLE they run and play basketball in one day. Haven't they heard of video games?

Beca wrote the following in May, but it fits here due to double duty for these two harriers today: *During basketball season, JP and I constantly talked about how the Lady hawk cross-country team is going to do at state in 2008. Our main goal is to trophy. There is some very tough competition coming from the eastern side of the state again, but we are also very tough competition. Last year the boys placed fourth, then came back and won state. We have the potential to do that as well. With the exception of Amanda Wood, we are all back for next season and stronger than ever. I think that our toughest challenge will be believing in ourselves, so mental strength is going to be very important throughout next season. We are going to do awesome.*

2-10-08: Matt finished his wrestling career yesterday in Billings. His season record was 31-11 with 28 pins. On Friday, he won both of his matches at State; unfortunately, Saturday he went 0-3, good enough for a sixth place finish. His best three years earned him a second, fourth, and sixth place individual finish.

Team Thompson Falls placed 11th in the state for wrestling.

Matt was extremely dedicated, including running a 1.6 mile loop everyday at lunch.

Today I am sure he is enjoying as much food as he wants!

I donated $1.26 (26 miles in a marathon) per pin to the wrestling program; this pledge was taken at the season's beginning; this cost me $35.28.

Nice work Matt – and good grades too!

Maybe he should spend more time on MySpace.com.

A John Hamilton article (*Sanders County Ledger* 1-14-08 issue).

Matt Hojem arrived in Thompson Falls in the fall of '05 after his father Randy was named District Ranger for the Plains/Thompson Falls office of the US Forest Service.

Relatively small and light for his age, Matt had not had the chance to wrestle competitively growing up in Wrangell, Alaska, where his father worked

By Andrew Gideon

as a forester and his mother Kathee as a school teacher, but he was quickly identified as a possible wrestler by members of the Blue Hawk team.

When winter arrived during his freshman year, wrestling came knocking and soon became a major part of his young life.

"The seniors on the team talked me into it; they needed some guys in the lighter weights," Matt said. "Pretty soon I was starting to like it. Over time it became a passion of mine."

Hojem went on to win his first divisional championship that winter at 105 pounds.

Holding that weight his sophomore season, Hojem rocked the Metra after winning his second straight Western B-C individual title, advancing all the way to the championship match before falling by a very slim margin in the title bout.

A casual grappler at first, Hojem became even more obsessed with wrestling after that, and working his rear end off, again maintained his weight at 105 and won second place in the division his junior year, followed by a fourth place medal at state.

Taking his ardor for grappling to an even higher level this past season, Matt went as far as to convert a room in his family home into his own personal wrestling room, using old mattresses to line the floor and lower walls, inviting teammates over for off-season workouts.

Running cross country to stay in shape and lifting weights and working out like a madman in the off season, Hojem started practice his senior year at 119 pounds.

Though he had a few ups and downs along the way, Matt went 31-11 this past season to finish his career with a fine 92-58 career record, and won a sixth place medal at State.

Hojem is grateful for the chance wrestling has given him, and the friends and mentors he has gained along the way.

"I want to thank coaches Cline and Allen especially," he said. "They liked to give me a bad time some but I was sure glad they were there to coach me."

And he thanked his teammates. "I want to give a special thanks to Jason (Shaw), Tate (Cavill) and John (Garrison) for being such great teammates this season," Matt said. "John sure had a good tournament last week and Tate, wow, what can you say about him?

"His story is really remarkable," he continued. "Coming back from that injury like he did and being able to compete at the level he did. It was just phenomenal what he was able to do this winter." (Author note – Tate received a spleen injury in the last football game of the season (11-3-07). He was airlifted to a hospital – his life was in limbo for a little while as he received emergency surgery; his wrestling career appeared over. Mercifully, he started competing ½ to 2/3 way through the season.)

Matt says he is probably done with wrestling competitively, but that he plans to take a more one-on-one approach while helping teach and coach Little Guy wrestling the next few months, perhaps hoping to give back to the sport that gave him so much.

But Hojem still hasn't let go of last week's State B-C either, those were matches that he thought he should have, at least could have won.

"I tried stoking' it," he said, "but couldn't quite get there."

To the contraire Matt, and I think anyone reading this will agree – you more than "got there" with the sport of wrestling... and a confident, poised young man where there once stood a young, unsure boy is the end result.

2-14-08: *Sanders County Ledger* article in the 2-14-08 edition

Ryan Sol –Accepted to U.S. Air Force Academy   *by Sandra Gubel*

Ryan Sol is headed into the wild blue yonder. The Thompson Falls High School senior has been accepted at the U.S. Air Force Academy in Colorado Springs, Colo.

The son of Julie and Scott Sol of Thompson Falls, Ryan heard the exciting news early this month. The opportunity for a full ride education and numerous career and military options became available after several months of investigating the option, and pursuing a lengthy application process.

"It was a lengthy process, but it wasn't overwhelming. We just worked on one thing at a time," he explained.

Ryan looks back on the process now and figures it was in junior high that he first remembers his grandfather, Joe Sol, a retired Montana Highway Patrol officer and Army veteran, say that going to the Air Force Academy "was a really good place to go."

While investigating college options and thinking about each of the military academies, Ryan looked at the areas of study that each had to offer, and decided he liked the Air Force's best, since being a commercial airline pilot in the future has peaked his interest.

Choosing the Air Force Academy also had another plus, he admitted. It's also the only one in the western U.S., which makes is somewhat close to home. A visit he made there in November sealed the deal–his choice of places to apply to. "It fit with what I want to do," Ryan said.

Between November and early February, Ryan, with the firm support of his mother Julie, went through each of the steps necessary to apply. He passed a physical fitness test administered by athletic coordinator Rick Dieterich. His application included his grades–a solid grade point average of 3.95; his ACT and SAT test scores; and his many extracurricular activities.

In addition to four years of cross-country and three years of track, Ryan has participated in one year of golf and three years of basketball. He's been on the National Honor Society three years, student council for four years, Envirothon team for four years, and Science Olympiad for four years.

The process also included going for an interview in Bozeman with Rep.

185

By Andrew Gideon

Denny Rehberg, but unfortunately, the Congressman didn't recommend him from amongst the large number of applicants lined up awaiting recommendations for all four military academies. Instead, both Senators Jon Tester and Max Baucus both saw his full application, and Sen. Tester made the recommendation.

Once Ryan had decided he wanted to pursue the Air Force Academy, he checked out the various career options. "I'd really like to be a pilot," he said, although he's not ruling anything out. About 60 percent of those who go to the academy pursue an aviation-related career, as a pilot or aeronautical engineer, or a field related to it. Some also pursue medical and other areas, Ryan said.

When Ryan enters the academy, his first year will include general courses, and in his sophomore he'll be asked to declare a major. He expects a very challenging academic environment. Fortunately, the academy offers lots of support, Ryan said.

After receiving what amounts to five years of college coursework in four years, Ryan will have a Bachelor of Science degree and will commission in the Air Force as a second lieutenant. He'll then have a five year commitment to the Air Force. After that, there are three more years where he could be called back if necessary.

He could begin a career as a commercial pilot if he wants. Or, he could decide after the five years, to remain in the Air Force.

No one in his family has been in the Air Force, although both his grandfathers served our country in the Army, Ryan said. He will be the first to chart this particular course.

Fortunately, all the hard work Ryan has done as a young man, particularly as a high school student, has paid off. And now, the sky's the limit.

My 9-09 entry included a letter written to Max Baucus. I also wrote one to Denny Rehberg. Apparently my writing and letters weren't good enough for Baucus or Rehberg to make the Ryan Sol recommendation to the Air Force.

We have to find who wrote a letter to Jon Tester – that person can write!

2-29-08: *Bird's Eye View* article (TFHS school paper), 2-29 edition. Yes, of course we had a leap year edition!

The first annual "Van broke down" half marathon
By Ryan Sol

On Saturday of last weekend, an inaugural race took place right here in Thompson Falls. For the first annual running of what was later dubbed the "Van broke down" half marathon, there was a quaint five runners who ran the race. Although this doesn't quite compare to the 625 runners that the Missoula Half Marathon brought in last July for its inaugural race, those who participated were very content with the small size.

The five runners who began the race were Jacob Naegeli, Mike Morris, Ryan Sol, Andrew Gideon and Cody White. However, only four finished, as Cody snuck off early to go eat an omelet.

There wasn't a single incident of death or heat stroke, unlike the Chicago marathon held in October, 2007, which resulted in one death and 49 runners taken to the hospital because of heat-related ailments.

The only notable incident was a small case of cold hands, due to two of the runners forgetting to wear gloves over the 14 mile course. These foolish individuals were none other than Mike Morris and Cody White. Both were seen utilizing such hand-warming techniques as the "armpit clamp" and the "breath-warmer."

However, none of this would have been possible if the Naegeli van hadn't had a faulty fuel pump that prevented the van from starting again once we had made it as far as the high school parking lot. The lack of a running vehicle or enough time to make it to Seeley Lake before the Snow Joke Half Marathon began left us with no choice but to cancel our previous plans and go with plan B, our own race. After all, who needs the crowded starting lines, annoying bib numbers, and worthless door prizes? The only thing really needed to have a "fun run" is a few companions and an open road. So, let's hope this is only the beginning of many "Van broke down" half marathons to come.

3-01-08: TFHS school year in review - there are approximately 46 teams in Class B in Montana.

Boys XC 1st at State, 3rd place Academic All-Team

Girls XC 4th at State, 4th place Academic All-Team

Girl's volleyball #13-16 at State,

Football #5-8 at State

Wrestling 11th place at State,

Boys basketball 9th place (8 make state, TFHS → only team to lose in a challenge game),

Girls basketball 25th-28th place at State (7th at 1 of 4 Divisionals)

Spring sports are track, golf, and girl's softball.

Looking at these sports, several ideas came to mind. Most thoughts (and even some writing) were edited out with running scissors. Here is what made the cut - in cross country, every harrier HAS TO WORK AND RUN. An athlete cannot hide behind the superstar or the team.

The great thing about XC is that times are evident for each athlete. Each runner is responsible for individual results. A supportive team helps motivate for improved performances, but it comes down to the individual.

Cross country is a hard sport – some individuals can handle the pain and go out – others play team sports where a small percentage of athletes are on the field at one time (examples: football 11 athletes are on the field at one time, while 40 are on the sidelines – basketball 5 on, 7 on the bench).

By Andrew Gideon

3-16 (Sunday): The black cloud of doom dissipated at 2:31 PM and 35 seconds.

Prom is over; cleanup just ended. Sunday afternoon, thank you sunshine. I can finally enjoy peace from the torture of being a junior class advisor.

Prom is a nightmare. I hated it when I was a kid, and now I hate it as an adult. Luckily I have matured – I hate it for different reasons now!

Mile 47 of a 50 mile Ultra-Marathon taught me to value Medical Marijuana; being a Prom advisor teaches me the same thing. NO, I don't smoke; It's an attempt at humor people.

Our original "Mardi Gras" theme was thrown out because of parental complaints. "Midnight Masquerade," with the same exact decorations as "Mardi Gras" had, was the theme.

What are we teaching kids with this party, dance, loud music, and prom premise? Spend hundreds of dollars on outfits/clothes, dinner, as well as mental thought stressing out over dates and dating and relationships – all to what.... Enjoy?? 4 hours from 9 PM to 1 AM.

Think about it - $100 dress, $50 dinner, $100 suit - $250 – at ten dollars per hour, someone would have to work 25 hours just to enjoy four hours.

We should be teaching the opposite. For example, part of the reason I run ½ hour daily on average is to enjoy the other 23 ½ hours. This works in nicely with an Asics advertisement.

Asics = sound mind and sound body (from Latin "**Anima Sana In Corpore Sano.**" (Information from any Asics apparel.) The specific advertisement I saw in *Runner's World* reads (sound body) x (sound mind) x (type A) = Type B.

In other words, exercise can turn a Type A personality (frenzied, high stress) into a Type B personality (more relaxed, easier paced). Plus, a person shows an appreciation for the blessing of health by using it in a positive way. Our society needs more running, not more Prozac.

How can prom's mental stress be calculated? For prom, think of all the kids (future adults) stressed out by relationships – should I hold her hand, should I ask her to dance, how close should I dance (sure, maybe this doesn't bother some kids like it used to!), etc – teenage angst in its finest form. By putting on proms, we teach kids to value that stress. Mental stress about relationships that will eventually take care of themselves is a big waste of time and energy.

Several girls said, "I have to starve myself (not eat all day) to fit into my prom dress." Yes, this is a healthy concept to enforce to our society. Just to understand, I didn't eat so I could fit into my suit that I wore to chaperone.

And then. . . high school students become adults and carry this over to funerals, I mean, weddings. We must, we must spend, spend, spend, and starve, starve, starve to look good because it is all about appearances, and have an absolutely perfect wedding, or else, o my gosh, I just might die, and I will cry, and my wedding will be ruined.

Shouldn't we teach that marriage – all 40 or 70 years of it - is of much more value than a wedding – a one day wedding? Too much emphasis is placed on big productions in our society.

I can't tell you how much class time was wasted with class meetings for organizing prom, how much money was spent on decorations that were torn down and thrown away (good old American waste). Yes, I was the junior class advisor (one of three). However, I am sure, with my attitude, that I was the worst of the three!!!! I did help out as needed; I did my job. Kak.

Another example of what we should be teaching – invest \$1000 in a stock or fund that will pay a dividend for life. One choice will lead to gains for the next 40-70 years as opposed to wasting / spending money on the must needed electronic accessory / toy, car / truck, or clothing.

I challenged the class of 2008 last year with the following. You spend \$40 per month on a cell phone, while I will purchase \$40 per month of Verizon stock. Currently I own 18 shares of VZ, while some people have spent at least \$600 (\$40 * 15). VZ is trading at \$34.02 as of 3-17-08, 11:36 am MST = \$612.36. The difference is not \$600, the difference is \$660 +\$612.36 + dividends earned + potential for stock price increase + future dividends.

My grading for school follows this theme. I give daily grades and challenge each person to work each day. I don't give one big test (one big prom, one big graduation, one big wedding, etc) to see whether progress has been made. Life is a daily battle, so we need to run daily. Yes, life has its big tests, but, for the most part, life is about competing on a smaller scale day to day. Each bit of daily exercise will be of more value than one longer workout. Running five days a week times five miles is better than one day a week at 25 miles.

Running and appreciating one's health is what our Hawk Harriers are all about; we set a future of better health and lower medical bills.

Game, Set, and Match – tennis terms to say that Prom is over, and that my point is made.

However, on the other hand, prom is not all bad.

Delcie, for the 2nd year in a row, made her own prom dress. This shows another creative side of her. Delcie, XC harrier, is to be complimented!

Bryant, for the 2nd consecutive year, welded a sculpture that became a prom decoration. Last year his upside-down octopus creature held balloons; this year two palm trees were made from recycled cans. Bryant, XC harrier! Nice!

RT wore an orange suit with an orange top hat. You da man RT, XC runner!

I suggested to Shane, Jacob, Ryan, Beca, and Delcie that we run a mile in our suits and dresses. The excitement I had for this idea did not flow to the rest of the crew, although they could have been one of the few high school students to ever run in suits and dresses at a prom. Where is their love of running?

Mariah, Cody, and Mike B all watched a movie at the Naegeli house. Where is their love of social customs?

By Andrew Gideon

3-17-08:   Mariah's Storm (famous race horse) fractured a bone and recovered. Our Mariah and other runners have had knee pain and somehow recover; Mariah is still working on keeping her knee healthy. Today at lunch we talked about several different strides. I have read that Elite African runners change strides, three different styles, every 200 meters or so in a marathon to help the body move more efficiently.

Mariah worked on this during her track workout and run. She felt good and Monica helped her by pointing out that her right foot was striking the ground harder than the left foot.

Runners simply don't whine as much as the average high school student.

3-18-08:   Gustavus Adolphus and money

Jacob visited Gustavus Adolphus College in Minnesota in February. The latest is that his charges will be $39,000/year for room/board/tuition/books, etc. Jacob currently has scholarship and aide for $33,000 of that. Most of that is renewable, so he is looking at $30,000 of debt or so by the time he finishes college. He is still trying for more scholarships.

If he decides to attend Earlham College in Indiana, his yearly charge would be $49,000. His aide would be approximately $26,000 per year. So he would owe $23,000 x 4 years.

3-26-08: Here is yet another letter written by this author/coach/teacher.

To: Body by Milk, SAMMY 2008

RE: Jacob Naegeli, one of the 500 semi-finalists

Jacob Naegeli has been selected as one of the 500 semi-finalists for the 2008 Scholar Athlete Milk Mustache of the Year (SAMMY) Awards.

Jacob Naegeli competed in cross country in the fall of 2007. Individually, he placed third in Montana Class B for the second straight year. Jacob was instrumental in helping his team win the State Championship for Montana Class B. The Thompson Falls Blue Hawks are State Champions because of Jacob's individual effort and his leadership. His personal best for the 3 mile cross country course is 16:02; this places him third all-time for Thompson Falls High School Cross Country. Jacob was one of the captains of the team.

Jacob is also competing for our track team. He has a main goal to establish the new school record in the 1600 meter run during this season. As of 3-26-08, Wednesday, we have not had any track meets. His personal best 1600 meter run is 4 minutes, 37 seconds. He has been elected a captain of the track team by his teammates.

Jacob Naegeli is deserving of the 2008 SAMMY Award.

Several weeks after writing this, I realized I didn't include that Jacob raises goats, cows, and chickens for their milk. He knows how to ranch and brand cows and squirrels – the *Body by Milk* judges needed this information – bad writer!

<u>3-28-08</u>:   Track cancellation.   Welcome to Montana – our 1st track meet tomorrow in Columbia Falls was cancelled due to snow/cold. No records will be broken, no laps run, and the vaulting poles will be silenced.

<u>4-4-08</u>:   *Missoulian* article - ***UGF cross country signs T. Falls' Donaldson***
GREAT FALLS (AP) - Thompson Falls distance runner Shane Donaldson has signed a letter of intent to join the cross country and track teams at the University of Great Falls.

Donaldson is a four-time all-state performer in cross country. He placed second at the State B championships as a junior and senior, with times of 15 minutes, 57 seconds and 16:44. Thompson Falls won the state meet in 2007.

Also last fall, Donaldson finished 10th overall at the Mountain West Classic cross country meetin Missoula with a time of 15:45.

UGF cross country and track coach Jim Brewer announced Donaldson's signing on Thursday.

Shane visited the College of Great Falls on March 24 and 25.   Shane asked for a letter of recommendation for the school on March 27. I am thankful he signed to go to a college. YeHaw, no more letters to write for Shane!!!!!

We had our first official track meet Thursday 4-3-08 in Missoula.

One of our harriers, who will remain nameless, was suspended 10 days for being at a party where alcohol was present. Therefore, she did not compete in our first meet of the year. Our perfect society and world crumbles. Boo Harrier.

Shane ran the 3200 and engaged in conversation most of the race with his arch rival from Darby. Shane took second to Paul Abrahamsen from Darby, just as he did in the State Championship last fall. 1.98 seconds separated him from first place. Maybe if he would have talked about his scholarship less and put his energy into running, then he might have won. Maybe next time Shane. Shane, quit talking, quit eating, time to run.

<u>4-12-08</u> Bigfork Track Meet

We met up with a former teammate. BM was the fastest freshman Class B boy at the State Cross Country Meet and finished 26th overall (our # 5 runner), transferred to Cut Bank. Cut Bank was at the same track meet as us today.

I am happy that two of our 800 runners beat him today. Mike Morris finished first in 2:08.56, Steve Block ran 2:09.42, and Bryce finished in 2:21. He was overheard saying that "he just dogged it." I asked him if he ever dogged it in TFHS XC; he assured me "never."

I spent some quality time discussing workouts with Mike Reynolds, the long-time Cut Bank coach. He won state in Girls Class B XC in 2006, yet we were both discussing ways to improve workouts and strategy. Mr. Reynolds has also won coach of the year awards and State B boys XC in 1993, as well as another State B Girls Title in 2001. Plus he coaches track and has been very successful in that for over a quarter of a century.

I guess we just don't know how to rest on our laurels.

191

Brian Schenavar, a pole vaulter I am currently coaching, moved his class B best vault to 14-0 today in this meet.

A bible quote from church yesterday, *"Set your minds on things above, not on earthly things."* That's why I like pole vault – setting the minds on things above, the sky is the limit, etc.

And in running, Mr. Reynolds continues to keep climbing that mountain, even though he has reached the top multiple times.

4-15-08 Further evidence of running's benefit

I sent out letters to parents discussing privacy concerns with <u>Harrier Hawks Fly High</u>. Respect for student privacy and information is important, so parental signatures, and opinions, were needed. I asked for comments, input, questions, and concerns. Here is a letter from Holly Hedley, Cody's mom.

"Wow! What a great idea. Thank you for investing your time on it. I couldn't be prouder of Cody's attitude, grades, physical bearing, and mental outlook since he started high school last year. Is it ironic that's when he started running? His grades keep improving, his physical stamina and get-up-and-go is usually in high gear. He's even keeping his room clean (ok, relatively). Argh, what have you done with my son?! He's the best Cody I've ever seen and you can tell he feels good about himself. That is priceless."

Now seems like a great time to write Cody's profile. Granted, Cody was given his information sheet back in October, but the middle of April is a good time to finally get it in. Hmmm, April 15, I wonder if Cody will procrastinate on his taxes until April 15 every year.

Benjamin Dakota White was born on 7-16-92. His due date might have been the 4th of July, but he was late, just like many of his assignments. That's not quite accurate, but it was an attempt at humor – Cody has a 3.714 overall GPA.

Cody is a team leader next season with the loss of all of our seniors (has beens). His GPA will help our harriers strive for the Academic All-Team award.

He stands 5'5" and weighs 142 pounds. Last week he pole vaulted 8 feet for a new personal record. His other bests (as a sophomore) include a 5:35 mile, a 12:47 3200, and a 21:35 cross country three mile. The distance times aren't that impressive, but Cody really only started running last summer. He came to a few summer workouts, got turned on by the endorphins, the challenge, the teammates, or something else. We shall see what these numbers look like in two years. Potential! He does have goals for running: *"lower my times! And coming home with another state title would be nice, too."*

Future plans include *"go to college, get married, and have 3 kids while directing movies."* His favorite movie is <u>Edward Scissorhands,</u> and his favorite celebrity is Harrison Ford. Maybe Cody can make a movie out of our XC team and star Harrison Ford as Mr. Gideon. My son Jaxon can star as Cody. His goals for life include *"marry the beautiful girl of my dreams, become rich, and have 3 kids – Ben, Abby, and Justin."*

Career possibilities are Film Editing or Architectural Design. Schools he thinks about include the U of Montana and the U of Oregon. His favorite food is cheeseburgers, and his best hobby is playing the guitar. Maybe he can do some guitar picking at college; otherwise his most liked food will become Top Ramen.

He has southern roots, but his attitude has been heading north. Holly Hedley (the letter writer above) was born in Mississippi, while Rob White, father, was born in Florida. Robby, his brother, is 16 and also a sophomore. However, they were born 1 year, 1 month, and 15 days apart. Robby is older. Two twin brothers are Curt and Colton, ages 7, and these twins both have autism, so that is another daily obstacle in life for this family. Cody's "real" father was killed in the towers of New York on 9-11. It's a small world.

Cody has advice; he is full of advice. In fact, he never shuts up giving advice! Okay younger students, listen up, *"study hard and go out for all kinds of sports."* Future runners need to *"be active, stay focused, drink lots of water."*

If Cody were to win $100,000,000, then he would *"give 90% to various charities, give 5% to my family, put 2.5 % of it in bank accounts for my kids to go to college, and blow the rest on various stuff nobody needs."*

Enough bribes (3rd quarter student of the quarter award for English 2, 7th period) have landed this author in the role of favorite coach/teacher. Maybe he just wants to improve his pole vault so he doesn't hurt himself. His least favorite workout is the Mule Pasture loop (2 miles of beautiful trails) – my favorite route.

Cody's favorite book is *Ice Reich* by William Dietrich. He enjoys the Wheel of Fortune and workouts with Bryce and Mike when they were allowed to make up their own routes.

Back in October, Cody, when this was due, Delcie wrote, *"very competitive. Loyal."*

4-15-08 Tax day deadline again

Maybe we are teaching kids to be true Americans. Today is the tax mailing deadline. Forms for runner profiles were due in October for this book. Not only did Cody turn in his form late, but Kyle did as well.

Oh well, last minute Americans, here is another profile: Kyle.

Kyle Breithaupt was born 11-2-91. Surely he wasn't 6'3" at birth like he is now.

He did use his 170 pound frame to run a PR of 18:54 this season at our home meet. Kyle dreams big – he has a goal of a 15:30. Hopefully he is running in the off-season as he did not joint track. It is hard to be a 15:30 XC three mile runner without putting in the mileage.

Kyle has future plans of running heavy equipment – and attending Cat Training school or Northwestern College. His life goals are to be a heavy equipment operator and equipment trainer. He works on ranches during the year in Philipsburg and the Yaak (near Troy, MT).

By Andrew Gideon

Advice to future runners and younger students is limited – "do your best" and "work hard." Kyle indeed worked hard during cross country as he improved from 252 miles during the 2006 season to 288 miles for the 2007 season. Next year he will be one of our top returning harriers, so hopefully summer mileage is on his to due list.

Kurt and Paula are his parents, and Keith, age 34, is an older sibling.

If he were to win $100,000,000, a big ranch would be purchased so that he could turn it into a money making ranch.

Kyle's least favorite workouts are the Tuesday Trials of Miles, while the shorter three mile days are his favorite. For the third paragraph out of seven in this profile, I hope Kyle learns to love punishing his body if he wants to lead us to success next year and achieve the lofty goal of 15:30. I would love to see this!

Favorites: Movie (*American Pie Beta House*), Food (Pizza), Hobby (Wood Working), Book (Harry Potter books), Class (Building Construction), Sport (XC), Teacher (Kegel), and Coach (Naegeli).

Based on his answers, working with wood, construction, and heavy equipment are Kyle's choices for happiness. I would gladly have him work on my house or with anything I needed with heavy construction. He has great aptitude for that; let's not talk about English!

Note added 5-13-08 ➔ Kyle B ran the mile in PE in 6:12. There is some running in Kyle's future if he desires a 15:30.

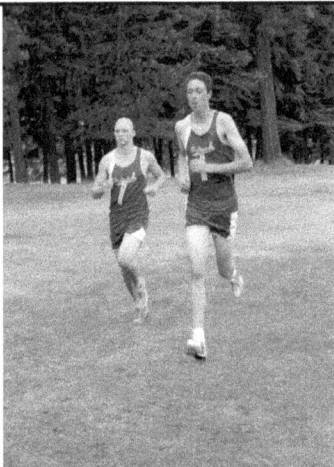

RT (bald) and Kyle B

Cody White, Homecoming

4-16-08

Coach Naegeli informed me that Coach Reall retired today. Bob called her and said last season took its toll; he is going out on top. Coach Bob volunteered his time for 10 years, all during his first retirement~!

So, we will be down to two coaches next season. Bob will be missed. I learned a lot from him and his 35 years of experience. The athletes appreciated his presence as well.

Beca G wrote the following, *"For all the years I've been a runner on our team, Bob has always been coaching us, along with Sarah, and later, Gideon. His favorite expression of 'Arms! ARMS!' is never far from our ears. However, I just found out that sadly, Bob won't be our coach next year. When our little group of girls first heard this news, we were crushed. What?! No Bob? No more 'back in Ohio . . . ' stories? No more meticulously-kept stats? No more perfectly-temped (temperature) ice baths? I suppose some of these things will still go on, but I want Bob to know that we are sincerely going to miss him and all the effort he puts into us and the team. I love the encouragement he gives, and I know when he tells me I'm doing something right, that I can take pride in that, because he tells it like it is."*

4-22-08 Top Ten Meet   **Best in the West**   By Brian Schenavar

Article for *the Bird's Eye View (TFHS school paper)*

Seven athletes from out Thompson Falls Track program went to represent our school at the 10th annual Russ Pilcher top ten meet on Tuesday April 22, 2008. Around 300 top athletes from approximately 40 western Montana schools performed at this selective meet.

Shane Donaldson received the nomination in not just one event but two events, the 1600 and the 3200, where he ran season bests in both events.

Beca Gunderson made it in the 1600 and posted her best season time.

Mike Morris ran a personal best by four seconds (2:04) in the 800 which gives him one of the best "B" marks in the state.

Rheanna Padden tossed the javelin 113' and took seventh place. The top eight places were separated by only 12 feet.

JF also threw the javelin and took third place with a toss of 176' 3".

JS earned fifth place with a heave of 49'9" in the shot put.

Brian Schenavar cleared 14'6" to win the pole vault.

All in all it was a very good showing for Thompson Falls High School.

Brian is a pole vaulter I am coaching. We are going for first place at State and a new Class B record. (The current one is 14-9.25.)

A real story: *Fuddruckers.* All 7 of our athletes ordered pounders.

Shane Donaldson did not defend his crown of being the first finisher – our shot put specialist beat him. Shane has lost his edge.

4-28-08 Monday, Oh, to be a Kenyan

On Sunday I ran 15 miles with three hard. This year I am using more hard/tempo stints into my long runs. Hopefully this will be the key to a more successful Missoula marathon on July 13. Dream: My name and 2:59.99 or less.

On Monday I ran 6 miles before school, 3 at lunch (with 1200, 800, 400 hard), and 3 more after school (same intervals) for a total of 12 on the day. If

Kenyans can do triple sessions, then so can I. My after school goal was to beat my lunch times in the 1200, 800, 400 – success.

I ran 27 miles in two days – a marathon in two days with 6 miles hard. Soon – a marathon in less than three hours with 26.214 miles hard.

UltraRunning – Ultra Living – yes, I still managed to teach, coach track, and spend three hours in the evening with my kids.

Work a little harder – just don't suggest that to school leaders. A statistic will be found to support lowering standards so Anywhere High School can meet graduation requirements for "No Child Left Behind."

Let me clarify: I ventured into the Principal's Office suggesting we an increase in our English credits from 4.0 to 4.5 for graduates of TFHS (for better writers). I was met with statistics indicating that other schools are dropping overall credits down to 20 for students to graduate. This will help schools meet the requirement for "No Child Left Behind" and increase graduation rates. So TFHS might follow suit and drop required graduation credits from 23 to 20. Kak and Blivits to that.

What a wonderful policy this would be. Let's not challenge students with higher standards. Let's take two years of Educational Leadership classes to earn $45,000 more per year than teachers and then make policies to make life easier for administrators. Our only 2010 graduation requirement: text your name on a cell phone. That is our only graduation requirement. 100% success! Make it easier on students now so life will be even easier post-graduation.

Here is an administrator coaching XC: Oh, you don't feel well today. Okay, take the next two days off, go home early, and here is a dollar to buy a Dr. Pepper on your way out the door. (Later, at state) I don't understand why our kids didn't run well; we babied them the whole season. Oh well, they can now call themselves athletes and graduate.

There is a saying, "don't bite the hand that feeds you."

Chomp.

Indigestion from these two philosophies: "No Child Left Behind" and "Love and Logic." I got the Runs.

Don't step in these educational philosophies.

4-29-08 Tuesday, State Champions

It was just announced over our school intercom that our Envirothon team won State for the second year out of three. This state sponsored event deals with the environment and science. The winning state team moves to Nationals in Flagstaff, AZ, in June 2008.

Look at four of the ten members of the Envirothon team: Jacob Naegeli, Ryan Sol, Beca Gunderson, and Mariah Naegeli. You've seen those names before and yes, in this book, and yes, DISTANCE RUNNERS.

Kudos to the area 4-H programs. Eight of the ten Envirothon team members have been or currently are part of a local 4-H program.

8:30 pm -9:30 pm the same evening, 4-29-08 Tuesday

Ryan, Beca, Mariah, and Jacob received a 2nd parade this school year. A police escort with lights and car horns honking led the team's bus to a bonfire at the high school. Ten cars joined the parade, while fourty people heated up at the bonfire. Don't tell child welfare services that Jaxon, 3 year old, sat in my lap and honked the horn in the parade.

It is good we celebrate academic deeds as well as athletic.

4-30-08 Oh, to be a Kenyan My title from 4-28-08 inspired my poetic voice.

Oh, to be a Kenyan
Running fast and free, away from political strife
Every step and stride = pain and strength
Swift as a cheetah
Endurance of eternity

Boston is a Kenyan victory stand
Cross country their choice game
Running to & from school & work
Since the age of three
Running enough to make an American lame

Kenyan coffee, purchased by me
Stretching to help their countries financial health
Caffeine to turn my feet into a Tasmanian Devil
A stretch it is to believe
Another runner, a life, saved by my penny.

Oh, to be a Kenyan
And feel the confident ground each stride
Running to achieve an Ultra Life
And heaven on Earth through
Endorphins, blisters, and VO^2 max.

I didn't say it was a good poem.

5-01-08 Letter of Complaint

Grammar 6.4 (Letter of Complaint) - Persuasive Writing assignment for English 2 *"From: Mike Barnett   To:Head Coach - Bluehawk XC*

On August 19, 2008, the cross-country team will be running a "speed workout," which may include a timed two, one, or a dreaded three mile. This is a problem because one of your new captains will be having their birthday on this day.

What a great present a timed three-mile will be! Good morning! Go run a timed two-mile! Please note my sarcasm.

Anyway, this will be the first week of the 2008 cross-country season. If it weren't for this year being a leap year, this Tuesday/Birthday coincidence would not occur. I'm sure you would not want one of your athletes to get heat exhaustion as a birthday present.   What I am proposing is that we schedule the speed work of this week for Wednesday and Friday. This could be an interesting mix up in our cross-country season. This could even turn out to be a positive change for our team. With this change, we could possibly win the State meet for the second year in a row!

Please consider the proposed solution. Thank you for your time and have a wonderful day. Sincerely, Mike Barnett"

5-4-08 Sunday, 17 miles

This morning I ran 17 miles as I prepare for yet another marathon: July 13, Missoula, in 10 weeks.

For 2 hours, 13 minutes, and 21 seconds thoughts raced through my brain. I am actively trying to improve VO^2 max with hard stints. Miles 4, 6, 12, and 16 were hard pushes today.

My thoughts drifted to Thursday's track meet in Libby where Delcie Peters tied the school record in the pole vault for at least seven minutes before another teammate had success at a higher height. At the beginning of the year, Delcie was one of five girls tied at 7-6. The record went to 7-8 and then 8-0. Thursday Delcie nailed her PR of 8 feet.

Our other vaulter, Rheanna Padden, then went 8-3, 8-6, and 8-9.

Records are made to be broken as progress continues. Some people strive to improve; it seems I fight to turn back time and resist the effects of aging!

My thoughts also drifted to Ryan (my running route passes his residence). In Saturday's track meet, he was a distant sixth place in the 3200 as far as our division goes. At his current pace, he won't make state. Yet, Ryan kept working through the finish line, through the end; he did all he could.

My wife commented that it is sad that such a great person and hard worker isn't blessed with the perfect physical ability to match his personality and effort. I responded that he was a key ingredient to our state championship team and he has an appointment to the Air Force Academy. That is a step above and beyond everyone else – even those running faster than him.

In Saturday's track meet, Ryan was on the back stretch as the gun lap started. In life, Ryan is through the tape before many others have started the race of life. Ryan has lapped quite a few high school kids in the race of life.

I also thought of anti-gravity pole vaulting poles. Brian Schenavar, TFHS vaulter, skied 14 feet, 10 inches yesterday. If he does that at State in three weeks, he owns the class B record. I hope it isn't a situation where he is tied with the record for seven minutes before someone else breaks it!

5-09-08 State Music Festival

Amanda Wood sang three duets at the state music festival. A student must qualify at an earlier event ("District" music festival) to sing there. These are MHSA sponsored events.

Amanda earned scores of 1, 1, and 2 on her duets. One is the highest possible score.

This is yet another demonstration of varied abilities of our XC team.

A side note – our band received average scores at the District music festival. This should mean that all members of band receive an appropriate grade of C (average) on report cards. What do you want to bet that that didn't happen!!

Amanda definitely deserves an A+ for choir, signifying superior efforts. Excellent and Superior work Amanda!!!!!!

5-10-08 District 8-B Track results

Hawk XC harriers performed well at the District track meet in Kalispell:

Boys: Mike Morris (1st 800, 2nd 1600), Jacob Naegeli (3rd 800, 3rd 1600), Shane Donaldson (1st 1600, 1st 3200), Ryan Sol (4th 1600, 2nd 3200), Mike Kidwiler (5th 110 hurdles, 2nd pole vault), and Mike Barnett (5th pole vault).

Girls: Jessie Drake (4th 200, 6th 400, 5th long jump), Beca Gunderson (2nd 800, 1st 1600, 1st 3200), Delcie Peters (4th 800, 2nd 1600, 2nd pole vault), Monica Conlin (3rd 1600, 3rd 3200, 3rd high jump), Mariah Naegeli (2nd 3200, 6th pole vault), Jeffreyanne Parker (1st 300 hurdles, 3rd triple jump, 4th pole vault).

Nice work Hawk harriers!

Another Hawk Harrier, BM, transferred to Cut Bank after our XC season. Our team met him at the Bigfork Track Meet on April 12. However, his name was found nowhere in the results from the District 1-B meet this weekend. Therefore, he did not place in the top six and did not move on. What happened to the #1 freshman boy Class B XC runner in the state after leaving our team?

5-12-08 Top Ten % ACT Test takers and MUS results

Congratulations to Ryan Sol, Shane Donaldson, and Katie Petteys (co-valedictorian, dating Jacob) who scored in the top 10% in the ACT in English, Math, Science, and Reading. This includes tests between Sept 06 and Feb 08. Two of the three who did this were in cross country. Runners are smarter!

Our MUS (Montana University System) writing scores came in this week. In 2006, our juniors scored 2.9 (6 is highest possible score) on the timed writing test. 2006 was my first year teaching here. In 2007, the juniors scored 3.6. That group includes our senior-laden Hawk Harriers. This year TFalls will earn a "School of Merit" commendation for having reached a school overall score of 3.8. 8000 juniors across Montana took this test; it replaces the writing portion of the ACT and/or SAT tests.

I had to write this so a reader knows I do my job in the classroom too. I teach and coach so I can be rich – I topped the $30,000 per year barrier last year in my 10th year of teaching. You are welcome.

5-13-08 Tuesday

The sophomore class (English 2) has to perform timed writing samples (40 minutes) six times per year. Lacey Wade wrote the following on Thur 5/8:

"Cross Country is a team sport. Each individual athlete contributes to the overall outcome of the team. I'm a proud participant on the Thompson Falls Cross Country team, and we are a very supportive, encouraging group. Whether a runner does bad or gets their personal best, they can expect a word of encouragement or praise. We push and motivate each other to succeed, each of

By Andrew Gideon

us inspiring in some way. The boys winning state this year was a memorable experience for me.

The whole team worked hard all season to achieve their dream. The majority of the boy's team had been working for four years to reach this goal - winning the Class B state championship. I saw determination in each and every one of the boys, especially those who were seniors. I admired them for all their hard work and not to mention their amazing running skills. They all had a great deal of inspiring character too.

My voice became almost hoarse from all the cheering I did. During the actual state race, the boys did their best; that I know. As the teams waited patiently for the results, I didn't know if their efforts paid off or not. Anticipation mounted from every team member, waiting for the award ceremony. It seemed like an eternity for the announcer to move up from 6th to 1st place. As the announcer climbed to 2nd place, we all finally knew that the boys had won the Championship, and the announcer called out Thompson Falls as multiple cheers and whoops filled the air. Hugs, tears, handshakes and pats on the back went around the Thompson Falls people like an infection. The boys had at last achieved their goal.

Being a part of this team, in and of itself has taught me many life values. But this win gave me motivation and inspiration for next year's season. I learned from this experience just how much character means. Talent will only get you so far. A positive mind set and determination will push a person the rest of the way. This counts for numerous aspects in life besides running. I took so much from this year's XC experience, and I will carry these values for the rest of my life.

I know the girl's team is capable of winning a trophy next year. This memorable experience will be forever imprinted on my brain."

5-14-08 The final words on the accident

These are the final words written on the car accident from the beginning of the year. This accident caused the final heartbeat (and runners understand heartbeats) of one person and has been in the community news for the entire year. Choices stay with us. (Reprinted from the latest *Sanders County Ledger*).

A proposed plea agreement for John Thomas Bennett will include 15 years with the Montana Department of Corrections said Defense Attorney John Putikka.

Bennett was the driver in a fatal accident in Thompson Falls in August of last year. Bennett allegedly lost control of the pickup he was driving and crashed on East Haley Avenue after leaving the roadway while heading down a hill at a high rate of speed.

A young woman was killed in the incident and another was injured slightly.

Both Bennett and the surviving passenger were treated at the scene, taken by ambulance to an area hospital and then released.

Bennett was originally charged with felony vehicular homicide while under the influence for allegedly ingesting or "huffing" chemicals from spray computer cleaner before the incident.

An amended information in the matter, to be filed as part of the plea agreement that will be formalized May 20, calls for a guilty plea to one charge of felony vehicular homicide and a guilty plea to one count of misdemeanor negligent vehicular assault.

Putikka said the plea agreement calls for 15 years with the Montana Department of Corrections with 10 years suspended, meaning Bennett will be sentenced to five years with the MDOC.

District Judge Kim Christopher told the parties to the matter Tuesday that she intended to set a trial date of June 30 for the matter. Putikka said with respect to the plea agreement that one matter still had to be resolved, and he felt that matter had been resolved "favorably to my client."

Bennett has been out on bail since shortly after being arrested.

5-15-08 State Golf

The boys golf team placed 3rd at State. There was high talk of a state championship for TFHS with this group. A 1st place trophy didn't come home.

Even with the right ingredients, winning State is hard. The boys XC team earned first, as did the Envirothon team. The Hawk Harriers were the nucleus of both of those teams.

The top golfer for Thompson Falls was RT Brown, yet another XC runner. He played a 77 and 77 (154 total) in the two rounds of golf at State in Bozeman to place 8th overall in the Montana Class B tourney Monday and Tuesday of this week.

Congratulations to RT – I am positive running helped his mental focus. The # 2 and #3 finishers for TFHS at State for boys golf might have been better golfers (based on scores during the season) and possibly even better athletes (who should have been running the 100, 200, and 400 relay for the track team), but, let's just write that the XC runner placed better at State Golf.

Instead of taking rainy days off, the golfers should have been running for better mental focus. Take that comment and run with it.

5-16-08 Friday, Day 1 at Divisionals = 9, nine, nine!!!

Thank you Shane Donaldson for running.

Two years ago Shane was an aide in my class. He earned a Blue Hawk Track and Field hat with the number 9 printed on the side. Each hat was numbered 1-24. I got the # 9 for Shane and told him that someday I would love to see Shane, the 3200, and the time of 9:xx.xx printed in the paper someday.

Someday was today - Shane Donaldson, 9:58.23, new school record.

Beca wrote on this subject, *"I am supposed to be writing mainly about cross-country. However, with State track less than a week away, sorry Mr. G, but I really can't focus on XC. It should be known that on Friday, Shane broke our school's 3200 meter record, previously 10:02, and now 9:58.*

By Andrew Gideon

Immediately after the race, Delcie and I noticed that we seemed much more pumped than he did. When we asked him why he didn't seem more excited, he said it was "just a time." I guess that's true, but...for some reason I think I would be very excited. But later, after Shane had recovered some, I think he was feeling pretty good.

"Also, Friday and Saturday were the hottest days we've had in weeks, just in time for the divisional track meet. ☹ I soaked my hair and uniform before the two-mile started, and by the time I was done I was dry. And despite the heat, Caitlin Stone of Seeley-Swan ran an amazing time of 10:53. (!!!!!!!!! is all I have to say about that.)"

Fact: (2006 National Federation of State High School Associations rulebook): The US record for 3200 is 9:48.59 by Kimberly Mortensen of Thousand Oaks HS in California (in 1996).

5-17-08 Day 2 at Divisionals, 1 point, hundredths of seconds, a game of inches.

Eureka 125, Thompson Falls 124 - final after 17 track and field events.

If Jacob Naegeli had run 0.14 faster in the 1600, we win.

If our 300 hurdler had run 0.01 seconds faster in the 300 hurdles, we win.

If a long jumper had jumped ½ inch further, we would have won.

If a Seeley-Swan sprinter had run 0.02 seconds faster in the 200, gold would be in the Hawk hands.

If any of the other lucky 13 events had changed slightly, we would have won.

If, if, if, if, reminds me of a poem by Rudyard Kipling.

> If you can keep your head when all about you
> Are losing theirs and blaming it on you;
> If you can trust yourself when all men doubt you,
> But make allowance for their doubting too;
> If you can wait and not be tired by waiting,
> Or, being lied about, don't deal in lies,
> Or, being hated, don't give way to hating,
> And yet don't look too good, nor talk too wise;
>
> If you can dream - and not make dreams your master;
> If you can think - and not make thoughts your aim;
> If you can meet with triumph and disaster
> And treat those two imposters just the same;
> If you can bear to hear the truth you've spoken
> Twisted by knaves to make a trap for fools,
> Or watch the things you gave your life to broken,
> And stoop and build 'em up with worn-out tools;
>
> If you can make one heap of all your winnings
> And risk it on one turn of pitch-and-toss,
> And lose, and start again at your beginnings
> And never breath a word about your loss;

Harrier Hawks Fly High
If you can force your heart and nerve and sinew
To serve your turn long after they are gone,
And so hold on when there is nothing in you
Except the Will which says to them: "Hold on";

If you can talk with crowds and keep your virtue,
Or walk with kings - nor lose the common touch;
If neither foes nor loving friends can hurt you;
If all men count with you, but none too much;
If you can fill the unforgiving minute
With sixty seconds' worth of distance run -
Yours is the Earth and everything that's in it,
And - which is more - you'll be a Man my son!

Eureka beat us; they battled slightly better than TFHS did. Win as a team, lose as a team.

In another division in Class B Montana: Malta 104.5, Glasgow 104. ½ point = ouch! Maybe they needed to be ¼ inch better or 0.001 seconds faster.

Sometimes it might not seem worth it, but if a person works hard, then improvements will come by hundredths of seconds and ¼ inches at a time. That's why some people don't challenge the self to be better. The difference doesn't matter to that individual.

As for me, it does matter, so I work a little harder. So will the students in the classrooms and the athletes that I coach.

5-20, Tuesday, Entry by Beca the Honorary Kenyan
"This is 10% luck, 20% skill, 15% concentrated power of will, 5% pleasure, 50% pain, And 100% reason to remember the name!" (Remember the Name Lyrics)

With State track coming up, I have no time to think about anything else. I'm trying to get mentally prepared (a.k.a. listen to music like the lyrics above) and visualize my races. You know that excited feeling you get in your stomach before something important? Every time I imagine lining up for the start of each race, butterflies play tag in my stomach. I'm not feeling nervous yet, but I am getting really wound up.

5-23 (Fri) and 5-24 (Sat) State Track – Bozeman, MT
Our boy thinclads earned a 3rd place trophy at the Class B State Track Meet.

Our only first was one of the only two records set in the state of Montana this year (State records can only be set at the State Meets). Brian Schenavar defied gravity to pole vault 14-9.5. This beat the old record by 0.25 inch. Brian set school, District, and Divisional records along the way. His fifteen foot vault at Kalispell is the new school record and was his season high.

I was blessed to be able to coach Brian in the pole vault this season. James 1:17 ➔ *"Every good and perfect gift is from above…"*

203

By Andrew Gideon

Some Hawk Harriers performed well at State – in rainy and windy conditions that didn't make running a perfectly enjoyable activity.

Shane Donaldson was on the State awards stand for the 1600 (4:38.32) and 3200 (10:13.05). He has a "9" after his name – his 9:58.23 is the new 3200 meter school record.

Beca Gunderson earned fifth place and a medal in the 800 (2:25.64).

What was impressive to watch was the girls 3200 late on Saturday. After seven hours of soaking and drenching rain, the downpour continued. Rain pelted the track, creating literally rivers of water in some areas. The cold wind didn't add to the "fun" of a 3200 meter, 8 lap, challenge of an event. However, Beca G and Mariah Naegeli battled the elements in grand fashion. Beca improved her PR by hundredths of seconds and Mariah came close.

Delcie vaulted a foot over last year's school record, but her 8-6 pole vault and 9th place finish at State placed her 6 inches under Rheanna Padden's new school record. Look for Rheanna and Delcie to become perfect 10's next season by vaulting 10 feet.

5-25-08 Memorial Day and championship softball

It is hard to win a State Championship.

The softball team at TFHS found this out the hard way. Despite four wins on Saturday, and a fierce determination to battle through the loser's bracket, a gold memory did not land in Hawk hands on this day.

TFHS was up by one run in the last inning with 2 outs. Two errors later and the Championship went to Columbus / Stillwater for a second straight year.

This is written about here to show just how hard it really is to win a State Championship – even with the right ingredients. The softball team had some players who dedicated a lot of summers playing and extra commitment, as I am sure Columbus / Stillwater did as well.

Our Hawk Harriers know that effort and determination (and luck?) were vital ingredients in the fall. Our willingness to prepare to win helped us win.

5-29-08 Last Day of School, bye bye seniors, from Beca

I would like to take this opportunity to tell the senior guys how much their friendships have meant to me over the last couple of years. I also want everyone else who reads this to know how awesome these guys are. (Don't let that go to your heads.) ☺

Our team has done a lot of stuff together, and made many fun memories. I don't have the room to write all of them, but for starters .....

At State cross-country last year we spent the whole evening before our races playing in the elevator at our motel, riding up and down. And at Montana Cup that year in Butte, we played "chicken" in the pool for hours, much to the frustration of that grouchy pool attendant.

Last summer some of you guys helped my family get hay, and I'm sure Ryan, Matt, and Shane remember going swimming in the middle of the night with me and Hannah. At the fair this past September, we spent a ton of time swimming in the river and hanging out at stalls, buying ice cream and watching the demolition derby.

Harrier Hawks Fly High

And of course I remember the home meet this year, when we were running our race and came across some familiar guys relaxing on a nice, grassy hill, all lined up like they had planned it or something.....good thing there were no race officials nearby. ☺

And most importantly, the everyday stuff, like the bus trips and meets we had together, whether it was cross-country or track. We had movie nights, and went running and swimming in the summer months. I had a blast.

But enough of that. There were some times where it was just me and you to remember an incident, so I have something I want to say about each of you. So, in no particular order, here are those famous state champs.

First of all, Jacob Naegeli. You are definitely like a brother to me, always teasing me and getting into arguments, *cough* I mean debates. ☺ At the fair you stayed up until midnight to help me put up decorations on my stalls, and ran with me basically every day. Come to think of it, you are always my running buddy, whether it's at 4H Congress, or Envirothon, etc. We had lots of long conversations on runs that were just the two of us. You were also my appointed "bodyguard" countless times on runs and other events. It's probably a good thing no one ever attacked us because I'm not so sure what our defense would be. We had a lot of unintentional innuendos as well, and I always appreciated your humor. And remember, running faster is probably not the solution to everything, although sometimes it may help. Thanks for being such a good brother / bodyguard / friend.

Next, RT Brown. I can't believe someone can drink Dr. Pepper as much as you do. Or chocolate milk, for that matter. ☺ You and I also debated about everything, although unlike me and Jacob, you and I tended to agree. We ran together a lot during cross-country practice, and you could hear us coming a mile away because of our clicking ankles. You and Matt moved cement parking blocks in front of and behind our cars after the state track meet, so that when we came home at 1:00 a.m. we would find a surprise. You also stuck around to help us move them away again. (Too bad that didn't prevent Jacob from driving over a couple of them anyway.) Thank you for being yourself (I'm thinking orange prom tux, here) and for being a great friend.

Now for Ryan Sol. Do you remember the day when you found me sitting on a fence down by Sandy Beach? I had stopped there in the middle of my run, and we sat on that fence for like an hour. You were also always running with me at things like Envirothon. Remember the letter we wrote to Jacob on his laptop on the trip home? You, Shane, and Jake were my companions at every track meet, and no matter how many times you try on my flip-flops, they're never gonna fit. ☺ There was also the time you showed up at my house on some random day, thinking that the team was running there. Instead you found me in the house, in pajama pants, eating a huge bowl of ice cream. I'm going to miss you, and you've been an awesome friend.

On to Matt Hojem, RT's partner in crime. I finally got to see you wrestle this year and I was so proud of you. You even baked me a cake when I was feeling sad. I also remember an early morning when I was getting ready to go to a meet and my dog got sprayed by a skunk. When I got on the bus, everyone woke up real quick asking what that smell was. ☺ You came up to sit with me, even though the smell was awful. (Later I made you move because I felt bad for you. ☺) You've always been a sweetheart and I want to thank you for being a good friend.

Next is Mike Morris. Although this was your first cross-country season with us, you fit right in. During the Christmas parade, I remember you stuffing a pocket full of

205

licorice and you and I ate it the whole time we went down Main Street. You also were the one who took to calling me "Gunderbuns" after hearing someone else say it, and I could count on hearing it from you during a race in track. Remember when I brought that giant bubble maker so that we could play with it after practice? I swear you were like a little kid, chasing after those bubbles to pop them. You always make me laugh with your teasing, and I'm so glad you were with us this year.

Now for Bryant Normandeau. You are also one of those 4H kids who are with me all the time, exactly like a brother. I can't help but laugh when I'm with you, no matter what we're doing. Your laugh is so infectious that pretty soon I'm laughing just as hard as you. One time at a 4H party, I remember everyone was playing some game with a little ball in the pool. We both grabbed it at the same time, and as I was trying my hardest to wrestle it away from you, you casually lifted me and the ball completely out of the water with one arm and started laughing. Needless to say, I gave up. ☺ You also were so supportive of me when I was trying to get approval from the Livestock committee to let me expand my sheep project. I really appreciate you standing up for me and speaking on my behalf. You have always been an amazing guy, and the best partner for playing "chicken" that anyone could ask for. Thanks for being such a terrific friend.

And finally, Shane Donaldson. I remember at the fair a couple years ago, you, CC, and me stood on a fire truck and watched the demo derby from over the fence. However, we found watching the policemen run into the beer garden more entertaining. You and Jacob always had a pack of cards at track meets, and always tried to make me play even though I was terrible at every game. As much as I don't like to admit it, ☺ I will probably miss playing cards next track season. I "debate" with you a lot too, but you always let me win, or at least think that I won. ☺ You have the biggest heart, in running and in life. As the most supportive kid I've ever met, you never fail to make me laugh or cheer me up. I have a special place in my heart for you, and I'm definitely going to miss you. Thank you for being my friend.

Above all, I wanted to tell each one of you that I am going to miss your crazy antics in the coming seasons. I know you are all going to do awesome after high school. As I was writing this, I kept catching myself grinning at the good times. I don't know what I would've done without you guys. By being around you, I learned to have confidence in who I am, and not care if the whole runner/science nerd combination isn't exactly the definition of the word "cool." I was able to be myself, because I was blessed enough to have you as friends. We had a lot of fun, and made awesome memories. Thank you for your friendships.   *Love,*   *Beca*

5-31-08 Finish Line, Graduation, Starting Line

Today was the finish line (again) for our Hawk Harriers.

On October 20th, our Hawk Harriers ran to the finish line of cross country before any other team. Today, Graduation 2008 for TFHS, our Hawk Harriers studied (worked, ran) to the finish line of high school ahead of the rest.

Eight of the 52 graduates (15%) were Hawk Harriers and achieved diplomas.

A total of $671,491 in scholarships were awarded. $533,171 of that went to members of our cross country team this fall. That's 79%.

Of course, Ryan Sol, scored $387,520 of that for an appointment to the United States Air Force Academy ($387,000) a $500 Envirothon scholarship, and a $20 Journalism scholarship. That $20 makes the difference.

Here is where our eight Hawk Harrier graduates are headed:

Shane Donaldson – U of Great Falls (Montana) (7 scholarships totaling $13,077)

Jacob Naegeli – Earlham College (Indiana) (12 scholarships = $108,274)

Ryan Sol – United States Air Force Academy (Colorado) ($387,520)

Mike Morris – University of Montana (Missoula, MT)

Bryant Normandeau – Montana Tech (Butte) (9 scholarships = $21,900)

Matt Hojem – University of Montana (4 scholarships totaling $2400)

RT Brown – Montana State University (Bozeman)

Amanda Wood – will start taking college classes online (graduated in 3 years)

Jacob was the co-Valedictorian and gave a speech about cracked eggs, friendship, family, and support. An egg also has gold in its middle.

The graduation speaker was John Hamilton of the *Sanders County Ledger*. He has several articles in this book, and his main topic was time. Time: How fitting for graduation and for a successful bunch of runners. Several quotes were *"time is precious, you'll realize that more as time goes by. . . we take time, we make time, we waste time. . . I didn't realize how much time flies."*

The time came on October 20th to run the last XC race of a successful high school career. Graduation time arrived. Both times our runners/harriers were prepared. I look forward to their successful use of future time.

We all have 24 hours in a day to spend as we choose. Running with this crew, writing this book, and loving the fact of being a Hawk Harrier XC runner was a good use of my time.

Lyrics that were played at graduation for a senior video included some words by Miley Cyrus. They were – *"I'm at the starting line / Of the rest of my life / As ready as I've ever been ' Got the hunger and stars in my eyes / The prize is mine to win."* Wonderful and fitting words.

I just heard the starter's gun for this team of winners.

6-01-08, Sunday, 101 miles in a week

More is always possible.

After every race, we require our runners to do anywhere from 1-4 miles of a cooldown. The work has been done, but the show will go on in the future, so some lactic acid needs to be run out of the system. Prepare for the next battle.

This is why I have rambled so long after the State Race has been won.

My final, final, final entry is 101 miles in a week. This was my week to end the school year: 21.25 on Monday (ran to rival town Plains), 15 Tuesday (saw a fox), 14.25 Wednesday, 15.5 Thursday (10.5 before school in 1:26:19, 5 at lunch with 1600 (6:42), 1200, 800 (3:13), 400, and 200 push intervals), 9.25 Friday, 14.25 Saturday (last 4 in 28:07), and 11.5 Sunday (saw elk).

My goal was 100 miles, yet I ran the extra mile.

I could have run another one; ask me why I was lazy!

By Andrew Gideon

That's my record week. One can always do more, but really it is time to edit and ship this off, and wait for the critics to respond.

Endurance runners outlast the Energizer Bunny; we are smarter too.

Beca, Coach G, Mariah after rainy State 3200

Ryan, Derek Naegeli, Shane, Jacob
Icing Blackfoot River after Missoula Marathon

Mo-Hawk!

Hawks Fly in Ronan 07!
At left is Paul A, Darby, State Champ

XC Pyramid, picture day

Beca, Ryan, Shane, Coach G stretching

Today, the first day of the rest of your life

The shoe is on the other foot – this means it is now the reader's turn to run, write, and motivate in the proper direction. The Hawk Harriers are a step ahead of you. Go run, NOW! With scissors please.

The Runner

The alarm rang at the usual hour of six. He picked up the telephone to find the line dead. He usually did this; his habit was so deeply ingrained for some odd reason that he couldn't change. The alarm would still be buzzing as his wife shrieked out in dismay to shut off the damn alarm. Then he would.

He crawled out of bed to start the day and the coffee. His wife lay in bed for another ten to fifteen minutes before clamoring up to occupy the bathroom. So he had his little time to utilize the bathroom as he pleased. Once in the bathroom he would realize he had forgotten his slippers yet again (and the floor was so cold). While urinating, he would wonder what the hell his wife could do in this God-forsaken room for 45 minutes every morning.

He wondered whether or not he should try to look at his wife's face again sometime before she woke. But he had learned his lesson before time and again. Sleeping Beauty? Let sleeping dogs lie? The correct version escaped his mind anyway. Why must he think these things to himself every single day? The same thoughts, habits, and every single thing occurred daily in exactly the same identical order. The routine was ingrained and had taken control. He never assumed he was the one in control.

In the kitchen he had his cup of coffee as he glanced at the paper from the previous day. He questioned why he always grabbed yesterday's afternoon paper to read. He knew he would put it down after realizing he had already read it. And he hated TV so it would be agonizing to try and watch the morning shows, wondering what truth was and what glorified TV crap was. Then he fretted and fumed over why he energized himself every morning to make breakfast for his damn wife. She never thanked him. Maybe it was because he hadn't improved one bit in ten years of making breakfast. But he had been pretty good in the first place.

She even complained about the breakfast to the egg. It wasn't the eggs fault. Hell, maybe she was just too picky. He ate what he cooked for breakfast. But he never really enjoyed food.

7:30 AM – the critic arrived.

He asked how she felt. She was fine and asked what inedible thing he cooked up for today (how nice).

He told her she looked nice. She said she knew she looked great because she was great-looking but hoped the food tastes as good as she looked. She remarked that the hash browns actually looked cooked for a change, but that they probably only looked good on the outside.

He laughed appeasingly and then sat down at the opposite end of the table with a headache. You look terrible she said this morning the same way she said it every morning. He remembered how he fell in love with her because she had made him feel so worthwhile as a person. I think she lost that loving feeling he thought to himself.

She asked how he felt. Didn't sleep well. Legs are still hurting. She musingly asked if he wanted to wear her extra support panty-hose for the day.

He again laughed appeasingly and stated with deep monotone that she was as amazingly funny as ever (Honey!). He hoped and told her to have a nice day at work. No she resisted with words, it will be hell as usual. Meetings twice today and presentations in both of them and why don't you get a job.

By Andrew Gideon

He held all thoughts to himself because he realized it was only ten minutes before she left for work. Time always dragged from here until she left. Ten minutes never went so slow in the history of school for a high-school kid with a head full of empty dreams with his wife menacingly staring at him and questioning his integrity. But he managed over it in his usual way. His way was to put it off and throw it out of his mind. For now.

She left for work. The burden lifted but only temporarily. She would be back.

The dishes were quickly washed, dried, and stored away. He then went into the bedroom and reset the alarm for ten. An hour all to himself. Once in a while he wished he possessed the energy to read or do something else. Anything else. But he went back to bed. At least in bed he could hopefully start to dream. However, his back was a magnet to the bed until the clock read ten anyway and dreams were shelved and undreamt again. He couldn't remember a dream. Ever.

The alarm rang. This time he turned it off without answering the phone. His legs ached from the bottom to the top. Ankles swollen, shins aching, and thighs burning, but he was on his way. Twenty minutes of stretching and rubbing eased his pain slightly. But easing doesn't erase. And erase he hoped for but it was deep malingering pain.

The doctors blathered time and again about surface pain needing time to heal. Time off his legs. But they didn't know what caused the swelling and the pain. He never told a soul. He wouldn't know what to do if he took time off. He couldn't stand the thought of it. He couldn't stand to think. Time heals all wounds, but the doctors didn't know how far down the pain traveled into his soul.

Ten-twenty, and he was out the door. It was nice to live in the suburbs where he could rent some peace. But the peace he wanted to himself was for everyone. He just borrowed it, although he rarely used it for what he could have. Even this suburb advantage didn't really give him the peace he really wanted. He wondered how life could work for so many people.

Step-by-step he agonizingly began. Each beginning step sent shivers of pain throughout his entire body. Right to the heart. And mind. And soul. It just didn't echo back.

With more pain and steps he tried to slowly increase his speed to outrun what was surely killing him. Pain shot through his ankles and shins and every sense and nerve became equally involved in helping to slowly numb and paralyze his center. That's why he ran. To paralyze his senses. To be numb and not feel a thing. The first two excruciating miles were his burden until slowly but surely endorphins began acting as his opiate to desensitize not only his legs but his entire body and psychological processes as well.

He started feeling better and better as the distance from home and the pain moved farther away. With separation, he slowly started to believe he was alive. Running to him was being alive. He didn't realize it but he wasn't running. He was running away, but not running. To be free and away from the forces or pain and the hurt associated with all of that was his way to live.

To run, he thought. To be free. Every single day he fought through physical pain for miles on end before his body and mind numbed and hindered him to thoughts that he was truly living.

Three miles in fifteen minutes and fourty seconds. He was running a little slow today. But he always started slow as he fought through the starting of a new day. His new day was a different route and distance, but it was all the same.

Four miles and into the park. The favorite part of his favorite run. And today as he was entering the park, the clouds parted slightly to send some rays of sun through to the lake. He began to feel nothing and loved every minute of it now that he believed he was running with freedom instead of running away. He was getting his high, right through the pain while the sun smiled to greet him today. He did not feel any of the sunshine because his timing was off. He slipped into the shade of the leafy trees as the small amount of light shone through to bless the day.

The overcast day quickly turned the ten minutes of minute sunshine into a paralyzing sliver of hope. The sliver was real and had been felt by many less than successful players before. Sitting the pine, riding out the bad moments, and realizing what it was not to be the star, but still blessed to be a part of it – that was the blessing he should have realized. But he skipped that and went straight into nothing.

Momentarily, the sun burst through the clouds now but he was running in the shade. He was in the thickest region of trees and bushes in the park. He didn't notice the sun anyway but this way his body didn't feel what the light could do. The body would love it, but not as much as the brain. The brain can find light in so many ways the sun can't even reach. Ease the pain was his effort and he felt he was doing that by running.

Six miles and a quarter of the way around the lake. The sun entered the last stage of real sunlight for the day (and it was only 10:52 am) before being swallowed up by smothering clouds. The dark oppressive clouds that could turn any smile around weren't doing that to the runner. He didn't have anything to turn around. He didn't even notice as a light trickle and drizzle of mist touched his brow. He was within his state of freedom and being alive and outside forces couldn't alter his world now.

Seven miles and the drizzle increased. He wiped his forehead with his shirt and thought through his clouded mind that he was doing less than sweating. Then he opened his eyes to the negative and saw a time of severe thunderstorms on the horizon as he looked up from his thoughts from deep within. But then he plunged straight back to his own hidden depths.

Step-by-agonizing step he came out of the tree sheltered area into a clearing as the clouds broke for good. His stride kept on pounding as rain pelted down upon him. The drops touched and splattered him everywhere but he felt nothing.

Ten miles and he was drenched. His legs felt nothing and he knew they were as happy then as they could be for the day. For today. Due to being indelibly numbed beyond feeling. Yet while running he felt so alive in this mental death.

Puddles formed on the beaten path where he ran. Each stride was an attempt to avoid the water. Quickly he stopped trying to avoid the splashes which were just wet and only affected the outside. Thin but thickening mud splashed and crawled its way up his socks to reach his thigh. Each stride bounced more mud on him. And it was crawling higher.

He went on blindly despite the clear, crisp feeling of the refreshing rain-water. The city had gone without rain for two months but to him the water was an obstacle to run through. He received the mud while the city received a refreshing baptism. It was a force that he could beat. But he was beating the good that he should have considered as help. And his help turned to murky splashes of mud on the legs and a soggy shirt.

211

By Andrew Gideon

As the rain cam down thicker and harder, he ran faster and harder. Trying to outrun the rain was something he unthinkingly tried to do. He needed to do this. He needed to outrun the rain but it couldn't be done. Not by anyone. And he really wanted to win and do this and put his legs to the test but even then they felt nothing and ignored him. His brain was willing something that wasn't getting through to his legs. And the legs were not successful now and were failing him more and more every day. Maybe he would realize it. A deeper puddle and his stride was straight to the center of the ring of water. And it came upon him the best it could.

Twelve miles in under fifty-nine minutes despite the wet grounds that had been dry for so many consecutive days. His lungs breathed mist from the throngs of icicles burning down from the sky. Even his lungs, despite being dulled, were telling a story that wasn't being heard by anything (or anyone). It was as bad as if he were smoking, but this wasn't the problem. But maybe that would have even been better.

Now nothing. His mind became blank. In his solitary world he was now alive! He was enjoying the run the best he could. He felt nothing.

Stride. Stride. Stride. The pace was even faster and more agonizing despite nothing being felt or sensed.

He was running close to world record pace and no one, except his lovely wife, knew that he even existed.

Stride. Stride. Stride. He plugged with his head down, on and on, and approached home for the first time but now that he was away from the park and heading home he never wanted to quit. Stride. He felt good now. Stride. He wondered why he had to go back home and stop. Stopping just drove the icicles of life deep to the center of nothing. Stride.

To stop would be Noon and then he had to wait until he ran later to feel the pain of his life. Stride. He didn't want to stop but knew his body needed food. Some energy and the hunger to go along with it was intense and he wanted to appease this feeling.

Stride. Stride. Stride. Two blocks away and his betraying mind was coercing his body to do opposite things. Should he continue to bypass the pain of stopping or stop and accept the agony of defeat (and the feet!)? He hurt and the suffering from his legs would bite at his heart and mind until he ran again later in the afternoon. And The Race wasn't until two weeks away.

He opened the door and ran straight for the shower. Tearing at his sopping clothes, he turned on the heat. Scalding hot to rid him of the chill and rain. Burn the bad out. His body didn't agree. He withstood intense pain from the piping hot water and accepted the cleansing from this water that was channeled through different systems of human cleansing. The cleansing that never seemed to (and couldn't) work and he was evidence of that fact now. It scalded him ruthlessly. Burning off the fresh rain water from his run and being subdued into the channel of thought that ran into the pipes and out his shower head. He didn't realize there was nothing wrong and everything right about the baptismal rain water that soaked him in the first place.

Now everything but nothing. Hurting and pain. He hobbled around the house naked after drying off. He ran to cover his naked body and put on his robe. The robe covered up his chest and torso down to his knees. His hair was dripping wet and his shins, ankles, and feet remained uncovered. The opening of the robe near his upper chest let some chill and homey air into his heart. All of it gripped at him intensely and told him to stop and look in the mirror but his senses were slightly dulled to begin with and now they were dulled even more. But the pain was too real to not be felt.

He gimped around in pain and the icy kitchen floor, but the chill and pain from his ankles and feet had come from deep within. His mind hurt endlessly as he looked into the fridge and tossed aside choices. To eat and appease his hunger from deep within almost ravaged his mind completely. He had an intense feeling of hunger but everything he touched turned undesirable. Everything he looked at burned holes through his stomach and burned at his heart. Nothing in the fridge containing everything could satisfy him now. He slammed the door and sat at the table with his head in his hands and cried into the nothingness on the plate before him.

His tears dried before they could splatter the plate. He sat for quite a while before realizing he was hungry again. The pains were for food this time and nothing else.

He opened the refrigerator door and found himself something to eat. He poured himself a tall glass of milk. He sat down to a meal that could hold him satisfied for a while.

The phone rang. Answer it or not? He knew it was his wife and he wanted to ignore the ringing in his ears. The rings were too loud and so he held the receiver to his ear.

It was his wife. What are you doing? Eating lunch.

Well go out and get a job and do something for once in your life she screamed. He said yeah maybe I should.

She advised no, do it now. Honey my legs hurt.

It's psychosomatic, nothing is wrong with you – the doctors told you that. And how can they hurt when you sit on your lazy ass all day. You're right darling and what time will you be home for dinner? Good I will make something you like.

Why not, I bought the food, I work, she complained and then slammed down the phone. And it could have been PERFECT he thought. She and I could have been perfect. We started that way.

He went back to the table and sat down to continue lunch. The milk tasted sour and old. The sandwich was dry. He got up and threw the uneaten portions away. His stomach rumbled with the little food he had taken in. The life was draining from his supply. Now he didn't feel hungry despite the rumblings of the stomach.

Two more hours and he could run again. Two weeks to the Race. His legs ached, bit, and scorched with intensity to match that burning of his head. He looked down to see swollen ankles. He reached down to roll his hands over and feel the swelling. To feel something he had caused and know the reason. He loved to run he thought; it's all I love. The pain is worth the price. The ankles will be okay. It's just the price you pay. The thighs were cramped but he felt he could run through it all.

The dishes were washed and placed away so no traces of his limited eating could be found. He took out the garbage as he did every day around now. He placed it in the neighbor's container.

Once back in the house he sat in the corner chair. His pride, his comfort, his favorite chair – and nothing could take it away. He sank into the soft seat cushions and began to feel so comfortable as to be floating in mid-air. He sank in and drifted, thoughts running on the soft air above him. He was swimming ever so effortlessly in nothing. His heavenly thoughts were of nothing. Only oblivion and nothing more. He felt at home. Softly swimming, ceremoniously dancing on air that held him aloft with space and warmth and comfort and nothing could lift him higher. And nothing was the only thing that lifted him at all.

The door banged. The doorbell clanged. And the mail came crashing through the slot and into his high and slammed to the floor as he was staggered back into his abysmal reality. He forgot he almost felt like entering a dream. He stood and gimped to the door on legs of splinters and needles. Each step harder than the step before and each with more agonizing pain than the previous. Someone somewhere was sticking pins into his thighs, shins, and ankles.

The door was opened; nobody was there. Damn mailman, can't he just put the mail into the slot like any normal mailman? No peace around here. Just leave me to myself he thought. That would make things right. He wondered where he could live alone and be free (and happy).

He picked up the mail and looked at nary a piece. He set the envelopes and magazines on the kitchen table in a neat pile. His legs throbbed and told macabre stories and nobody listened.

He sat in the kitchen chair and watched out the window at the trees and the wind blowing everything. Everything moving somewhere but the wind didn't really exist. Touch it, grab it, hold it, he thought. A leaf blew off the tree to its death and burial on the ground. He scoffed at the beauty of nature. He knew things in nature just died so why all the shouts of beauty and happiness for what would soon be dead?

The sky remained dark and held no hope. He wouldn't have noticed anyway.

2 pm – Time to run. His hopes were blown past with the wind he couldn't hold anyway. His legs said no. His head ached and told him no. His heart pierced with the pain of each step and again the message was negative. He blocked out all the messages.

He had his clothes on and began stretching. Stretching hurt, but he fought through it. But what was he fighting? What was he going through?

Outside in the cold, brisk wind he began. His legs shocked, swelled, and swayed but held him upright. He moved disconnectedly down the street. Bones called for help, and muscles responded with exaggerated stubbornness. But he moved forward.

He lurched and wobbled and found the intense pain he captured earlier. It was approaching death and he loved the thought of life for a brief moment in running time.

This time he ran away from the park. His favorite spot to run and he was running away from it. With each step he felt worse. He wanted to go back and start the run again and go the other direction but he felt it was too late. He couldn't turn around now. He had set his path. And each step twinged his body with a remorse ness of infallible messages of stepping over a crucial line and knowing you can't go back.

The runner's high finally came to him after ten miles. It was starting later and taking longer each time to numb what he barely felt. At eleven miles his heart and head felt nothing from his legs. He knew he was moving. Moving somewhere slowly (Ten miles in a SLOW 62 minutes). Moving somewhere slowly. Or maybe just running. Away.

His motion was steady but jerky at that. Stride. Stride. Stride. He swayed when he should have swooned. Icicles pricked cold icy pins deep into every body part. Colder and more. Each time they were sharper. And pushed a little farther in. Each time he knew he had his high until he stopped. He hoped the numbness would get him past a line of no return.

He was nearing home.

The Race was two weeks away.

As a child he ran a race and won. He had run home to tell his parents he loved that he won the race and the door was locked. The only race he ever ran – his first triumph! – And when he had come home the door to home was locked. He didn't have a key. He went around to the back door and burst excitedly through the unlocked boundary.

Mom! Dad! He yelled triumphantly out his tired lungs to an answering echo. Then he heard them. His parents fighting and screaming once more, but this time at the highest intensity that could only stop with a burst bubble of life. The top of their lungs. Some blood, broken furniture. The parents didn't hear the son. They continued to yell about the boy.

The boy stopped and froze and listened. Unfortunately for him he didn't hear the beginning or the end of the battle. He heard many negative things, just as he had before, but this time put the turtle into the shell to stay.

Life. Work. The Boy. Love. Affair. Money. Tears now flowing non-stop out of his young ignorant eyes. The tears splashing the figurative divorce papers separating life and soul.

Bittersweet victory of a race just minutes ago vanished from his head forever.

The parents were fighting over what was right for their son and both of them had a legitimate argument. Neither would know a race was won.

Both parents separate ideas could be fused into one fantastic home. The fuse, however, was lit, and the bomb blast still echoed in his soul today as he returned home from his second long run of the day.

A slow death grabbed hold of a bright and talented hope-filled future with iron claws of destruction.

The parents ended the discussion of the end, but it was never over; the memory remained.

The son had raced out of the house (he could RUN) fast, a sprint really, away from the bitter words which reeked despair into his not understanding mind. His vision of perfection shattered – an incomprehensible version of reality.

He vowed perfection in his own world and grew distant from others. He slowly closed himself off from his parents despite their love and affection and he fought and battled and lost every day. His world of perfection shattered for good when his wife turned her attitude just slightly after marriage. The steamroller continued over the top of him.

The boy had run out of his house to the park where he won the race earlier that day and fell to the grass. Some walkers found him there asleep that night with a horrid look on his face. He was transported home to a different world for the rest of his life.

A dim ray of hope emerged to his soul with the race two weeks away.

Now, back in his current life, he fell to the grass in the front yard after completing his second long "victorious" run of the day. 28 miles greeted him with wet, cold grass from the rain earlier in the day and chilled his body. Sweat and dirt stains covered him. He tore out clumps of grass and tossed them into the nonexistent wind – they landed back on top of him.

Cars drove by but nobody noticed someone who had just run his daily 28 miles in a phenomenal world record training time. A police car cruised by, sped up, and turned on the lights for a real emergency somewhere else in the city. Probably a kitten stuck in a tree somewhere.

His tears dried before they fell and even had a chance to mesh with the wet on the ground. A dog came running by – stopped, growled, and moved on. The dog found a fire hydrant close by and released his mark of property.

His legs begged forgiveness but there wasn't a soul around to hear. His heart scolded his legs and they burned more. But the burning didn't melt the icicles pricking holes and freezing everything but his senses. His legs were always running even after they stopped. They hadn't healed yet.

Inside the house he tore off his clothes and showered. The steam from the red hot, scalding water covered the mirrors. He felt nothing while the water burned away everything it could. He struggled to get out of the shower stall. He dried himself off and peeked at the steam covered mirror. He didn't wipe it off.

He dressed and threw all the sweaty, dirty, frustrating memories of running clothes into the washer. His wife never questioned why her clothes from the day before were always cleaned and folded. They were placed away neatly in their proper spots.

He began dinner. He could cook anything. Nothing was very good so his wife said. He could never eat much but was always hungry. Yet his hunger was never satisfied in the right way and he slowly was withering away – crawling into his protective turtle shell.

Energy left him not from his body, but from his head. His head was drained, yet his heart contained enough to pump blood for 28 stellar miles a day. A physical specimen, but valentines for soul support never found the right mailbox in his heart.

6 PM and the critic arrived.

How was your day honey? She replied with a what's for dinner and it better be good. Then she asked if he did anything with himself today.

No, he answered; he didn't mention his legs.

Do something, anything, she said. He told her dinner was ready and her laundry was clean.

She ate and complained but she knew it was good.

They read the paper after dinner. She read what she wanted and he fit in behind, picking up the scraps shredded from the critic. She talked of the day's events at work and he listened intently.

She turned on the TV and watched it silently until she went to bed. He went in and washed the dishes and silent tears away, then played solitaire until it was too late.

The Race was two weeks away but he would never run in a race again. He could have raced the game of life and won, but his miles would stay silent.

The alarm rang at the usual hour of six. . .

January 1991, slight editing 2008

This story isn't about a rude wife or unhappiness in marriage.

Rather, it contemplates what Henry David Thoreau said, "Most men lead lives of quiet desperation."

It is about the fact that try as people might, there are always secrets and thoughts that hold humans back from greatness. The journey of a 1000 miles begins with one step and too many times that one step is never taken (or taken in the wrong direction). We need to run *The Race of Life* – make the choice – and move with this choice (work), letting our dreams and lives take flight.

Hebrews 12:1 ➔ "*. . . and let us run with perseverance the race marked out for us.*"

The grammar and choppy sentence structure of the story drives me nuts. However, the man in the story has choices and attitudes that intentionally drive me batty. The unnamed man's thought patterns are as poor as the grammar and sentence structure.

Another point of the story is that he who has to have the story explained to him has (1) read a bad author, or (2) missed the point, so why don't we just explain it! Point next: we can never truly know what is in each other's hearts – our communication gaps, cultural differences, age differences, and brains don't say the right words at the right time. We can only hope that enough of our good (and our intentions) shines through to make a difference in people's lives.

Surrounding oneself with *Harrier Hawks who fly High* is a great place to start. We all need to give each other a lift into the wind and spread our wings and dreams over the world.

These Thompson Falls student-athletes (their running and their lives – one step at a time) are the right first step to a great world.

I was proud to be a part of this team, and I am honored to be involved in the lives of these Harrier Hawks.

In 1991, when I wrote this story, I was anti-Christian, anti-God. In 1993 I started reading the Bible daily. In 1997 I was baptized. One thing that can be noticed in this story is a lack of love and a lack of appreciation; the story is surely deficient! Maybe The Runner needs a dose of the Bible and the Father, the Son, and the Holy Spirit.

Done – the American Way – I can smoke a cigar, sit in my Lazy-Boy chair, and have a beer. Go ahead – as for me and my habits, I'm going for a run.

2 Timothy 4:7 ➔ I have fought the good fight, I have finished the race, I have kept the faith.

At State, we were one 'right' step ahead of the competition

Shane battles for the # 1 spot	Ryan a step ahead of a Poplar runner

Jacob two steps ahead of a Poplar runner	Mike M a step ahead of a Poplar runner

217

Epilogue

The prologue of <u>Harrier Hawks fly High</u> started with the 2007 yearbook article; the epilogue might as well use the 2008 yearbook article as an ending.

Cross Country Fall 2007

State Champions: 2007 Class B Boys Cross Country – Thompson Falls High School.

It is in the history books and will be, well, forever!

No words can express the effort, but commitment, fun, challenge, and bright smiles all give an idea of what the phrase "State Champions" might mean.

Shane Donaldson (2nd), Jacob Naegeli (3rd), Mike Morris (9th), Ryan Sol (25th), and Bryce Miller (26th) scored the team's 65 points at State to beat 2nd place Poplar by 13 points and bronze trophy Darby by 26. However, the team is more than just the scoring athletes. Patrick Jamison, Mike Kidwiler, Matt Hojem, RT Brown, and Bryant Normandeau will have their names inscribed on the first place trophy for their efforts, along with coaches Sarah Naegeli, Bob Reall, and Andrew Gideon.

The girl's team also did a phenomenal job this fall 2007 also. The Lady Hawks finished 4th at State, the highest finish in the history of TFHS. Beca Gunderson placed 22nd and led the team. Ciara Normandeau, Monica Conlin, Mariah Naegeli, and Delcie Peters were the scoring members at State. Three other runners earned varsity letters: Jeffreyanne Parker, Amanda Wood, and Lacey Wade.

The cross country team (twenty-two TFHS XC harriers in all) ran a combined 7035.0001 miles in the ten week 2007 season. Check out the cross country page at www.thompsonfalls.net for more XC information.

Grades – The varsity boys had a 3.333 GPA for fall 2007 first quarter grades, while the girl's team scored a combined 3.494. These runners define the term student-athlete.

Seven members of the team are also on the Science Olympiad team, while nine members are part of the National Honor Society. These Hawk Harriers are involved in 4-H, Envirothon, and Student Council. In fact, Jacob Naegeli is the Student Body President, while Bryant is the senior class President. Meanwhile, Ryan, RT, Beca, and Mariah are Vice-Presidents. Five other members are also involved in the student council.

These runners are leaders.

These Harrier Hawks are also State Champions.

2 Timothy 4:7 is a good Bible verse to end on → *I have fought the good fight, I have finished the race, I have kept the faith.*

About the Author

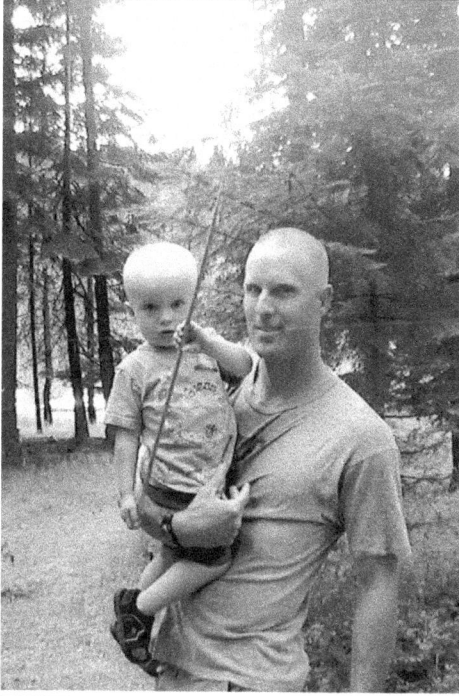

Andrew Gideon and Jaxon, 7-4-06	Deborah & Kaden, Homecoming Parade 07

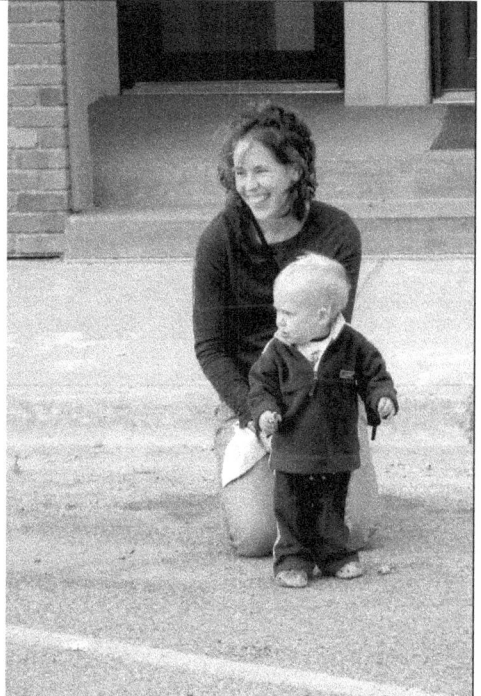

Andrew Gideon went to school for seven quarters at the University of Montana, but graduated from Jamestown College, North Dakota. Gideon has his Secondary Education certification, with a major in English, and minors in Mathematics and Psychology.

Gideon was born 1-17-68 in Madison, Wisconsin, and will probably be able to live the life of luxury with the proceeds of this novel.

The 2007-2008 school year was his 11th year of teaching and his third year at Thompson Falls High School. Eleven years of teaching down, 39 to go until retirement. In 40 years of life, 31 have been spent in the classroom. This may be why he runs so much.

Gideon lives in Thompson Falls. He has been married to Deborah since August 6, 2000. Deborah and Andrew have two amazing children: Jaxon Isiah (born 9-16-04) and Kaden James (born 6-9-06).

Now you have enough information to steal my identity. Good luck with that!

By Andrew Gideon